International Workplace Sexual Harassment Laws and Developments for the Multinational Employer

As the #MeToo movement has become an increasingly global and significant workplace matter, a timely resource compiling must-know international workplace sexual harassment laws for the multinational employer is clearly needed.

This book provides a comprehensive compilation of global sexual harassment laws, clearly necessary in this climate but not currently existing until now. It presents legislation addressing workplace sexual harassment in over 50 countries in the European Region, Asia Pacific, Americas, and the Middle East and Africa. Within each region, the laws of individual countries are set forth, as well as some cultural context and recent developments to indicate present and future trends in workplace sexual harassment regulation.

Written in clear, plain English for anyone without a legal background to understand, this book is essential reading and a key resource for employment and business attorneys, global employers, managers, human resources professionals, and occupational health and safety professionals. Academics, practitioners, union members, employees, NGOs, and those in the human rights field will also benefit from this timely resource.

Ellen Pinkos Cobb, attorney and author of *Workplace Bullying and Harassment: New Developments in International Law* has turned her international workplace law expertise to sexual harassment. In addition to a decade of tracking international laws and developments in workplace bullying and harassment, publishing work, and presenting on these topics, she has years of experience in the employment discrimination and occupational health and safety fields.

International Workplace Sexual Harassment Laws and Developments for the Multinational Employer

Ellen Pinkos Cobb

Routledge
Taylor & Francis Group
LONDON AND NEW YORK

First published 2020
by Routledge
2 Park Square, Milton Park, Abingdon, Oxon OX14 4RN

and by Routledge
52 Vanderbilt Avenue, New York, NY 10017

Routledge is an imprint of the Taylor & Francis Group, an informa business

British Library Cataloguing-in-Publication Data
A catalogue record for this book is available from the British Library

Library of Congress Cataloging-in-Publication Data
Names: Cobb, Ellen Pinkos, 1958-author.
Title: International workplace sexual harassment laws and developments for the multinational employer / Ellen Pinkos Cobb.
Description: Milton Park, Abingdon, Oxon; New York, NY: Routledge, 2020. |
Includes bibliographical references and index.
Identifiers: LCCN 2019041133 (print) | LCCN 2019041134 (ebook) |
ISBN 9780367192761 (hardback) | ISBN 9780429201530 (ebook)
Subjects: LCSH: Sexual harassment–Law and legislation. |
Sex discrimination in employment–Law and legislation.
Classification: LCC K1770 .C627 2020 (print) | LCC K1770 (ebook) |
DDC 345/.0253–dc23
LC record available at https://lccn.loc.gov/2019041133
LC ebook record available at https://lccn.loc.gov/2019041134

ISBN: 978-0-367-19276-1 (hbk)
ISBN: 978-0-429-20153-0 (ebk)

Typeset in ITC New Baskerville and Helvetica
by Deanta Global Publishing Services, Chennai, India

Contents

Acknowledgments

Many thanks to, of course, my family. You're the best.

Thanks also to The Isosceles Group, my employer, for giving me the time and space to write this book, and to Amy Laurens, Senior Editor at Routledge, a Taylor & Francis Group, for her support and excellent suggestion of adding a cultural context. Thanks too to the copy editor for their sharp eyes and astute observations.

More thanks to the multitude of others, in all their capacities, who raise awareness of the destructiveness of sexual harassment and other abusive conduct in the workplace.

Finally, advance thanks to the multinational employers and others that are informed by the laws contained herein, and by the measures they take to ensure the health and safety of their employees.

Disclaimer

This book is intended to serve only as general information about workplace sexual laws and regulations addressing the covered countries. The information is not intended to serve as guidance or legal advice in connection with any particular problem, issue, or transaction arising thereunder. Legal information is provided for guidance only and should not be regarded as an authoritative statement of the law, which can only be made by reference to the particular circumstances which apply.

As many of the laws and regulations were translated from their original language, these translated texts may contain errors and omissions that may have been inadvertently incorporated into this document. Although all web links presented were checked for accuracy or working condition prior to publication, they may have subsequently changed or become inoperative. No warranty or guaranty is made about the accuracy or completeness of any information set forth herein; laws around the world are constantly changing. In some cases, because of these changes, links contained within the report may direct the reader to incorrect material, or may not work, or may contain time-sensitive material.

Links to websites do not imply an endorsement of the materials disseminated by publishers at those websites or verification of the accuracy of any information contained on the web pages. The existence of a link to another site does not imply that the organization or person publishing at that site endorses any of the materials in this report. Additionally, opinions expressed and conclusions reached in this report are from sources used and referred to by the author and do not represent the opinions or conclusions of the author.

Any user of this book should consult with the appropriate officials in the covered country for the most current information and should also consult with counsel who is familiar with the laws of the covered country prior to taking any action. Users should also consult the actual text of any laws or regulations summarized or discussed herein.

In many instances, non-US punctuation or non-US spelling variants, such as "labour," are retained.

Introduction

Sexual harassment in the workplace is not a new issue, and is legally prohibited in a majority of the world's countries. However, on October 15, 2017, Alyssa Milano tweeted, "If you've been sexually harassed or assaulted write 'me too' as a reply to this tweet," in order to show support for those who asserted they were sexually harassed or assaulted by Harvey Weinstein, and to seek to illustrate the magnitude of the problem. Within 24 hours, the tweet generated more than 12 million retweets, posts, and reactions. The present #MeToo movement took flight.[1] (Note: Tarana Burke founded the #MeToo movement in 2006, using the phrase "me too" to raise awareness of the pervasiveness of sexual abuse and assault in society and to let women of color who had survived sexual assault know that they were not alone.)

The #MeToo movement subsequently spread around much of the world, known by various terms in other countries but with similar connotations. Its significant and ongoing impact on multinational employers and workplace culture has brought the prevalence and destructiveness of sexual harassment to the forefront, bringing with it increased responsibility for employers.

With many businesses operating globally, it is imperative that businesses know the applicable sexual harassment laws. From the International Labour Organization's 2019 adoption of a new Convention and Recommendation to Combat Violence and Harassment in The Workplace, to Saudi Arabia's 2018 enactment of a harassment law which includes sexual harassment, this issue remains very much at the forefront of today's workplace. No industry is immune.

A comprehensive compilation of global sexual harassment laws is imperative for multinational employers and has not existed until now. This book fills a void, presenting laws and developments addressing sexual harassment in Europe, Asia Pacific, the Americas, and the Middle East and Africa.

Applicable workplace laws in over 50 countries, provinces, territories, and states are provided, including sexual harassment definitions, employer requirements and liabilities, and other relevant information such as statistics and guidance. In cases where recent and relevant information concerning sexual harassment at work in a cultural context is available, a country is introduced with this information to offer insight into the present climate.

Preventing sexual harassment in the workplace is not only legally required in the countries addressed in this book; it is good business. Employers who fail to prevent and respond to sexual harassment risk harm to their workplace climate and to their company's reputation. Their workforce may suffer lower morale, higher turnover, and reduced productivity, not to mention legal claims, with the possibility of the employer's own vicarious liability being on the line.

As an attorney who has worked in the employment discrimination field at the state and federal agency level for many years and has researched and published on workplace bullying and harassment over the last decade (see my book, *International Workplace Bullying and Harassment: New Developments in International Law*, Routledge, 2017), I have long been aware of the prevalence and destructiveness of sexual harassment at work. I am honored to be writing this timely book.

It is hoped this work brings together timely information to better inform the workplace as a whole, serve as a useful tool for organizations, employers, human resource and legal professionals, employee organizations and employees, and academics, and contribute to continuing the discussion of global sexual harassment.

A caveat: it is a challenging and fine line to provide select information from comprehensive laws in numerous languages without detracting from or changing their meaning on the one hand, or bogging down the reader with too much detail or legalese on the other. With much legislation, almost every word counts for meaning, and every phrase is crafted based on both a history and a future intent. Following are the best efforts to capture an appropriate amount of essential information for the reader.

NOTE

1 The Telegraph, The #MeToo shockwave: how the movement has reverberated around the world, by By Louise Burke, March 9, 2018. Available at https://www.telegraph.co.uk/news/world/metoo-shockwave/. Accessed August 22, 2019.

1 Workplace sexual harassment

The big picture, the role of culture, and the global view

SEXUAL HARASSMENT BASICS

- *Sexual harassment* is frequently defined as involving unwanted sex-related behavior. While no universal definition exists, most legal understandings include similar elements, such as descriptions of the conduct as unwanted or unwelcome, with the purpose or effect of being intimidating, hostile, degrading, humiliating, or offensive (Source: *14 International Journal of Management Reviews* 1, 2, 2011. "Workplace sexual harassment 30 years on: a review of the literature," by Paula McDonald; *31 Nova Law Review* 225, 226–227, 2007. "Directions in sexual harassment law," by Catharine MacKinnon).
- *Sexual harassment is sex discrimination*: many countries regard sexual harassment as sex discrimination, as is shown in this book's country-by-country legislation. Sexual harassment is not gender-specific, but a large majority of its victims are women.
- *Types of sexual harassment*: the two types of sexual harassment are known as "quid pro quo" and "hostile working environment."

  Sexual harassment is a form of sexual violence that commonly occurs in the world of work, and it is frequently categorized in two ways: "quid pro quo" or "hostile working environment." Quid pro quo sexual harassment is when a worker is asked for a sexual favour, and submitting to or rejecting that request is used to make a decision about that worker's job. Hostile working environment harassment covers conduct that creates an intimidating, hostile, or humiliating working environment (Source: *International Labour Organization*, International Labour Conference, 2018. "Ending violence and harassment against women and men in the world of work").

Quid pro quo means "this for that." *Quid pro quo harassment* occurs when "submission to or rejection of such conduct by an individual is used as the basis for employment decisions affecting such individual," and when expressed or implied demands for sexual favors are implied or offered by someone in a position of power over another in exchange for some benefit (e.g., a promotion), or to avoid some detriment (e.g., termination), in the workplace. Unwelcome sexual conduct constitutes sexual harassment when "submission to such conduct is made either explicitly or implicitly a term or condition of an individual's employment" (Source: US Government Publishing Office. Code of Federal Regulations. 29 C.F.R § 1604.11(a)(1), (2), and (3)).

Hostile working environment harassment occurs when speech or conduct is so severe and pervasive that it creates an intimidating or demeaning environment or situation that negatively affects a person's job performance. The harassing conduct may be perpetrated by anyone in the work environment, including a coworker, supervisor, customer, or contractor.

According to the International Labour Organization, the most common way to define sexual harassment is to include both the quid pro quo and the hostile working environment categories.

TYPES OF WORKPLACE LAWS WHICH INCLUDE SEXUAL HARASSMENT PROVISIONS

Around the world, laws addressing sexual harassment are included in anti-discrimination, equality, and equal opportunity laws; criminal codes; labor codes; health and safety legislation; and laws on psychosocial risks. In some countries, definitions of sexual harassment include gender-based harassment, or harassment based on gender identity. Some laws address psychosocial risks and regulate sexual harassment as a psychosocial risk. (Workplace factors that cause stress are referred to as psychosocial risks or hazards. Sexual harassment is one of the working conditions leading to psychological risk.)

IMPACT OF WORKPLACE SEXUAL HARASSMENT

Sexual harassment significantly affects organizations, with consequences which include increased employee use of sick leave, higher turnover, training and development costs, possible litigation, and harm to reputation. For a sexually harassed employee, there may be reduced job satisfaction, commitment, and productivity, as well as the possibilities of anxiety, depression, anxiety, and other physical and psychological health issues.

WORKPLACE SEXUAL HARASSMENT RECOGNITION AND PREVENTION BY INTERNATIONAL ORGANIZATIONS

A global movement and response of global bodies

> The United Nations and regional treaty systems have recognized sexual harassment as a form of discrimination and violence against women.
>
> International statements of law and principle provide an important starting point in drafting legislation that prohibits sexual harassment.

The Convention on the Elimination of all Forms of Discrimination Against Women (CEDAW), adopted by the UN General Assembly in 1979, directs States Parties to take appropriate measures to eliminate discrimination against women in all fields, specifically including equality under law and in governance and politics, the workplace, education, healthcare, and other areas of public and social life (Arts. 7–16). It entered into force as an international treaty on September 3, 1981 after the twentieth country had ratified it. By the tenth anniversary of the Convention in 1989, almost one hundred nations had agreed to be bound by its provisions. The implementation of the Convention is monitored by the Committee on the Elimination of Discrimination Against Women (CEDAW).

Additionally, in 1993, the UN General Assembly Resolution 48/104 on the Declaration on the Elimination of Violence Against Women defined violence against women as including sexual harassment, which is prohibited at work, and encouraged development of penal, civil or other administrative sanctions, as well as preventative approaches, to eliminate violence against women (Art. 4(d–f)).

International Labour Organization (ILO): the ILO is a tripartite UN agency which brings together governments, employers, and workers of 187 Member States to set labor standards, develop policies, and devise programs promoting decent work for all women and men.

The ILO defines sexual harassment as follows:

[Sexual harassment is] a sex-based behaviour that is unwelcome and offensive to its recipient. For sexual harassment to exist these two conditions must be present.

Sexual harassment may take two forms:

1) Quid Pro Quo, when a job benefit—such as a pay rise, a promotion, or even continued employment—is made conditional on the victim acceding to demands to engage in some form of sexual behaviour; or;
2) Hostile working environment in which the conduct creates conditions that are intimidating or humiliating for the victim.

Behaviour that qualifies as sexual harassment:

PHYSICAL: Physical violence, touching, unnecessary close proximity
VERBAL: Comments and questions about appearance, lifestyle, sexual orientation, offensive phone calls
NON-VERBAL: Whistling, sexually-suggestive gestures, display of sexual materials

2019 ILO CONVENTION AND RECOMMENDATION TO COMBAT VIOLENCE AND HARASSMENT IN THE WORKPLACE

On June 21, 2019, the ILO adopted a new *Convention and Recommendation to Combat Violence and Harassment in the Workplace* at the International Labour Conference (ILC) annual meeting. (Conventions are legally binding international treaties that may be ratified by member States, while Recommendations provide advice and guidance.) Before adoption of the Convention, there had been no international legal standard that addressed violence and harassment in the workplace and provided a definition and scope for it. Article 1 of the Convention states the following:

For the purposes of this Convention:

(a) The term "violence and harassment" in the world of work refers to a range of unacceptable behaviours and practices, or threats thereof, whether a single occurrence or repeated, that aim at, result in, or are likely to result in physical, psychological, sexual or economic harm, and includes gender-based violence and harassment;
(b) The term "gender-based violence and harassment" means violence and harassment directed at persons because of their sex or gender, or affecting persons of a particular sex or gender disproportionately, and includes sexual harassment.

The Convention recognizes that violence and harassment in the world of work "can constitute a human rights violation or abuse...is a threat to equal opportunities, is unacceptable and incompatible with decent work."

The new international labour standard aims to protect workers and employees, irrespective of their contractual status, and includes persons in training, interns and apprentices, workers whose employment has been terminated, volunteers, jobseekers and job applicants. It recognizes that "individuals exercising the authority, duties or responsibilities of an employer" can also be subjected to violence and harassment.

The standard covers violence and harassment occurring in the workplace; in places where a worker is paid, takes a rest or meal break, or uses sanitary, washing or changing facilities; during work-related trips, travel, training, events or social activities; in work-related communications (including through information and communication technologies); in employer-provided accommodation; and when commuting to and from work. It also recognizes that violence and harassment may involve third parties.

WORKPLACE SEXUAL HARASSMENT IN A CULTURAL CONTEXT

> Cultural differences in perception and communication can and do lead to different frames of reference and accepted behaviors with regard to workplace sexual harassment.

The culture of a country influences such things as its definition of sexual harassment, its response, awareness, and acknowledgment thereof, the reaction of the employer and employee, and the legislative response.

The following factors may play into the means by which sexual harassment is addressed in the workplace and are important to consider when implementing legal requirements to address, inform, stop/prevent, and investigate workplace sexual harassment:

- The culture of the region/country;
- The culture of the workplace;
- Existing legislation; and
- Enforcement of laws.

Multinational and/or multicultural work environments may lead to misunderstandings in the workplace over many issues, no less so than when sexual harassment is being considered.

Further, the culture of an individual workplace plays a major role in a company's response to sexual harassment. The tone set at the top with regard to intolerance of sexual harassment is key to creating a workplace culture for the entire organization.

The existence of legislation is a factor in the occurrence and treatment of sexual harassment, setting out the employer's responsibilities. These responsibilities may include creating and implementing a sexual harassment policy and procedure, providing training, promoting awareness, assigning a confidential advisor, implementing confidential and impartial investigation processes and measures for sharing findings, prohibiting retaliation with regard to those who lodge complaints or participate in investigations, and remedies and measures for when sexual harassment is found to have occurred.

Whether existing laws are enforced in a country, though related to this issue, is beyond the scope of this book.

Finally, it is difficult and often ill-advised to generalize about a region or country; moreover, when this characterization is in the context of its treatment of workplace sexual harassment, it becomes a potentially even more inflammatory subject. However, where it is helpful to set the stage for gaining understanding of the context of sexual harassment, or of developments in light of the #MeToo era that have brought about new or enhanced legislation, brief characterizations of such a region or country may be offered.

COUNTRIES WITHOUT SEXUAL HARASSMENT LAWS

Not all countries have workplace sexual harassment laws.

Although new and amended legislation has become effective in numerous countries, sexual harassment in the workplace remains unacknowledged and unaddressed in numerous countries. According to "Preventing Gender-Based Workplace Discrimination And Sexual Harassment: New Data On 193 Countries," a report by the World Policy Analysis Center, of the 193 countries reported on, more than 68 do not have any workplace-specific prohibitions of sexual harassment in place. This means that more than one-third of the world's countries do not have any laws prohibiting sexual harassment at work, and nearly 235 million women worldwide lack legal protection from sexual harassment at work.

BIBLIOGRAPHY

International Labour Conference, June 2019. Text of the Convention Concerning the Elimination of Violence and Harassment in the World of Work. Available at: https://www.ilo.org/wcmsp5/groups/public/---ed_norm/---relconf/documents/meetingdocument/wcms_711242.pdf. Accessed June 22, 2019

International Labour Organization, International Labour Conference, 2018. Ending Violence and Harassment against Women and Men in the World of Work. Available at https://www.ilo.org/wcmsp5/groups/public/---ed_norm/---relconf/documents/meetingdocument/wcms_553577.pdf. Accessed June 7, 2019

ILO, Sexual Harassment at Work Fact Sheet, April 9, 2007. Available at: https://www.ilo.org/wcmsp5/groups/public/---ed_norm/---declaration/documents/publication/wcms_decl_fs_96_en.pdf. Accessed June 7, 2019

UCLA Fielding School of Public Health, 2019. WORLD Policy Analysis Center. Is Sexual Harassment Explicitly Prohibited in the Workplace? Available at: https://ph.ucla.edu/sexual-harassment-explicitly-prohibited-workplace and https://www.worldpolicycenter.org/policies/is-sexual-harassment-explicitly-prohibited-in-the-workplace. Accessed June 25, 2019

UN General Assembly, 1993. 48/104. Declaration on the Elimination of Violence against Women. Available at: https://www.un.org/documents/ga/res/48/a48r104.htm. Accessed June 7, 2019

UN Human Rights Office of the High Commissioner, Convention on the Elimination of All Forms of Discrimination against Women, 1979. Available at: https://www.ohchr.org/EN/ProfessionalInterest/Pages/CEDAW.aspx. Accessed August 27, 2019

UN Women, 2011. Sources of International Law Related to Sexual Harassment, January 13, 2011. Available at: http://www.endvawnow.org/en/articles/492-sources-of-international-law-related-to-sexual-harassment.html. Accessed June 7, 2019

US Government Publishing Office. Code of Federal Regulations. 29 C.F.R § 1604.11(a)(1), (2), and (3). Available at: https://www.govinfo.gov/app/details/CFR-2009-title29-vol4/CFR-2009-title29-vol4-sec1604-11. Accessed August 19, 2019

2017 WORLD Policy Analysis Center. Preventing Gender-Based Workplace Discrimination and Sexual Harassment: New Data on 193 Countries. Available at: https://ph.ucla.edu/news/press-release/2017/oct/nearly-235-million-women-worldwide-lack-legal-protections-sexual#map1. Accessed June 25, 2019

2017 WORLD Policy Analysis Center. UCLA Fielding School of Public Health. Preventing Gender-Based Workplace Discrimination and Sexual Harassment: New Data on 193 Countries. Available at: https://www.worldpolicycenter.org/sites/default/files/WORLD%20Discrimination%20at%20Work%20Report.pdf. Accessed May 31, 2019

2 Sexual Harassment in the European Union

The role of dignity and directives

The role of dignity: the concept of a worker's dignity provided for in the Charter of Fundamental Rights of the European Union is a foundation of numerous EU sexual harassment laws. The word "dignity" is included in the language of over a dozen EU country laws which address workplace sexual harassment.

In much of Europe, there is the recognition, reflected in legislation, that a component of health and safety at work is taking the dignity of the worker into consideration. The European Union's bill of rights, the Charter of Fundamental Rights of the European Union (2000/C 364/01) ("Charter"), states: "Human dignity is inviolable. It must be respected and protected" (Article 1).

It also states: "Every worker has the right to working conditions which respect his or her health, safety and dignity" (Article 31(1)).

Further, the Istanbul Convention on Violence Against Women (the Council of Europe Convention on preventing and combatting violence against women) defines sexual harassment in Article 40 as "any form of unwanted verbal, non-verbal or physical conduct of a sexual nature with the purpose or effect of violating the dignity of a person." Article 40 furthermore states that: Parties shall take the necessary legislative or other measures to ensure that any form of unwanted verbal, non-verbal or physical conduct of a sexual nature with the purpose or effect of violating the dignity of a person, in particular when creating an intimidating, hostile, degrading, humiliating or offensive environment, is subject to criminal or other legal sanction.

In 1991, the EU adopted a non-binding recommendation on the dignity of men and women at work and a Code of Practice on measures to combat sexual harassment.

The first legally binding legislation defining *sexual harassment* was adopted in 2002 as the European Union Parliament passed legislation that for the first time set forth a legal definition of sexual harassment applicable throughout the European Union (EU).

EUROPEAN DIRECTIVES

What is a Directive?

> A Directive is a legislative act that sets out a goal that all EU countries must achieve. However, it is up to the individual countries to devise their own laws on how to reach these goals. Definitions provided in the EU Directives constitute the common basis for most EU national legislation.
>
> Although there is no international consensus on the definition of sexual harassment, many countries have definitions based on the EU Directives.

An EU Directive is a legal act provided for in an EU Treaty. EU Directives are legally binding and have to be transposed into national laws by Member States within a set deadline. EU Directives set out minimum requirements and fundamental principles, such as the principle of prevention and risk assessment, as well as the responsibilities of employers and employees. A directive enters into force once it is published in the Official Journal of the EU.

EU Directive 2002/73/EC (equal treatment in access to employment) defines *sexual harassment* as a situation:

> where any form of unwanted verbal, non-verbal or physical conduct of sexual nature occurs, with a purpose or effect of violating the dignity of a person, in particular when creating and intimidating, hostile, degrading, humiliating or offensive environment.

Directive 2004/113/EC of 13 December 2004 on implementing the principle of equal treatment between men and women in the access to and supply of goods and services provides a definition of sexual harassment, stated in Article 2, "Definitions":

> *sexual harassment*: where any form of unwanted physical, verbal, non-verbal or physical conduct of a sexual nature occurs, with the

> purpose or effect of violating the dignity of a person, in particular when creating an intimidating, hostile, degrading, humiliating or offensive environment.

Article 4, "Principle of equal treatment," states:

> Harassment and sexual harassment within the meaning of this Directive shall be deemed to be discrimination on the grounds of sex and therefore prohibited. A person's rejection of, or submission to, such conduct may not be used as a basis for a decision affecting that person.

Directive 2006/54/EC of 5 July 2006 on the implementation of the principle of equal opportunities and equal treatment of men and women in matters of employment and occupation (recast) contains the same EU definition of sexual harassment as is set out in the 2002 Directive:

> ...where any form of unwanted verbal, non-verbal or physical conduct of a sexual nature occurs, with the purpose or effect of violating the dignity of a person, in particular when creating an intimidating, hostile, degrading, humiliating or offensive environment.

The Directive defines sexual harassment as discrimination on the grounds of sex.

SEXUAL HARASSMENT AS A PSYCHOSOCIAL RISK AND AS WORK-RELATED STRESS

> Psychosocial risks arise from poor work design, organization, and management, as well as a poor social context of work, and they may result in negative psychological, physical, and social outcomes such as work-related stress, burnout, or depression. Some examples of working conditions leading to psychosocial risks include psychological and sexual harassment.
>
> Psychosocial risks and work-related stress are among the most challenging issues in occupational safety and health. They impact significantly on the health of individuals, organizations, and national economies.

PRESENT-DAY SNAPSHOT OF EU SEXUAL HARASSMENT

A 2018 report, "Bullying and sexual harassment at the workplace, in public spaces, and political life in the EU," by Helge Hoel and Maarit Vartia, commissioned by the European Parliament's Policy Department for Citizens' Rights and Constitutional Affairs at the request of the Committee on Women's Rights and Gender Equality (FEMM), offers insights and findings on sexual harassment in EU workplaces by providing a broad account and an in-depth analysis of bullying and sexual harassment in the workplace, in public spaces, and in political life.

Relevant excerpts include the following:

- Whilst considerable agreement exists regarding the general definition of sexual harassment, more uncertainty and disagreement remain with respect to the less serious offences associated with it, although in light of the current debates (including #metoo) boundaries for what is considered unacceptable behaviour are being redrawn. (p. 8)
- Prevalence figures for sexual harassment are uncertain with large discrepancies emerging between studies, and the recent public debate suggests that real figures are higher than often suggested. (p. 8)
- Tolerance towards sexual harassment is a key factor in maintaining and reproducing the problem. It varies between EU countries, even between countries which in other respects are economically and culturally very similar, including with respect to perceived gender equality. (p. 8)
- Sexual harassment should be recognised as a severe psychosocial stressor with impact on targets' health and wellbeing, organisational functioning and career prospects. However, sexual harassment cannot be reduced to an occupational hazard alone, but must be understood in the light of (male) power and wider gender equality. (p. 9)

BIBLIOGRAPHY

Council of Europe Convention on Preventing and Combating Violence against Women and Domestic Violence, 2011. Available at: https://rm.coe.int/CoERMPublicCommonSearchServices/DisplayDCTMContent?documentId=090000168046031c.

Council of Europe, 2014. Available at: https://www.coe.int/en/web/istanbul-convention/about-the-convention.

Directive 2004/113/EC of 13 December 2004. Available at: https://eur-lex.europa.eu/eli/dir/2004/113/oj. Accessed August 22, 2019

Directive 2006/54/EC of 5 July 2006. Available at https://eur-lex.europa.eu/legal-content/EN/TXT/?uri=CELEX:32006L0054. Accessed August 22, 2019

Directorate General for Internal Policies Policy Department for Citizens' Rights and Constitutional Affairs, 2018. Women's Rights & Gender Equality, Bullying and Sexual Harassment at the Workplace, in Public Spaces, and Political Life in the EU, by Helge HOEL, Maarit Varta, Commissioned by the European Parliament's Policy Department for Citizens' Rights and Constitutional Affairs at the Request of the Committee on Women's Rights and Gender Equality (FEMM). Available at: http://www.europarl.europa.eu/RegData/etudes/STUD/2018/604949/IPOL_STU(2018)604949_EN.pdf. Accessed August 21, 2019

European Agency for Safety and Health at Work, n.d. Psychosocial Risks and Stress at Work. Available at: https://osha.europa.eu/en/themes/psychosocial-risks-and-stress. Accessed May 30, 2019

European Agency for Safety and Health at Work, n.d. Safety and Health Legislation. Available at: https://osha.europa.eu/en/safety-and-health-legislation. Accessed May 13, 2019

European Parliament, 18 July 2018. PE 620.941v02-00 A8-0265/2018. Report on Measures to Prevent and Combat Mobbing and Sexual Harassment at Workplace, in Public Spaces, and Political Life in the EU (2018/2055(INI)). Committee on Women's Rights and Gender Equality. Available at: http://www.europarl.europa.eu/sides/getDoc.do?pubRef=-//EP//TEXT+REPORT+A8-2018-0265+0+DOC+XML+V0//EN. Accessed June 23, 2019

EU-Directive 2002/73/EC, 2002. Available at: https://eur-lex.europa.eu/LexUriServ/LexUriServ.do?uri=CELEX:32002L0073:EN:HTML. Accessed August 22, 2019

International Labour Organization, 2016. pp. 1–2. Workplace Stress a Collective Challenge. Available at: http://www.ilo.org/wcmsp5/groups/public/---ed_protect/---protrav/---safework/documents/publication/wcms_466547.pdf. Accessed March 15, 2019

Signatures and Ratifications, 2011. Available at: https://www.coe.int/en/web/istanbul-convention/text-of-the-convention.

3 Sexual harassment laws in European countries

National legislation of European countries addressing *sexual harassment* consists of the implementation of applicable EU Directives and the creation of country-specific laws, regulations, and guidance.

Sexual harassment provisions in European countries are included in a variety of laws. Most frequently, equal treatment or equality laws address and prohibit sexual harassment, but occupational health and safety laws, labor laws, anti-discrimination laws, and criminal and/or penal codes also cover sexual harassment matters.

Even between European countries, understanding of what constitutes sexual harassment varies greatly:[1] although there is no consensus on the definition of sexual harassment, many EU countries have definitions based on those in the EU Directives. However, while EU legislation has led to some consistency in the Member States' sexual harassment laws, there are also significant differences, as definitions and boundaries of what is considered sexual harassment differ from one European country to another.

Recent sexual harassment legislation or developments discussed in this chapter indicate that while laws in some countries in Europe have been impacted by the #MeToo movement, others have not.

A significant paradox regarding countries reporting higher levels of sexual harassment: an indication of understandings of what constitutes sexual harassment varying greatly and differing levels of sexual harassment between countries was demonstrated by a major study in 2014 by the European Agency for Fundamental Rights Violence Against Women, an EU-wide survey that included 42,000 women from all 28 EU member states.

Chapter Six of the survey, "Sexual harassment," includes tables of varying degrees of sexual harassment among countries. It found that higher prevalence rates are generally found in northern Member States than in southern Member States. The report indicates three reasons for the observed differences between Member States: the exposure to adverse social behavior relates to variations in the actual prevalence of adverse social behavior; cultural differences with regard to the type of behavior considered adverse; and country differences in the likelihood of people reporting that they were subjected to any of these types of behavior, based on factors including the different level of acknowledgement of sexual harassment in national legislation and policies (Source: European Agency for Fundamental Rights, 2015. "Violence against women: an EU-wide survey").

Figures reflect the self-labelling nature of the survey which shows low figures for national contexts where the phenomenon is little discussed or acknowledged. Thus, the true figures for some of the lowest scoring countries are likely to be considerably higher (Source: 2018/2055(INI), 2018. "Report on measures to prevent and combat mobbing and sexual harassment at workplace, in public spaces, and political life in the EU").

NOTE

1 European Agency for Fundamental Rights, Violence against women: An EU-wide survey https://fra.europa.eu/sites/default/files/fra_uploads/fra-2014-vaw-survey-main-results-apr14_en.pdf. Accessed April 13, 2019

BIBLIOGRAPHY

Eurofound. European Foundation for the Improvement of Living and Working Conditions, 2015. Violence and Harassment in European Workplaces: Causes, Impacts and Policies. By Mario Giaccone, M. and Di Nunzio, D. Available at: http://www.eurofound.europa.eu/sites/default/files/ef_comparative_analytical_report/field_ef_documents/ef1473en.pdf. Accessed March 15, 2019

European Parliament, 18 July 2018. PE 620.941v02-00 A8-0265/2018. Report on Measures to Prevent and Combat Mobbing and Sexual Harassment At Workplace, in Public Spaces, and Political Life in the EU (2018/2055(INI), 2018). Committee on Women's Rights and Gender Equality, p. 19. Available at: http://www.europarl.europa.eu/RegData/etudes/STUD/2018/604949/IPOL_STU(2018)604949_EN.pdf. Accessed August 25, 2019

FRA-European Union Agency for Fundamental Rights, Violence Against Women; An EU- Wide Study 2015. Available at: https://fra.europa.eu/sites/default/files/fra_uploads/fra-2014-vaw-survey-main-results-apr14_en.pdf. Accessed August 23, 2019

AUSTRIA

Under Austrian law, sexual harassment in the workplace is considered a form of discrimination. Laws for the private sector and public sector treat sexual harassment similarly.

Austria's Federal Equal Treatment Act is applicable to the private sector; the Federal Equal Treatment Act of 1993 is applicable to the public sector. The offender may be the employer, another employee, or a third party. The law applies not only to harassment that takes place during the employment relationship but also before or after.

Legislation

- Equal Treatment Act (BGBl. I—2004), as amended
- Equal Treatment Act (public sector)
- Employee Protection Act—ASchG

Title of legislation	Equal Treatment Act BGBl. I, 2004, as amended

The *Equal Treatment Act BGBl. I, 2004, as amended,* addresses sexual harassment in Part 1, "Equal treatment of women and men in the world of work," under Section 6.

Section 6, titled Sexual Harassment, states as follows:

(1) Discrimination based on sex also occurs when a person is being sexually harassed by the employer, or is discriminated against by the employer by culpably failing, in the case of sexual harassment by a third party, to remedy a situation which is appropriate on the basis of legal provisions, collective law or employment contract, or is harassed by a third party in connection with his/her employment relationship, or is harassed by third parties outside an employment relationship.

(2) Sexual harassment occurs when a sexual-related behavior is committed that interferes with or has the purpose of interfering with the dignity of a person; is undesirable, inappropriate or offensive to the person concerned; and creates or intends to create an intimidating, hostile or humiliating work environment for the data subject. It also occurs when the data subject rejects or condones a behavior

that is a part of the sexual sphere on the part of the employer or of supervisors or colleagues, expressly or tacitly becoming the basis for a decision affecting that person's access to vocational training, employment, employment, promotion or remuneration, or as the basis for another decision in the world of work.

(3) There is also discrimination in the case of instructions for the sexual harassment of a person.

(4) Discrimination also occurs when a person is sexually harassed because of their close relationship with a person because of their sex.

Sexual harassment occurs when a behavior related to the sexual sphere is used which interferes with or has the purpose of violating the dignity of a person, is undesirable, inappropriate, or offensive to the person concerned, and

- Creates, or intends to, an intimidating, hostile, or humiliating work environment for the person concerned.
- The fact that the person concerned rejects or condones a behavior that is a part of the sexual sphere on the part of the employer or superiors or colleagues, expressly or tacitly becoming the basis of a decision affecting that person's access to vocational training, employment, employment, promotion or remuneration, or as the basis for another decision in the world of work.
- There is also discrimination in the case of instructions for sexual harassment of a person.
- Discrimination also occurs when a person is sexually harassed because of their close relationship with a person because of their sex.

The employer's duty of care towards his or her employees obliges the employer to take appropriate measures upon learning of sexual harassment in order that the employee is not exposed to any further attacks.

The *Federal Act on Equal Treatment* I No. 66/2004, as amended, applies to the public sector. It prohibits *sexual harassment* and gender-related harassment with regard to a working climate generally hostile to women or men. Harassment or sexual harassment on these grounds is also deemed to be discrimination.

Harassment by the employer himself/herself or by third persons (e.g. colleagues, customers, suppliers, etc.) is prohibited. If an employee is being harassed by third persons, the employer is obligated to intervene and to take appropriate measures.

The prohibition of *sexual harassment* is addressed to colleagues and superiors as well as to employers, whether the employer commits the harassment or negligently fails to take action against harassment by third persons. Sexual harassment also occurs if committed by third persons, such as customers, in connection with the employment relationship. The employer has a defense to liability when steps are taken designed to protect the harassed person from further harassment, and by so doing fulfil his or her duty of care as an employer.

Title of legislation	Employee Protection Act—(ASchG), as amended

Austria's Federal Law on Safety and Health at Work (Employee Protection Act—ASchG), as amended, does not contain provisions on sexual harassment but does require that employers ensure the safety and health of workers in relation to all aspects of the work. The costs must under no circumstances be borne by the employees. Employers must take the necessary measures to protect life, health, integrity and dignity… (§ 3. (1)).

BIBLIOGRAPHY

2018. Federal Ministry for Digitization and Business Location. Federal Law on Equal Treatment (Gleichbehandlungsgesetz—GlBG). Available at: https://www.ris.bka.gv.at/GeltendeFassung.wxe?Abfrage=Bundesnormen&Gesetzesnummer=20003395. Accessed December 13, 2018

2019. Federal Ministry for Digitization and Business Location. Federal Law on Safety and Health at Work. (Employee Protection Act—ASchG). Available at: https://www.ris.bka.gv.at/GeltendeFassung.wxe?Abfrage=Bundesnormen&Gesetzesnummer=10008910. Accessed June 25, 2019

BALKAN PENINSULA

Balkan Countries: Albania, Bosnia and Herzegovina, Bulgaria, Croatia, Greece, Romania, Serbia, Slovenia

In general, the #MeToo campaign has not gained traction in Balkan countries.

Consideration of the paradox regarding countries reporting higher levels of sexual harassment, and with regard to observed differences between Member States concerning the exposure to adverse social behavior, relates to variations in the actual prevalence of adverse social behavior; cultural differences with regard to the type of behavior considered adverse; and country differences in the likelihood of people reporting that they were subjected to any of these types of behavior, based on factors including the different level of acknowledgement of sexual harassment in national legislation and policies.

In this context, sexual harassment at times appears least common and lowest in countries such as Romania, Slovenia, and Bulgaria. However, these low figures may result from the phenomenon being little discussed or acknowledged. Thus, the actual figures for some of the lowest scoring countries are likely to be considerably higher (Source: European Parliament, July 18, 2018. Committee on Women's Rights and Gender Equality. "Report on measures to prevent and combat mobbing and sexual harassment at workplace, in public spaces, and political life in the EU").

BIBLIOGRAPHY

European Parliament. Committee on Women's Rights and Gender Equality, July 18, 2018. Report on Measures to Prevent and Combat Mobbing and Sexual Harassment At Workplace, in Public Spaces, and Political Life in the EU (2018/2055(INI)), p. 19. Available at: http://www.europarl.europa.eu/RegData/etudes/STUD/2018/604949/IPOL_STU(2018)604949_EN.pdf. Accessed August 25, 2019

ALBANIA

Legislation

- Law No 7961, 12.07.1995 Code of Labor of the Republic of Albania, as amended
- Anti-Discrimination Law, 2010
- Gender Equality in Society No. 9970, 24.07.2008

Title of legislation	Law No 7961, dated 12.07.1995 Code of Labor of the Republic of Albania, as amended

Law No. 7961, 12.07.1995 Code of Labor of The Republic of Albania, as amended, forbids the employer from carrying out any action of *sexual harassment* against the employee. *Sexual harassment* means any nuisance that considerably harms the psychological state of the employee because of sex. This Article, Article 32, also states that the employer shall prevent any attitude that threatens the employee's dignity.

Title of legislation	Anti-Discrimination Law, 2010

Albania's *Anti-Discrimination Law,* adopted on February 4, 2010, states, in reference to sexual harassment in the context of sexual annoyance, that "annoyance" is defined:

> ...as that form of discrimination that occurs in the case of an undesirable conduct, when it is related to any of the causes mentioned in article 1 of this law, which has the purpose or effect of violating the dignity of a person and the creation of an intimidating, hostile, degrading, humiliating or offensive environment for that person, as well as in the case of a less favourable treatment performed as a result of an objection or failure to submit by the person affected by such a behaviour.

3Tr. note: The Albanian word translated here (*shqetësim*) has a number of closely related meanings; the concept aimed at is "(sexual) harassment." The law "On gender equality in society" (No. 9970 dated 24 July, 2008) has two separate definitions in this area; one uses this word (with the adjective "sexual") and the other uses a different word with a stronger connotation (*ngacmim*), which is often translated as "harassment." To preserve the difference *shqetësim* is translated as "annoyance."

Every kind of annoyance is prohibited, including sexual annoyance, by an employer against an employee or an applicant for work or between employees.

The employer is obliged under this law as follows:

- To implement, protect and encourage the principle of equality and the prohibition of every kind of discrimination;
- To take necessary measures, including disciplinary measures, for the protection of employees from discrimination and victimisation, within one month from receiving knowledge [of them];
- To respond effectively and in compliance with this law to complaints received because of discrimination committed by his employees, within one month from receiving them; and
- To raise consciousness about this law by posting it in public premises of the workplace as well as enabling a full understanding of it by his own means or with the assistance of specialized subjects.

Title of legislation	Gender Equality in Society No. 9970, 24.07.2008

The *Gender Equality in Society No. 9970, 24.07.2008* prohibits *sexual harassment* in the workplace.

- *Gender-based harassment* is any kind of unwelcome conduct relating to the gender of one person and aiming and/or resulting in violating personal dignity or creating a threatening, hostile, humiliating, disparaging or insulting environment. (Article 4)
- *Sexual harassment* is any kind of unwelcome conduct, by means of words or actions, physical or symbolic, of a sexual character, which intends or leads to violating personal dignity, specifically when it creates a threatening, hostile, humiliating, disparaging or insulting environment constitutes. (Article 4)

Article 16 requires that the employer and any other individual acting on behalf of the employee do the following:

- Take measures to stop sexual harassment towards employees; and

- Not place in a disfavoured position or take disciplinary measures against an employee rejecting or complaining of sexual harassment or any employee witnessing sexual harassment done by the employer or other employees.

Article 18 sets forth the employer's responsibilities for protecting the employee from *sexual harassment,* requiring that the employer take preventive measures and define disciplinary measures (sanctions) in the internal regulations concerning prevention of sexual harassment towards the employees, in compliance with this law:

- If the employer comes to know indirectly or in cases where he or she receives information or a complaint from an employee who claims to have been sexually harassed by another employee, after being convinced of this, the employer should take the proper organizational measures to stop the sexual harassment and apply the disciplinary sanctions;
- Inform all employees on the prohibition of sexual harassment in the working place.

BIBLIOGRAPHY

International Labour Organization, 1995. Law No. 7961, 12.07.1995 Code of Labor of The Republic of Albania, without the December 2015 amendment. Available at: http://www.ilo.org/dyn/natlex/docs/SERIAL/41344/63433/. Accessed February 22, 2019

LegislationOnLine, Anti-Discrimination Law, 2010. Available at: https://www.ilo.org/wcmsp5/groups/public/---ed_protect/---protrav/---ilo_aids/documents/legaldocument/wcms_178702.pdf. Accessed February 22, 2019

LegislationOnLine, 2008. Gender Equality in Society No. 9970. Available at: https://www.legislationline.org/documents/id/16425. Accessed February 22, 2019

BOSNIA AND HERZEGOVINA

Legislation

- Law on the Prohibition of Discrimination, 2009
- Gender Equality Law, No. 16/2003, as amended

Title of legislation	Law on the Prohibition of Discrimination, 2009

The *Law on the Prohibition of Discrimination, 2009* covers employment, labor and working conditions, promotions, and dismissals. Under this law, *sexual harassment* means any form of unwanted verbal, nonverbal, or physical conduct of a sexual nature with the aim or effect of harming the dignity of persons, especially when it creates an intimidating, hostile, degrading, humiliating, or offensive environment.

Title of legislation	Law on Gender Equality, 2003, as amended

The *Law On Gender Equality in Bosnia And Herzegovina* ("Gender Equality Law") defines *sexual harassment* as any behavior that in word, action, or psychological effect of a sexual nature in intent or effect inflicts injury on the dignity of a person or gives rise to intimidation, hostility, or demeaning, threatening or similar situations and which is motivated by belonging to another gender or different sexual orientation and which to the victim represents inappropriate physical, verbal, suggestive, or other behavior.

An employer must take effective measures to prevent *sexual harassment* in employment.

BIBLIOGRAPHY

Agency for Gender Equality of Bosnia and Herzegovina, 2010. Law on Gender Equality in Bosnia and Herzegovina Consolidated Version 2010. Available at: http://arsbih.gov.ba/wp-content/uploads/2014/02/GEL_32_10_E.pdf. Accessed May 7, 2019

refworld UNHCR The UN Refugee Agency, 2009. Law on the Prohibition of Discrimination. Available at: http://www.refworld.org/pdfid/4d302a9f2.pdf. Accessed May 7, 2019

BULGARIA

Sexual harassment is deemed to be discrimination.

Legislation

- Protection Against Discrimination Act, 2004, as amended

Title of legislation	Protection Against Discrimination Act, 2004, as amended

The *Protection Against Discrimination Act, 2004,* as amended, prohibits all forms of discrimination. *Sexual harassment and harassment on the grounds of sex* is deemed to be discrimination.

Sexual harassment and harassment related to sex are defined consistently with the EU's Equal Treatment Directive. Definitions cover both quid pro quo and hostile work environment sexual harassment.

Sexual harassment means any unwanted conduct of a sexual nature expressed physically, verbally, or in any other manner, which violates the dignity or honor of a person or creates a hostile, degrading, humiliating, or offensive environment, attitude or practice, in particular when the refusal to accept such conduct or the pressure to accept it could influence the taking of decisions affecting the person.

An employer who receives a complaint of sexual harassment at the workplace from an employee must immediately carry out an investigation, take measures to stop the harassment, and impose disciplinary sanction in cases where the harassment has been committed by another worker or employee.

BIBLIOGRAPHY

refworld UNHCR The UN Refugee Agency, 2006. Protection Against Discrimination Act, 2004 as amended. Available at: http://www.refworld.org/publisher,NATLEGBOD,LEGISLATION,BGR,44ae58d62d5,0.html. Accessed May 25, 2019

CROATIA

Sexual harassment, among other forms of harassment, is discussed in the context of protection of a worker's dignity under applicable Croatian legislation.

Legislation

- Labour Act, 2014
- Anti-Discrimination Act, 2009, as amended
- Gender Equality Act, 2008
- Criminal Code, 2011

Title of legislation Labour Act, 2014

The *Labour Act* regulates employment relationships in the Republic of Croatia unless otherwise provided for by another law or a published and valid international agreement, as concluded and ratified in accordance with the Constitution of the Republic of Croatia.

Sexual harassment is discussed in the context of a worker's dignity (Article 134) and is prohibited. (Chapter 5)

Article 134, the Protection of Workers' Dignity, states that the procedure and measures for the protection of workers' dignity from *sexual harassment* shall be regulated by special legislation, collective agreement, agreement between the works council, and the employer or working regulations.

This article requires the following:

- The employer employing at least 20 workers must appoint a person who would, in addition to him/her, be authorized to receive and deal with complaints related to the protection of the workers' dignity.
- The employer or person referred to above shall, within the time limit prescribed by the collective agreement, the agreement between the works council and the employer or working regulations, and within a maximum of eight days from the day of the filing of the complaint, examine the complaint and take all the necessary measures appropriate for a particular case to stop the sexual harassment, if he/she has established that harassment has taken place.
- Where the employer fails to take measures for the prevention of sexual harassment within the time limit referred to above, or if the

measures taken are clearly inappropriate, the worker who is a victim of sexual harassment shall have the right to stop working until he/she is ensured protection, provided that he/she sought protection in the court that has jurisdiction, within the following eight days.

- If there are circumstances under which it is not reasonable to expect that the employer will protect a worker's dignity, the worker shall not be obliged to file a complaint with the employer and shall have the right to stop working, provided that he/she sought protection before the competent court and notified the employer thereof, within eight days of the date of work interruption.
- During the period of interruption of work, the worker shall be entitled to remuneration in the amount he/she would have earned if he/she had actually worked.
- In the event of a valid judicial decision ruling that the worker's dignity was not violated, the employer may request the refund of remuneration.
- All information collected in the procedure for the protection of workers' dignity shall be confidential.
- The worker's behavior constituting sexual harassment shall be regarded as the breach of obligations arising from employment.
- The worker's resistance to the behavior constituting sexual harassment shall not be regarded as the breach of obligations arising from employment and must not be grounds for discrimination against the worker.

Title of legislation Anti-Discrimination Act, 2009, as amended

The *Antidiscrimination Act* covers *sexual harassment,* defining it as any verbal, non-verbal, or physical unwanted conduct of a sexual nature with the purpose or effect of violating the dignity of a person, and of creating an intimidating, hostile, degrading, or offensive environment. Provisions of the Act referring to discrimination apply accordingly to sexual harassment (Article 3). The Act does not set out specific requirements for the employer with regard to policies, training, or investigation.

Title of legislation Gender Equality Act, 2008

The *Gender Equality Act* defines the concept of discrimination based on gender and prohibits *sexual harassment*. Under Article 8, *sexual harassment* shall be considered discrimination.

Sexual harassment shall include any form of unwanted verbal or non-verbal, that is, physical behavior of sexual nature, which aims at or actually constitutes violation of the personal dignity and creates an unpleasant, unfriendly, humiliating, or insulting atmosphere.

The employer must provide a work environment free of sexual harassment, as well as a structure for handling complaints.

Title of legislation Criminal Code, 2011

In Croatia's Criminal Code, *Sexual Harassment* is addressed in Article 156 as follows:

(1) Whoever sexually harasses another person who is his or her subordinate or who is in a situation of dependence with respect to him or her or who is especially vulnerable due to age, illness, disability, addiction, pregnancy, or a severe physical or mental disability shall be punished by imprisonment not exceeding one year.
(2) Sexual harassment shall mean any form of unwanted verbal, non-verbal, or physical conduct of a sexual nature which aims at or effectively constitutes a violation of the dignity of a person, which creates an intimidating, hostile, degrading, or offensive environment.
(3) The criminal offence referred to in paragraph 1 of this Article shall be prosecuted upon request.

Workplace mistreatment is also provided for in Article 133, as follows:

(1) Whoever insults, humiliates, mistreats or otherwise disturbs another in the workplace or in relation to work and by doing so damages his or her health or violates his or her rights shall be punished by imprisonment not exceeding two years.
(2) The criminal offence referred to in paragraph 1 of this Article shall be prosecuted upon request.

BIBLIOGRAPHY

Croatian Parliament, 2008. The Anti-Discrimination Act. Available at: http://www.prs.hr/attachments/article/2127/Croatian%20Anti-discrimination%20Act.pdf. Accessed September 8, 2018

Croatian Parlimanent, 2011. Criminal Code. Available at: http://www.mvep.hr/files/file/dokumenti/prevodenje/zakoni/kazneni-zakon-nn-125-11-eng.pdf. Accessed August 25, 2019

Croatian Parliament, 2014. Labour Act. Available at: http://www.mrms.hr/wp-content/uploads/2015/03/labour-act.pdf. Accessed September 8, 2018

International Labour Organization, 2008. Gender Equality Act. Available at: http://www.ilo.org/wcmsp5/groups/public/---ed_protect/---protrav/---ilo_aids/documents/legaldocument/wcms_127456.pdf. Accessed September 8, 2018

GREECE

Greek laws states that sexual harassment is sex discrimination, which is prohibited.

Article 337(6) of the Greek Penal Code defines sexual abuse as a crime, and states anyone who is sexually harassing by exploiting the work position of the victim shall be liable to imprisonment of up to three years and a pecuniary penalty of at least 1,000 euros. Lewd gestures or suggestions for lewd acts may constitute a crime. (Note: in June 2019, a new Criminal Code and Criminal Procedure Code were ratified. Information on these new Codes is not contained here.)

Legislation

- Law No. 3896 of 2010 Concerning the Application of the Principle of Equal Opportunity and Treatment of Men and Women in Terms of Employment

Title of legislation	Law No. 3896 of 2010 Concerning the Application of the Principle of Equal Opportunity and Treatment of Men and Women in Terms of Employment

Law No. 3896 of 2010 Concerning the Application of the Principle of Equal Opportunity and Treatment of Men and Women in Terms of Employment (Law 3896/2010) states that termination of an employment contract is prohibited if based on reasons of sex or marital status or on retaliation by the employer, because of the non-compliance of the employee in sexual or other harassment against him or her.

BIBLIOGRAPHY

Greek Ombudsman, 2010. Law No. 3896 of 2010 Concerning the Application of the Principle of Equal Opportunity and Treatment of Men and Women in Terms of Employment. Available at (in Greek): https://www.ilo.org/dyn/natlex/docs/SERIAL/86905/98642/F412846679/2010-207.pdf. Accessed May 25, 2019

ROMANIA

Sexual harassment is considered gender-based discrimination under the Equal Opportunities Law.

Legislation

- Law No. 202/2002, republished 2010 On Equal Opportunities Between Women and Men
- Criminal Code

Title of legislation	Law No. 202/2002 On Equal Opportunities Between Women and Men, 2002, as amended

Under *Law No. 202/2002 On Equal Opportunities Between Women and Men, as amended* and republished 2010, *sexual harassment* is considered gender-based discrimination and defined as unwanted conduct of a sexual nature expressed physically, verbally, or nonverbally, with the purpose or effect of violating the dignity of a person, in particular when creating an intimidating, hostile, degrading, humiliating, or offensive environment. (Article 4)

Sexual harassment includes behavior having as its purpose to create at the workplace an atmosphere of intimidation, hostility or discouragement for the affected person; to negatively influence the situation of the employed person as regards the vocational promotion, wage or revenues of any nature or the access to vocational training or retraining, in the case of his or her refusal to accept an undesired behavior.

Under Article 12, to prevent and eliminate all behavior defined as gender-based discrimination, the employer shall:

- Provide internal regulations for employees infringing the personal dignity of other employees, by creating degrading, intimidating, hostile, humiliation or offending environments by committing the discriminatory actions as defined;
- Ensure the information of all employees on the prohibition of harassment and sexual harassment at the workplace, including by posting in visible places the internal regulations to prevent any act of gender-based discrimination; and

- Inform, immediately after the complaint, the public authorities in charge with implementation and control of the enforcement of the legislation on equal opportunities between women and men.

The employer's responsibilities also include informing all employees that harassment and sexual harassment are prohibited in the workplace. Company rules and regulations must include disciplinary sanctions for employees who violate the dignity of other employees;

Cases of sexual harassment are considered breaches of the law for which fines run as high as ROL 15–150 million (EUR 415–4,150).

Title of legislation Criminal Code

The *Criminal Code* defines *sexual harassment* under Article 223 as:

(1) Repeatedly soliciting sexual favors as part of an employment relationship or a similar relationship, if by so doing the victim was intimidated or placed in a humiliating situation, shall be punishable by no less than three months and no more than one year of imprisonment or by a fine.
(2) Criminal action shall be initiated based on a prior complaint filed by the victim.

Title of legislation Labour Code, No. 53/2003, as amended

The *Labour Code, No. 53/2003* prohibits discrimination including sex discrimination, but does not specifically refer to sexual harassment. Under Article 241, the employer shall draw up the internal regulations after consultations with the trade union or the employees' representatives, as applicable, which shall include rules on compliance with the principle of non-discrimination and removal of any form of dignity violation.

BIBLIOGRAPHY

Centre for Human Rights and Migration, 2007. Romanian Ordinance on Preventing and Punishing All Forms of Discrimination. Available at: http://cdom.rau.ro/download/Materiale%20didactice/Scoli%20Intensive/2016-Me

diation_Alternative_Dispute/ROMANIAN%20Anti%20Discrimination%20Ordinance%20and%20Amendments.pdf. Accessed February 14, 2019
International Labour Organization, 2002. Equal Opportunities Law 202/2002, as amended and Republished 2010. Available at: http://www.ilo.org/dyn/travail/docs/1532/LEGE%20%20%20Nr.%20202-2002%20equal%20opportunities%20betw.%20men%20and%20women.pdf. Accessed on May 25, 2019
Legislation Online. Criminal Code. Available at: https://www.legislationline.org/documents/section/criminal-codes/country/8/Romania/show. Accessed May 27, 2019
The Parliament. Labour Code. Available at: https://www.ilo.org/dyn/travail/docs/1530/Labour%20Code%20-%20last%20version.pdf. Accessed May 27, 2019

SERBIA

Three Serbian laws address sexual harassment in the workplace, discussed below. The country is in the process of adopting a new Gender Equality Law to replace the 2009 Gender Equality Law. Serbia's National Assembly discussed the draft of the new law in June 2018 (Source: National Assembly of the Republic of Serbia, 2018).

The first high-profile #MeToo trial in the Balkans: a secretary publicly accused the mayor of her small Serbian town of repeated sexual assault and harassment in the workplace. A year later, the mayor resigned after being charged by police and the former secretary is facing down mobs of men outside court and small-town power politics in the first high-profile #MeToo trial in the Balkans. Although the trial opened in February 2019, four of the five hearings so far have been postponed (Source: France 24, June 21, 2019. "Serbia's first #MeToo trial proves a lonely path").

Legislation

- Law on Prevention of Abuse at Work, 2010
- Labour Code, 2005, as amended
- Law on Gender Equality, 2009

Title of legislation	Law on the Prevention of Abuse at Work, 2010

The *Law on Prevention of Abuse at Work No. 36/10* regulates the prohibition of abuse at work and the procedure for the protection of persons exposed to *harassment* at work and other issues of importance for the prevention and protection harassment at work (Articles 1, 5). The law applies to employers and employees, including part-time employees, and its provisions apply to cases of *sexual harassment.*

The employer is required to organize the work in a way that as far as possible prevents the occurrence of abuse at work and provides the employees working conditions where they will not be exposed to abuse at work by an employer or employee. (Article 4)

Harassment shall include any active or passive conduct at work or related to work against an employee or group of employees, which recurs, aiming at or representing a violation of dignity, reputation, personal and professional integrity, health, or the employee's position, and which causes fear or creates an unfriendly, humiliating, or offensive environment, aggravates the working conditions or results in isolation of the employee, or leads the employee to terminate the contract of employment or another type of contract upon his own initiative. (Article 6)

The employer must protect the employee from harassment by protecting employees from abuse by measures which include providing an employee, prior to coming to work, written notice of the prohibition of abuse and exercise the rights, duties and responsibilities of the employee and employer regarding the prohibition of abuse; and implementing measures to inform and train employees and their representatives to identify the causes, forms and consequences of carrying out abuse. (Articles 7, 8)

The employer is responsible for the damage that the responsible person or employee performing the abuse causes another employee with the same employer (Article 9). Employers may be given fines up to 800,000 dinar (7,500 EUR).

Proceedings for protection from abuse are set forth in Articles 13–21. The right to apply for protection from abuse by the employer shall expire within six months from the day the assault was committed. (Article 22)

Title of legislation Labour Law, 2005, as amended

Serbia's *Labor Law No 24/05, as amended,* prohibits *sexual harassment* under Article 21. *Sexual harassment* is defined as "any verbal, non-verbal or physical behavior aimed at or representing violation of dignity of a person seeking employment or employee in the area of sexual life, causing fear or breeding adverse, humiliating or insulting environment." There is no other reference to sexual harassment.

Title of legislation Law on Gender Equality

A new Gender Equality Law will replace the *Law on Gender Equality No 104/2009.* As of June 2019 it was still a draft law.

Sexual harassment is "any unwanted verbal, non-verbal or physical act of a sexual nature, committed with the aim or with the purpose to violate personal dignity, establishment of intimidating, hostile, humiliating, degrading or offensive environment, which is based on sex." (Article 10(7))

The new law would define it as "any unwanted verbal, non-verbal or physical act of a sexual nature that is aimed at or constitutes a violation of personal dignity, and in particular if it creates fear, hostility, degrading or offensive environment."

Harassment, sexual harassment, or sexual blackmail at work or related to work, which is committed by an employee to another employee, is considered a violation of duties at work and as grounds to terminate the employment contract, as well as to expel the employee from work. An employee shall inform the employer in writing about the circumstances indicating his or her exposure to harassment, sexual harassment or sexual blackmail and request efficient protection. (Article 18)

The initiation of proceedings by an employee for gender-based discrimination, harassment, sexual harassment or sexual blackmail may not be considered a justified reason to terminate or discontinue the employment contract. (Article 20)

Pursuant to Article 54, a fine ranging from RSD 10,000 to 100,000 shall be imposed if the employer does not undertake measures to protect an employee from harassment, sexual harassment or sexual blackmail. (Article 18)

BIBLIOGRAPHY

France 24, June 21, 2019, Serbia's First #MeToo Trial Proves a Lonely Path. Available at: https://www.france24.com/en/20190621-serbias-first-metoo-trial-proves-lonely-path. Accessed August 27, 2019

International Labour Organization, 2005. Labor Law. Available at: http://www.ilo.org/dyn/travail/docs/2403/Labour%20Law%20Republic%20of%20Serbia.pdf. Accessed May 23, 2019 and 2014 amendment. Available at: https://www.ilo.org/wcmsp5/groups/public/---ed_protect/---protrav/---ilo_aids/documents/legaldocument/wcms_388397.pdf Accessed May 23, 2109

International Labour Organization, 2010. Law on Prevention of Abuse at Work No. 36/10). Available at (in Serbian): http://www.ilo.org/aids/legislation/WCMS_170961/lang--en/index.htm. Accessed May 23, 2019

http://www.legislationline.org, 2009. Law on Gender Equality. Available at: http://www.legislationline.org/documents/action/popup/id/16015. Accessed May 23, 2019

Ministry of Labor, Employment, Veterans' Affairs and Social Affairs. Sector for Anti-Discrimination Policy and Promotion of Gender Equality, Report on the Status of Protection and Gender Equality in 2018. Available at: https://

www.minrzs.gov.rs/sr/dokumenti/zakoni/sektor-za-antidiskriminacionu-politiku-i-unapredjenje-rodne-ravnopravnosti. Accessed June 18, 2019
National Assembly of the Republic of Serbia, 2018. Available at: http://www.parlament.gov.rs/Public_Debate_on_Gender_Equality_Draft_Law:at_National_Assembly.34380.537.html. Accessed June 18, 2019.

SLOVENIA

Legislation

- Employment Relationships Act, 2013
- Health and Safety at Work Act, 2011
- Criminal Code

Title of legislation Employment Relationships Act, 2013

The *Employment Relationships Act* considers *sexual harassment* discriminatory and prohibits it.

Sexual harassment is any form of undesired verbal, non-verbal or physical action or behavior of a sexual nature with the effect or intent of adversely affecting the dignity of a person, especially where this involves the creation of an intimidating, hateful, degrading, shaming or insulting environment.

Under Article 229, a fine of not less than SIT 1,000,000 shall be imposed on the employer or legal person if he has not provided protection against sexual harassment in accordance with Paragraph 1 of Article 45 of this Act. Article 45 (1) states that the employer shall provide a working environment in which none of the workers is subjected to sexual harassment on the part of the employer, a superior, or co-workers. To this end the employer must take appropriate steps to protect workers from sexual harassment in the workplace.

Title of legislation Health and Safety at Work Act, 2011

The *Health and Safety at Work Act,* 2011 sets forth measures to ensure health and safety at work. The employer shall adopt measures to prevent, eliminate, and manage, cases of violence, mobbing, harassment, and other forms of psychosocial risks at the workplace which can pose a threat to workers' health. A fine amounting from 2,000 to 40,000 EUR shall be imposed on an employer who fails to adopt measures to prevent, eliminate and manage cases of violence, mobbing, harassment and other forms of psychosocial risks at the workplace which can pose a threat to workers' health (Article 24). Psychosocial risks and harassment are not defined, nor is sexual harassment specifically mentioned.

Title of legislation	Criminal Code

The *Criminal Code,* Article 197: (1) Whoever degrades or frightens another person at the workplace or in relation to work with *sexual harassment,* physical violence, ill-treatment or unequal treatment shall be sentenced to imprisonment for not more than two years. (2) If the offence under the preceding paragraph results in psychological, psychosomatic or physical illness or reduction of work productivity of an employee, the perpetrator shall be sentenced to imprisonment for not more than three years.

BIBLIOGRAPHY

Criminal Code of the Republic of Slovakia. Available at: https://www.wipo.int/edocs/lexdocs/laws/en/si/si045en.pdf. Accessed May 25, 2019

Ministry of Labour, Family, Social Affairs and Equal Opportunities, 2013. Employment Relationships Act. Available http://www.mddsz.gov.si/en/legislation/. Accessed May 25, 2019

Ministry of Labour, Family, Social Affairs and Equal Opportunities, 2011. Law on Health and Safety at Work Act. Available at http://www.mddsz.gov.si/en/legislation/. Accessed May 7, 2019

BALTIC AND NORDIC COUNTRIES

> In the wake of #MeToo, many countries in the Nordic and Baltic regions have strengthened their legislation concerning abuse, harassment, and sexual violence against women.

A survey called "Initiatives and action in the Nordic and Baltic countries" was developed on the initiative of the Swedish presidency of the Nordic Council of Ministers in 2018. The material was compiled by NIKK and is based on data from these countries and supplemental interviews with key individuals. NIKK's survey highlights various initiatives that have been taken in the Nordic and Baltic countries (Source: NIKK, Nordic Information on Gender, 2018. "Initiatives and action in the wake of the Me Too movement").

The new survey entitled "One year after Me Too – Initiatives and action in the Nordic and Baltic countries" was developed on the initiative of the Swedish presidency of the Nordic Council of Ministers in 2018. The material was compiled by NIKK and is based on data from these countries and supplemental interviews with key individuals (Source: Nordic Information on Gender, 2018. "One year after Me Too – Initiatives and action in the Nordic and Baltic countries").

BIBLIOGRAPHY

NIKK - Nordic Information on Gender, 2018. Initiatives and Action in the Wake of the Me Too Movement. Available at: https://www.nikk.no/en/news/initiatives-and-action-in-the-wake-of-the-me-too-movement/. Accessed May 28, 2019

NIKK - Nordic Information on Gender, 2018. New Survey from NIKK: One Year after Me Too – Initiatives and Action in the Nordic and Baltic Countries which are Denmark, Estonia, Finland, Iceland, Latvia, Lithuania, Norway and Sweden. Nordic Information on Gender, One Year after Me Too – Initiatives and Action in the Nordic and Baltic Countries. Survey Is Produced by NIKK, Nordic Information on Gender, Text by Ida Måwe Gothenburg. Available at: https://www.nikk.no/en/publications/one-year-after-me-too/. Accessed August 19, 2019

BALTIC STATES

Laws in Estonia, Latvia, and Lithuania treat sexual harassment as a violation of work responsibilities, and permit dismissal of employees at fault without notice or severance payment.

ESTONIA

Sexual harassment is addressed in the Gender Equality Act. Additionally, Estonia amended in its Penal Code in 2017 to introduce sexual harassment as a separate category of offence.

Legislation

- The Gender Equality Act, 2004, as amended
- Labour Law, 2002
- Penal Code

Title of legislation The Gender Equality Act, 2004, as amended

The *Gender Equality Act*, 2004, as amended, prohibits direct discrimination, which includes *sexual harassment.*

In the words of the law:

> *sexual harassment* occurs when any unwanted verbal, non-verbal or physical sexual behavior or activity, the object or effect of which is to diminish the dignity of a person, in particular by creating a disturbing, intimidating, hostile, degrading, humiliating or offensive atmosphere.

It further mores states:

> gender harassment occurs when there is unwanted sex-related behavior or activity whose purpose or actual effect is to diminish the dignity of the person and to create a disturbing, intimidating, hostile, degrading, humiliating or offensive environment.

The employer shall ensure that employees are protected from sexual harassment in the working environment.

An employer discriminates if he or she harasses a person by reason of his or her sex or sexual activity or fails to perform the obligation provided for in clause 11 (1) (4) of this Act. Pursuant to section 6 (5), the employer is responsible for failure to comply with the duty of care if he or she knew or should have known about the occurrence of gender or sexual harassment and did not take the necessary measures to end the harassment.

Title of legislation	Penal Code, 2002, as amended

The 2017 amendment to the *Penal Code* added §153, "Sexual harassment," which states:

(1) An intentional physical act of sexual nature against the will of another person committed against him or her with degrading objectives or consequences is punishable by a fine of up to 300 fine units or by detention.
(2) The same act, if committed by a legal person, is punishable by a fine of up to 2,000 EUR.

BIBLIOGRAPHY

Gender Equality Act, 2004, as amended. https://www.genderportal.eu/sites/default/files/resource_pool/estonia_gender_equality_act_english_0.pdf. Accessed May 26, 2019

Riigi Teataja. Penal Code. Available at: https://www.riigiteataja.ee/en/eli/508092017002/consolide. Accessed February 17, 2019

LATVIA

Sexual harassment is viewed as a violation of a person's dignity in the Labour Law in Latvia.

Legislation

- Labour Law 2001, as amended

Title of legislation Labour Law 2001, as amended

The Labour Law, 2001, as amended, regulates employment issues and obligates employers to ensure fair and safe working conditions that are not harmful to health. It does not impose any duties on employers specifically related to sexual harassment; any duties imposed on employers relate to discrimination generally. The law states:

> Harassment of a person and instructions to discriminate against him or her shall also be deemed to be discrimination within the meaning of this Law.

Although *sexual harassment* is not expressly mentioned or defined, Article 29 prohibits differential treatment. In the words of the law (Article 29 (7) and (8)):

> Infringement of a person within the meaning of this Law is the subordination of a person to such undesirable behavior related to his or her affiliation to a particular sex, including sexual acts, if the purpose or result of such action is the violation of the dignity of the person and intimidating, hostile, hateful, or creating a degrading, degrading or offensive environment. In the event of a violation of the prohibition of differential treatment and the prohibition of adverse consequences, an employee has the right to claim damages and compensation for non-pecuniary damage in addition to other rights specified in this Law. In the event of a dispute, the court determines the amount of compensation for moral damages at its own discretion.

BIBLIOGRAPHY

Acts of the Republic of Latvia, 2001. Labour Law. https://likumi.lv/ta/en/id/26019-labour-law. Accessed May 29, 2019

http://likumi.lv/, 2001. Labour Law. Available at: https://likumi.lv/doc.php?id=26019. Accessed February 17, 2019

LITHUANIA

Sexual harassment constitutes discrimination on the grounds of gender in Lithuania.

Legislation

- Law on Equal Treatment, 2003, as amended
- Gender Equality Law, 1998, as amended
- Labour Code, 2017

Title of legislation	Law on Equal Treatment, 2003, as amended

The *Law on Equal Treatment* (2003 November 18 d. No. IX–1826), as amended, imposes a duty on the employer to take measures to prevent sexual harassment against any employee or civil servant (Article 5). The law does not refer to sexual harassment beyond this provision and does not oblige an employer to adopt a sexual harassment policy.

Title of legislation	Law on Equal Opportunities for Men and Women, 1998 as amended

The *Law on Equal Opportunities for Men and Women (1998 December 1 d. No. VIII–947)*, as amended, prohibits discrimination, which includes *sexual harassment.*

Sexual harassment shall mean any form of unwanted and insulting verbal, written or physical conduct of a sexual nature with a person with the purpose or effect of violating the dignity of a person, in particular when creating an intimidating, hostile, humiliating or offensive environment. (Article 1(6))

When implementing equal rights for women and men at the workplace, the employer must take appropriate measures to prevent sexual harassment or harassment of the employees (Article 5). The Equal Opportunities Ombudsperson shall investigate the complaints related to sexual harassment and shall provide objective and unbiased consultations. (Article 12)

A person who has suffered sexual harassment shall have the right to demand that the guilty persons reimburse the pecuniary and non-pecuniary damage in the manner prescribed by the Civil Code of the Republic of Lithuania. (Article 24)

Title of legislation Labour Code, 2017

The *Labour Code* prohibits sexual harassment. The employer is required to take measures to ensure that the employee does not experience sexual harassment at the workplace and that the employee is protected if he or she files a complaint. The employer shall have the right to terminate the contract without notice and not to pay the severance pay, if the employee commits sexual harassment.

Title of legislation Criminal Code, 2017

The *Criminal Code of the Republic of Lithuania* provides that a person who, in seeking sexual contact or satisfaction, harasses a person subordinate to him or her at the workplace or otherwise by vulgar or comparable actions or by making offers or hints will be considered to have committed a misdemeanor and may be punished by a fine or by imprisonment or by arrest. A person shall be held liable for an act provided for in this Article only subject to a complaint filed by the victim or a statement by his authorised representative or at the prosecutor's request. (Article 152 of the Criminal Code of the Republic of Lithuania)

BIBLIOGRAPHY

International Labour Organization, 2010. Law on Safety and Health at Work. Available at: http://www.ilo.org/wcmsp5/groups/public/---ed_protect/---protrav/---ilo_aids/documents/legaldocument/wcms_242329.pdf. Accessed February 17, 2019

Ministry of Social Security and Labour, 1 December 1998 No VIII–94, As Last amended on 15 July 2014 No XII–1023. Republic of Lithuania Law on Equal Opportunities for Women and Men. Available at: https://e-seimas.lrs.lt/portal/legalAct/lt/TAD/488fe061a7c611e59010bea026bdb259?jfwid=q8i8817y0. Accessed February 17, 2019

Republic of Lithuania, 2003. Law on Equal Treatment. Available at: https://www.lygybe.lt/data/public/uploads/2016/10/law-on-equal-treatment_no.-ix-1826.pdf. Accessed February 17, 2019

United Nations Office of Drugs and Crime. Criminal Code. Available at: https://sherloc.unodc.org/res/cld/document/ltu/criminal_code_of_lithuania_html/Lithuania_Criminal_Code_2000_as_amd_2010.pdf. Accessed April 13, 2019

Seimas of the Republic of Lithuania, 2002. Labour Code, as amended 2017. Available at: https://socmin.lrv.lt/en/activities/labour-and-employment/labour-law/presentation-of-the-labour-code.

Seimas of the Republic of Lithuania. Labour Code. Available at: https://www.ilo.org/dyn/natlex/docs/ELECTRONIC/104719/127853/F725248113/new%20Labour%20Code%20Lith%20as%20of%2014%20Sept2016.pdf. Accessed February 17, 2019

NORDIC COUNTRIES

Sexual harassment in the workplace is illegal in all Nordic countries. The employer has responsibility for creating a work environment free from sexual harassment. But despite employers' far-reaching responsibilities, reports of violations remain disturbingly common. One problem, say experts, is that the laws are not followed.

(Source: NIKK, Nordic Information on Gender, January 21, 2018. "Review: sexual harassment in the workplace remains widespread in the Nordic countries")

BIBLIOGRAPHY

NIKK - Nordic Information on Gender, January 21, 2018. Review: Sexual Harassment in the Workplace Remains Widespread in the Nordic Countries. Available at: https://www.nikk.no/en/news/review-sexual-harassment-in-the-workplace-remains-widespread-in-the-nordic-countries/. Accessed August 28, 2019

DENMARK

> Denmark's Ministry of Employment enacted a Bill amending the Danish Act on Equal Treatment of Men and Women in relation to sexual harassment, effective January 1, 2019.

Although sexual harassment was already prohibited under the Act, the amendment specifies that sexual harassment is prohibited, addressing it as a specific offense rather than a form of gender discrimination.

In the Explanatory Notes to the Bill, it is stated that the amendment of the Act is intended to specify that "casual," "informal" or "bantering" workplace behaviour or language does not mean that employees must generally put up with offensive behaviour or language, explaining that the tone of communication or conduct at the workplace was not chosen by the individual employee. For this reason, tone or conduct should not form part of the assessment of whether the prohibition on sexual harassment has been violated. This means that in the future, the courts must take into account the nature of the event(s) and assess whether particular behaviour or communication would have been regarded as unacceptable at a workplace with a "more professional or restrictive tone of communication." This is a change from the prior approach to what constitutes sexual harassment, which was more subjective, taking into account the general culture of a workplace.

Since 2008, municipal and regional workplaces in Denmark have been required to actively prepare guidelines for how to prevent harassment, including sexual harassment, and violence based on the Social Partners securing the commitment of municipalities and regions in terms of preventing, identifying, and managing, harassment and violence, including sexual harassment, at work (Source: "Social partners behind the 2008 agreement: local government Denmark, Danish Regions and the Danish Association of Local Government Employees' Organisations").

Legislation

- Working Environment Act, 2010, as amended
- Executive Order on the Performance of Work, 2004, as amended
- Equal Treatment of Men and Women as regards Access to Employment, Consolidation Act No. 734 of 28 June 2006, as amended
- Act on Gender Equality of Women and Men, 2013, as amended

Title of legislation	Working Environment Act, 2010, as amended

The *Working Environment Act* is a framework Act which lays down general provisions. The Act is implemented through executive orders. It lays down the general objectives and requirements in relation to the working environment and covers physical and psychological work. It emphasizes that individual workplaces should be designed in a way which will prevent employees from being forced to leave the labour market due to attrition and stress. Factors which in the short or long term may lead to health risks of a physical or mental character must be remedied.

The Working Environment Act states that it is the employer's duty to ensure that the working environment is free of harassment. The employer must prepare a written workplace assessment, which must include the issue of *sexual harassment.* If an employee feels that he or she is the object of harassment, the employer is obliged to discuss the problem in the occupational safety organization or the liaison committee.

The employer may be liable for sexual harassment by a worker's superiors, peers, and clients. An employer is liable if the employer is aware of the harassment and does not take action to deal with it. The employer is not liable for the sexual harassment if he or she is not aware of it.

Title of legislation	Executive Order on the Performance of Work, as amended

The *Executive Order on the Performance of Work, 2004, as amended,* applies to any work performed for an employer.

9a. In connection with the performance of work, it shall be ensured that the work does not involve a risk of physical or mental impairment to health as a result of bullying, including sexual harassment.

The obligations under this executive order shall rest on employers, business managers, supervisors and other employees, suppliers, project planners, repairers, etc. in accordance with the general rules laid down by the Working Environment Act.

Title of legislation	Consolidation Act on Equal Treatment of Men and Women as regards

Access to Employment, 2006

Consolidation Act No. 734/2006 consolidated the *Act on Equal Treatment of Men and Women as Regards Access to Employment,* and prohibits discrimination on the basis of sex.

Part 1 on the scope of the Act defines *sexual harassment* and harassment as "discrimination on the ground of sex," stating that it is prohibited. It continues: "Any person's rejection of or consent to that type of conduct must not be used as grounds for a decision concerning the person in question."

Specific definitions are as follows:

(5) Harassment shall be understood as taking place when any form of unwanted verbal, nonverbal or physical conduct is exhibited in relation to one person's sex for the purpose or effect of violating the dignity of a person and of creating an intimidating, hostile, degrading, humiliating or offensive environment.
(6) Harassment shall be understood as taking place when any form of unwanted verbal, nonverbal or physical conduct with sexual undertones is exhibited for the purpose or effect of violating the dignity of a person, in particular by creating an intimidating, hostile, degrading, humiliating or offensive environment.

Denmark's Ministry of Employment enacted a Bill to amend the Danish Act on Equal Treatment of Men and Women in relation to sexual harassment, effective January 1, 2019. Sexual harassment had been classified as a form of gender discrimination under the Danish Equal Treatment Act and consequently prohibited, but (as noted in the introduction) the Act was amended to state that sexual harassment is prohibited in the workplace as a specific offense and that workplace culture should not be a factor in assessing whether a breach has occurred. Compensation awards were also increased.

The bill specified that employers' obligations to provide equal employment terms for men and women also includes a prohibition on sexual harassment. This aspect of the amendment is meant to set out the prohibition on sexual harassment that is already contained in the Danish Act on Equal Treatment of Men and Women.

Title of legislation	Act on Gender Equality of Women and Men, 2007, as amended

The *Act on Gender Equality of Women and Men, 2007, as amended,* states that its purpose is also to counteract direct and indirect discrimination on the grounds of gender and to counteract *sexual harassment.* Persons who are exposed to sexual harassment may be awarded compensation.

In this connection, special regard shall be paid to whether a relationship of dependence has existed between the person who has been exposed to the harassment and the person who has exercised it.

BIBLIOGRAPHY

Arbejdsmiljo, n.d. What Is Sexual Harassment. Available at: https://amid.dk/viden-og-forebyggelse/psykisk-arbejdsmiljoe/seksuel-chikane/viden-om/hvad-er-seksuel-chikane/. Accessed May 28, 2019

Danish Working Environment Authority, 2010. Working Environment Act. Available at: https://amid.dk/da/regler/love-og-eu-forordninger/arbejdsmiljoe-sam-1084/. Accessed February 22, 2019

Danish Working Environment Authority, 2010. Executive Order on the Working Environment Act. Available at: http://arbejdstilsynet.dk/da/regler/love/sam-1072-arbejdsmiljoloven.

Danish Working Environment Authority, 2004. Executive Order on the Performance of Work. Available at: http://engelsk.arbejdstilsynet.dk/en/regulations/executive-orders/559-performance-of-work. Accessed February 22, 2019

http://www.kl.dk/, 2010. Avoiding Harassment and Violence in Danish Municipal and Regional Workplaces. Available at: http://www.kl.dk/ImageVaultFiles/id_46479/cf_202/Avoiding_Harassment_and_Violence.PDF. Accessed February 22, 2019

Ministry of Employment, 2006. Consolidation Act on Equal Treatment of Men and Women as Regards Access to Employment. Available at: https://www.legislationline.org/documents/id/20335. Accessed March 5, 2019

Working Environment Information Centre, n.d. Psychosocial Work. Available at: http://www.arbejdsmiljoviden.dk/Emner/Psykosocialt-arbejdsmiljo. Accessed March 5, 2019

Ministry of Gender Equality, 2013. Executive Order on the Gender Equality Act. Available at: https://www.retsinformation.dk/Forms/R0710.aspx?id=160578. Accessed May 27, 2019

Act on Gender Equality, 2000. Available at: https://www.wcwonline.org/pdf/lawcompilation/Denmark-genderequality.pdf. Accessed May 28, 2019

KL, 2010. Avoiding Harassment and Violence in Danish Municipal and Regional Workplaces. Available at https://www.kl.dk/ImageVaultFiles/id_46479/cf_202/Avoiding_Harassment_and_Violence.PDF/. Accessed February 22, 2019.

FINLAND

> Sexual harassment is considered discrimination under Finland's Equality Act.

A January 2018 survey commissioned by the Confederation of Finnish Industries (EK) about sexual harassment in the workplace found that employees who have been harassed are often afraid of not being taken seriously if they speak up. The survey (by pollster Taloustutkimus) asked approximately 2,100 people between 18 and 64 years old whether they had faced sexual harassment, who the harasser was, and whether the victim faced further harassment after the first incident.

Thirty-eight percent of female respondents said they had experienced sexual harassment at work while 9 percent of male respondents also reported having experienced workplace sexual harassment. Only a quarter of workplace sexual harassment incidents in Finland end up being reported to supervisors or other company representatives.

The survey found that sexual harassment is most often carried out by a client against a company employee, with 60 percent of sexual harassment incidents involving customers. However, supervisors and coworkers also carried out some of the incidents (Source: Uutiset News, February 13, 2018. "#metoo: vast majority of workplace sexual harassment in Finland goes unreported").

Legislation

- Act on Equality Between Women and Men No. 609/1986, as amended
- Criminal Code, 1989, as amended
- The Occupational Health and Safety Act, No. 738/2002, as amended

Title of legislation	Act on Equality Between Women and Men No. 609/1986, as amended

The *Act of Equality between Women and Men No. 609/1986* ("Act"), *as amended,* also called the Equality Act, is the primary legislation addressing sexual harassment.

It prohibits *sexual harassment* and gender-based harassment. *Sexual harassment* is defined as:

> verbal, non-verbal or physical unwanted conduct of a sexual nature by which a person's psychological or physical integrity is violated

> intentionally or factually, in particular by creating an intimidating, hostile, degrading, humiliating or offensive atmosphere. In this Act, gender-based harassment means unwanted conduct that is not of a sexual nature but which is related to the gender of a person, their gender identity or gender expression, and by which the person's psychological or physical integrity is intentionally or factually violated and an intimidating, hostile, degrading, humiliating or offensive atmosphere is created.
>
> *(Section 7)*

Section 8d (232/2005) Harassment in the workplace states as follows:

> The action of an employer shall be deemed to constitute discrimination prohibited under this Act if, upon receiving information that an employee has been a victim of sexual or other gender-based harassment in the workplace, the employer neglects to take the steps available to eliminate the harassment.

Title of legislation	Criminal Code, 1989, as amended

The *Criminal Code, 1989, as amended,* states that *sexual harassment* may also be punished under the Criminal Code.

Section 5(a)—Sexual harassment (509/2014) goes on to say that a person who, by touching, commits a sexual act towards another person that is conducive to violating the right of this person to sexual self-determination, shall be sentenced, unless punishment is provided elsewhere in this Chapter for the act, for *sexual harassment* to a fine or to imprisonment for at most six months.

Title of legislation	The Occupational Health and Safety Act, No. 738/2002, as amended

The Occupational Health and Safety Act, No. 738/2002, as amended, covers physical and psychological violence, including *sexual harassment.*

Although *sexual harassment* is not expressly defined, the employer is required to protect employees from violence and the threat of violence.

Definitions include:

- Physical violence: the use of physical force against another person or group that results in physical, sexual or psychological harm.

- Psychological violence: intentional use of power against another person or group that can result in harm to physical, mental, spiritual, moral or social development.
- Violence: a long-term recurring bullying, oppression, degradation or other negative behavior designed to make another person feel defenseless.

If harassment or other inappropriate treatment of an employee occurs at work and causes hazards or risks to the employee's health, the employer, after becoming aware of the matter, shall take available measures for remedying the situation. (Section 28)

Title of legislation	Non-Discrimination Act No. 1325/2014

Finland's *Non-Discrimination Act (1325/2014)* increased requirements for preventing workplace discrimination. Direct and indirect discrimination includes harassment and is prohibited. Harassment occurs if the offensive behavior is related to prohibited grounds of discrimination and behaviors are degrading or humiliating or intimidating to a person, and create a hostile or offensive environment (Section 14). However, the grounds of prohibited discrimination do not include sex or gender nor is sexual harassment specifically mentioned.

BIBLIOGRAPHY

Uutiset News, #Metoo: Vast Majority of Workplace Sexual Harassment in Finland Goes Unreported, February 13, 2018. Available at: https://yle.fi/uutiset/osasto/news/metoo_vast_majority_of_workplace_sexual_harassment_in_finland_goes_unreported/10073601. Accessed August 13, 2019

Ministry of Social Affairs and Health, Finland Act on Equality Between Women and Men, 1986. No. 609/1986 (Act) as amended. Available at: https://www.finlex.fi/en/laki/kaannokset/1986/en19860609_20160915.pdf. Accessed February 27, 2019

Ministry of Justice, 2015. Criminal Code of Finland (39/1889, amendments up to 766/2015 Included). Available at: http://www.finlex.fi/en/laki/kaannokset/1889/en18890039.pdf. Accessed March 19, 2019

Ministry of Justice, 2014. Non-Discrimination Act. Available at: http://finlex.fi/fi/laki/ajantasa/2014/20141325#L6P29. Accessed February 27, 2019

Ministry of Social Affairs and Health, 2002. Occupational Safety and Health Act. Available at: https://www.finlex.fi/en/laki/kaannokset/2002/en20020738_20060053.pdf. Accessed March 5, 2019

NORWAY

Legislation

- Act Relating to Equality and a Prohibition Against Discrimination (Equality and Anti-Discrimination Act), 2018
- The Working Environment Act, No. 62/2005, as amended

Title of legislation	Act Relating to Equality and a Prohibition Against Discrimination (Equality and Anti-Discrimination Act)

The *Act Relating to Equality and Anti-discrimination* (Equality and Anti-discrimination Act) was approved in 2017. The four previous laws—the Gender Equality Act and the three anti-discrimination acts—were replaced by this law, effective January 1, 2018. The Equality and Discrimination Act 2017, as amended, applies to all employers.

The prohibition against harassment prohibits *sexual harassment,* defined in Section 13 as "any form of unwanted sexual attention that has the purpose or effect of being offensive, frightening, hostile, degrading, humiliating or troublesome."

Employers and managers of organizations must prevent and stop harassment and sexual harassment in their area of responsibility.

Title of legislation	The Working Environment Act, No. 62/2005 as amended

The Act relating to working environment, working hours, and employment protection, etc. (*Working Environment Act No. 62/2005,* as amended) covers the *psychosocial work environment.* The employer is responsible for ensuring that the working environment is fully satisfactory regarding employees' physical and mental health and welfare and for ensuring equality.

Although sexual harassment is not specifically referred to, this law should be recognized by an employer, as the psychosocial work environment can include sexual harassment.

Working Environment Act, 2005 (amended 2019) Section 4–3 contains the requirements regarding the psychosocial working environment. It states:

(1) The work shall be arranged so as to preserve the employees' integrity and dignity.
(2) Efforts shall be made to arrange the work so as to enable contact and communication with other employees of the undertaking.
(3) Employees shall not be subjected to harassment or other improper conduct.
(4) Employees shall, as far as possible, be protected against violence, threats and undesirable strain as a result of contact with other persons.

BIBLIOGRAPHY

Ministry of Children and Equality, 2018. Act Relating to Equality and a Prohibition against Discrimination (Equality and Anti-Discrimination Act). Available at https://lovdata.no/dokument/NLE/lov/2017-06-16-51#KAPITTEL_1. Accessed May 28, 2019

Ministry of Labour and Social Affairs, 2017. Working Environment Act 2017, as amended. Available at: https://lovdata.no/dokument/NLE/lov/2005-06-17-62. Accessed May 28, 2019

SWEDEN

> The Government of Sweden takes action against sexual violence and harassment: The #MeToo movement in Sweden strongly demonstrates that more needs to be done to combat sexual harassment and sexual violence in workplaces and society at large.

The Swedish Government requires all employers to take responsibility for a secure work environment. In the area of work environment and discrimination there are already many tools and relevant legislation, but the power and size of the petitions show that there are deficiencies in compliance with the regulations. For this reason, Minister for Employment Ylva Johansson and Minister for Gender Equality Åsa Regnér have met with the labour market and union partners, and several ministers have convened meetings with heads of government agencies and business leaders in order to focus on the responsibility of employers to counteract sexual violence and harassment (Source: Government Offices of Sweden, January 3, 2018. "The Government of Sweden takes action against sexual violence and harassment").

Further, Culture and Democracy Minister Alice Bah Kuhnke says she "totally changed [her] agenda" at the end of last year to make sexual harassment issues a priority. Looking forward, one clear goal she has in mind is continuing work to strengthen Sweden's Discrimination Act (Source: The Local, December 10, 2018. "Sweden in focus: one year on, what did #MeToo achieve in Sweden?" by Catherine Edwards).

#MeToo industry-specific developments: the culture sector has seen some of the most radical changes, after the #tystnadtagning letter in which hundreds of women detailed sexual abuse in the industry inspired over 60 further industry-specific "#MeToo initiatives." Specifically, in late 2017, 456 Swedish theatre stars shared stories of sex harassment (Source: The Local, December 10, 2018. "Sweden in focus: one year on, what did #MeToo achieve in Sweden?" by Catherine Edwards).

Additionally, Sweden's #Teknisktfel movement exposes sexual harassment in the tech industry. #MeToo has rapidly spread across Sweden with over 65 industry-specific callouts (ranging from the culinary world to doctors and medical students to opera singers). Petitions have been signed by some 60,000 women in the country (Source: Public Radio International, June 11, 2018. "Sweden's #Teknisktfel movement exposes sexual harassment in the tech industry," by Karis Hustad).

The Employer's Responsibility—A 2018 brochure: "Sexual harassment—between the person being exposed and the person who exposes you (ADI 713)" was produced by the Swedish Work Environment Authority and the Discrimination Ombudsman to help the employer know his or her responsibility as an employer. It contains an introduction on what sexual harassment is and what legislation exists, a section on preventive work, and a section on how the employer is expected to act if sexual harassment still occurs at the workplace. Employers are responsible for working preventively against sexual harassment and acting to stop it if it nevertheless arises (Source: "Sexual harassment—between the victim and the victim you stand (ADI 713)").

Legislation

- Discrimination Act, No. 567/2008, as amended
- Victimization at Work, 1994
- Organisational and Social Work Environment (AFS 2015:4), 2016

Title of legislation	Discrimination Act, No. 567/2008, as amended 2017

The *Discrimination Act* defines *sexual harassment* as discrimination and as conduct of a sexual nature that violates someone's dignity. An employer may not discriminate against his or her employees, applicants, or those performing work as temporary or borrowed labour.

If the employer becomes aware that an employee considers that he or she has been subjected in connection with work to *sexual harassment* by someone performing work or carrying out a traineeship at the employer's establishment, the employer must investigate the circumstances surrounding the alleged harassment and where appropriate take the measures that can reasonably be demanded to prevent harassment in the future. This obligation also applies with respect to a person carrying out a traineeship or performing work as temporary or borrowed labour.

Section 18 states that an employer may not expose an employee to retaliation because the employee has rejected the employer's sexual harassment.

Title of legislation	Ordinance of the Swedish National Board of Occupational Safety and Health Containing Provisions on Measures Against Victimization at Work, 1994

The *Ordinance of the Swedish National Board of Occupational Safety and Health*, effective 1994, applies to all activities in which employees can be subjected to victimization at work.

Victimization is defined in Section 1 as recurrent reprehensible or distinctly negative actions which are directed against individual employees in an offensive manner and can result in those employees being placed outside the workplace community.

Guidance on Section 1 states as follows:

> Victimization in the form of various kinds of reprehensible behaviour can be committed both by employees and by the employer personally or his representatives. The phenomena commonly referred to, for example, as adult bullying, mental violence, social rejection and harassment—including sexual harassment—have come to be seen more and more as problems of working life in their own right and will be collectively referred to here as victimization.

Instances of victimization can include persecution in various forms, threats, and the inspiration of fear or degradation such as *sexual harassment.*

The Act places the onus on the employer to plan and organize work so as to prevent victimization and to make it clear to employees that victimization is not acceptable. The employer is responsible for the early detection of signs of victimization, prompt counter measures to deal with victimization, and making support available to employees who have been targeted. (Sections 2–6)

Title of legislation	Organisational and Social Work Environment (AFS 2015:4), 2016

The Swedish Work Environment Authority has issued provisions on the *Organisational and social work environment (AFS 2015:4)*, effective March 31, 2016, pursuant to the Work Environment Ordinance (SFS 1997:1166) in order to establish general recommendations designed to promote a good working environment at workplaces in Sweden.

Provisions on victimization are included. Victimization is defined as actions directed against one or more employees in an abusive manner, which could lead to ill health or their being placed outside the community of the workplace.

Section 6 states that the employer shall see to it that managers and supervisors have knowledge on how to prevent and handle victimization and that there are prerequisites for putting this knowledge into practice, such as by providing training, preferably for managers, supervisors and safety representatives together. Training can be provided by occupational health services or other resource with competence in the field.

The employer is required to make it clear that victimization will not be tolerated at work and shall take measures to counteract conditions in the work environment that could give rise to such victimization. This clarification is best done in a written policy. Managers and supervisory staff have a particular responsibility as regards preventing, noticing and dealing with victimization. (Section 13)

Section 14 states:

> The employer shall ensure that there are procedures for how victimization is to be handled. The procedures should indicate who receives information that victimization is occurring; what the recipient is to do with the information; and how and where victims can quickly receive help. The employer shall make these procedures known to all employees.

BIBLIOGRAPHY

Government Offices of Sweden, January 3, 2018. The Government of Sweden Takes Action against Sexual Violence and Harassment. Available at https://www.government.se/articles/2018/01/the-government-of-sweden-takes-action-against-sexual-violence-and-harassment/. Accessed August 21, 2019

The Local Sweden in Focus: One Year on, What Did #MeToo Achieve in Sweden? by Catherine Edwards, December 10, 2018. Available at: https://www.thelocal.se/20181210/one-year-on-what-did-metoo-achieve-in-sweden. Accessed August 21, 2019

Public Radio International (PRI), June 11, 2018. Sweden's #Teknisktfel Movement Exposes Sexual Harassment in the Tech Industry, by Karis Hustad. Available at: https://www.pri.org/stories/2018-06-11/swedens-teknisktfel-movement-exposes-sexual-harassment-tech-industry. Accessed August 25, 2019

Swedish Work Environment Authority, 2018. Sexual Harassment - between the Victim and the Victim You Stand (ADI 713), Brochure. Available at: https://www.av.se/arbetsmiljoarbete-och-inspektioner/publikationer/broschyrer/sexuella-trakasserier---mellan-den-som-utsatts-och-den-som-utsatter-star-du/. Accessed August 25, 2019

Government Offices of Sweden, 2014. Discrimination Act, 2008, as amended 2017. Available at: http://www.riksdagen.se/sv/dokument-lagar/dokument/svensk-

forfattningssamling/diskrimineringslag-2008567_sfs-2008-567. Accessed May 28, 2019
Statute Book of the Swedish National Board of Occupational Safety and Health, 1993. Ordinance AFS 1993:17, Victimization At Work. Available at: https://www.av.se/globalassets/filer/publikationer/foreskrifter/engelska/victimization-at-work-provisions-1993-17.pdf. Accessed February 3, 2019
Swedish Work Environment Authority, 2015. 2015 Provisions and General Recommendations on Organisational and Social Work Environment. Available at: https://www.av.se/globalassets/filer/publikationer/foreskrifter/engelska/organisational-and-social-work-environment-afs2015-4.pdf. Accessed February 3, 2019
Swedish Work Environment Authority. The Organisational and Social Work Environment – Key Pieces of the Puzzle in Shaping a Good Work Environment. Guide for Implementation of the Swedish Work Environment Authority's Provisions Concerning the Organisational and Social Work Environment, AFS 2015:4 Available at: https://www.av.se/globalassets/filer/publikationer/bocker/books/the-organisational-and-social-work-environment-h457.pdf. Accessed February 3, 2019

BELGIUM

> Sexual harassment in Belgium is principally dealt with under provisions on psychosocial risks in the workplace.

Sexual harassment is treated legally as one of a number of psychosocial risks under the law on wellbeing at work, which addresses employee health and safety. Rather than being limited to violence, harassment, and sexual harassment at work, all psychosocial risks that could lead to stress became covered pursuant to September 2014 legislation, which requires that employers must recognize them as they do other risks to employees' health. Regulations relating to the prevention of psychosocial risks are very comprehensive.

A business or company is required to take measures to prevent sexual harassment. Such measures must be based on a risk analysis and will differ from one business to another, taking into account factors such as the activities, the context, and whether it is a large or small organization. Employers also need to implement internal procedures to enable employees who have been sexually harassed to contact a neutral and objective person of trust and/or a specialized prevention counsellor (usually someone who is external to the company and a certified psychologist). Employees who use these internal procedures are protected against dismissal. Finally, employers should provide psychological assistance and support to victims.

Sexual harassment at work is considered a crime under Belgium's Social Criminal Code. Companies and businesses which do not comply with the legislation on psychosocial risks at work risk criminal penalties and can be ordered to pay damages to employees who have been victims. The harasser can also be liable under both the civil and criminal law.

Legislation

- Act of 4 August 1996 on Welfare of Workers in the Performance of their Work, as amended
- Social Criminal Code, 2011, as amended

Title of legislation	Act of 4 August 1996 on Welfare of Workers in the Performance of their Work, as amended

The Act of 4 August 1996 ("Welfare Act") on the welfare of workers when carrying out their work, also known as *the Welfare Law,* and subsequent Royal Decrees, make up the *Code on Welfare at Work* ("Code"), the basis for the legislation on health and safety at work. The Welfare Act lists the general obligations of for all employers in Belgium, requiring them to take the necessary measures to promote workers' wellbeing, including the prevention of psychosocial risks at work, one of which is *sexual harassment.* In addition, implementing decrees have been enacted. These provisions are brought together in the Code, with Chapter V entitled "Measures for the prevention of psychosocial risks at work." 2014 legislation significantly changed the provisions of the Law of 4 August 1996, setting out a general framework for the prevention of psychosocial risks at work where previously it concerned only violence, bullying, and sexual harassment at work.

Employers, workers, and those who come into contact with the workers in the execution of their work shall refrain from any act of sexual harassment at work.

Sexual harassment at work means any form of unwanted verbal, non-verbal, or physical behaviour with a sexual connotation, the goal or consequence of which is a compromise of the dignity of a person, or the creation of a threatening, hostile, insulting, or injurious environment.

Chapter V bis.—Special provisions regarding the prevention of psychological risks at work, including stress, violence, harassment, and sexual harassment at work

Section 1.—General, Sub-section 1.—Definition of psychosocial risks at work

Article 32/1 states:

> For the purposes of this Act, psychosocial risks at work shall mean the probability that one or more worker(s) suffer(s) a psychological damage, which can also be accompanied by physical damage, resulting from exposure to some elements of the work organisation, job content, working conditions, living conditions at work and interpersonal relationships at work, on which the employer has an influence and which objectively involve a danger.

Article 32/2 § 1. The employer is required to identify situations that can lead to psychosocial risks at work and determine and assess these risks, and shall determine which measures must be taken to prevent violence, harassment, and sexual harassment at work. He or she shall determine these prevention measures based on a risk analysis and take into account the nature of the activities and the size of the enterprise.

The employer shall take, insofar as he or she has an influence on the danger, the necessary preventive measures in order to prevent situations and actions that can lead to psychosocial risks at work and to prevent or limit the damage.

Whenever the employer is informed of acts of sexual harassment at work, he or she shall take appropriate measures, in accordance with the provisions of this Chapter.

The role of the prevention advisor: the law requires that the employer establish an internal procedure to handle harassment complaints by employees, in part through appointing a prevention advisor who specializes in psychosocial problems and through setting up an internal service for prevention and protection at work. The employer decides whether the tasks assigned to the prevention advisor will be carried out by the internal service for prevention and protection at work or by an external service for prevention and protection at work. Only a limited number of organizations in Belgium have their own in-house specialists.

Prevention advisors are called in where a case of undesirable behavior is suspected in the workplace. They can be assisted by what are known as confidential mediators, appointed by employers from members of staff. These are people employees can turn to if they feel they have become a victim of bullying, sexual harassment, or violence. In all organizations, an in-company procedure has to be put in place to ensure the prevention advisors and the confidential mediators play a central role. Requests for a psychosocial intervention can be informal or formal, and can be made by an individual or on a collective basis. The prevention advisor on psychosocial issues shall conduct an investigation and determine written proposals for preventive and corrective measures. The anonymity of the employee or employees involved in the complaint should be guaranteed as far as possible (Source: European Foundation for the Improvement of Living and Working Conditions).

Title of legislation Social Criminal Code, 2011 as amended

The *Social Criminal Code*, 2011, amended by the Act of 29 February 2016, amending the Social Criminal Code in terms of psychosocial risks at work, addresses prevention of psychosocial risks at, such as *sexual harassment*. The Code states that acts of violence and moral or sexual harassment at work will be punished with a Level 4 sanction; it applies to anyone who comes into contact with workers during execution of their work and which, in contravention of the Law of 4 August 1996 on the welfare of during the performance of their work, commits an act of violence or moral harassment or sexual at work (Article 119). Further, failure to comply with the procedures laid down in the Act on wellbeing with regard to a formal psychosocial intervention request, failure to appoint a health and safety advisor specializing in psychosocial aspects and a person of trust, and non-compliance with the obligations regarding psychosocial risk prevention in general may result in a criminal fine of 600 to 6,000 EUR or an administrative fine of 300 to 3,000 EUR.

BIBLIOGRAPHY

Federal Public Service Employment, Labor and Social Consultation, 1996. Code on Welfare At Work, 1996 as amended. Available at: http://www.employment.belgium.be/WorkArea/showcontent.aspx?id=1896. and http://www.employment.belgium.be/defaultTab.aspx?id=556. Accessed March 6, 2019

European Foundation for the Improvement of Living and Working Conditions, n.d. Belgium: New legislation on Preventing Psychosocial Risks. Available at: http://www.eurofound.europa.eu/observatories/eurwork/articles/working-conditions/belgium-new-legislation-on-preventing-psychosocial-risks. Accessed March 6, 2019

Federal Public Service Employment, n.d. Psychosocial Risks At Work. Available at: http://www.emploi.belgique.be/defaultTab.aspx?id=45949#sexuel. Accessed March 6, 2019

Emploi, Travail Et Concertation Sociale, April 28, 2017. Royal Decree Establishing Book I General Principles of the Code of Well-Being At Work. Available at: http://www.ejustice.just.fgov.be/cgi_loi/change_lg.pl?language=fr&la=F&table_name=loi&cn=2017042826. Accessed May 30, 2019

International Labour Organization, 2016. Social Criminal Code. Available at: https://www.ilo.org/dyn/natlex/docs/ELECTRONIC/84094/93283/F921770394/BEL-84094.pdf. (In French) Accessed March 6, 2019

CYPRUS

In Cyprus, sexual harassment is prohibited under the Equal Treatment Act.

A 2015 European foundation for the Improvement of Living and Working Conditions (Eurofound) report, "Cyprus: sexual harassment in the workplace," states that although sexual harassment in the workplace:

> ...is recognised and a relatively full and adequate institutional framework exists and is being gradually supplemented and amended in line with EU provisions, women tend to conceal the problem. This concealment also explains the extremely small number of cases brought to justice. The two main reasons for victims' failure to exploit their opportunities to recourse to justice are: fear of the consequences; the difficulty of proving sexual harassment.
>
> *(Source: European Foundation for the Improvement of Living and Working Conditions, February 26, 2015. "Cyprus: sexual harassment in the workplace," by Eva Soumeli)*

Sexual Harassment Conviction: On August 7, 2014, a decision (Case No. 758/2005) issued by the Nicosia Industrial Disputes Tribunal concluded that a female employee at the General Hospital of Nicosia had been the victim of systematic sexual harassment by a male colleague which had lasted for almost 12 months. The Industrial Disputes Tribunal has exclusive jurisdiction to determine cases of unequal treatment or sexual harassment in the workplace. The case highlighted the obligation of employers and their representatives to take all available and timely measures to prevent sexual harassment in the workplace. For the first time, a Cypriot court not only recognized this obligation but also ruled that the employer was fully and jointly responsible for the sexual harassment along with the defendant (Source: European Foundation for the Improvement of Living and Working Conditions, February 26, 2015. "Cyprus: sexual harassment in the workplace").

Cyprus' Equality Authority has published a two-part *Code of good practice for the prevention of sexual harassment in employment.* The Code provides practical guidance to employers and employees aiming at securing appropriate procedures to deal with sexual harassment and harassment incidents. The second part of the Code for combating sexual harassment and harassment in employment provides useful advice and directions for employees and their employers with regard to effective prevention and a strong response to sexual harassment and harassment in the field of employment (Source: Cyprus Ombudsman, 2007. "Code of practice for combating of sexual harassment and harassment in employment").

Legislation

- The Equal Treatment for Men and Women in Employment and Vocational Training Law, No. 205/2002, as amended

Title of legislation	The Equal Treatment for Men and Women in Employment and Vocational Training Law, No. 205/2002, as amended

The Equal Treatment for Men and Women in Employment and Vocational Training Law, No. 205/2002, as amended, applies to all employees and defines discrimination as including *sexual harassment.*

Sexual harassment:

> ...is any unwanted by the recipient behavior of sexual nature, which is expressed verbally or physically, with the purpose or effect of infringing the dignity of the recipient, especially when creating an intimidating, hostile, humiliating or offensive environment in employment or professional education or training or in access to employment or professional education or training.

It also states:

> Any act that constitutes sexual harassment or causes direct or indirect discriminatory treatment shall be prohibited. Employers and representatives of legal entities or their supervisor, or the person competent/responsible, shall abstain from such an act, whether isolated or repeated.

The employer must take all appropriate measures against sexual harassment as soon as sexual harassment comes to his or her attention to take all appropriate measures to stop it and ensure that it does not re-occur. The employer is liable for the offence of sexual harassment if he or she fails to take all necessary precautions to protect his or her employees. Further, the employer is liable irrespective of whether he or she was aware that an offence occurred.

BIBLIOGRAPHY

Republic of Cyprus Department of Labour, 2002. The Equal Treatment of Men and Women in Employment and Vocational Training Law, No. 205(I)/2002. Available at: http://www.mlsi.gov.cy/mlsi/dl/dl.nsf/All/4F1DB719F3AA8A73C22581CB0041B58A?OpenDocument. Accessed March 1, 2019

Cyprus Ombudsman, 2011. Code of Practice for Combating of Sexual Harassment and Harassment in Employment, 2007 (First Part). Available at: http://www.ombudsman.gov.cy/Ombudsman/ombudsman.nsf/All/F44ACFD138A8C8B2C2257E7E003F4A24?OpenDocument. Accessed March 1, 2019

Cyprus Ombudsman, 2011. Code of Practice for Combating of Sexual Harassment and Harassment in Employment (Second Part). Available at: http://www.ombudsman.gov.cy/Ombudsman/ombudsman.nsf/All/2348CE8BA625D720C2257E8100412689?OpenDocument Accessed March 1, 2019

European Foundation for the Improvement of Living and Working Conditions, 2015. Cyprus: Sexual Harassment in the Workplace, by Soumeli, Eva February 26, 2015. Available at: http://www.eurofound.europa.eu/observatories/eurwork/articles/working-conditions/cyprus-sexual-harassment-in-the-workplace. Accessed March 1, 2019

CZECH REPUBLIC

In the Czech Republic, sexual harassment constitutes a form of discrimination and is prohibited in national law in the Antidiscrimination Act.

Legislation

- The Act on Equal Treatment and Legal Remedies of Protection against Discrimination No. 198/2009 Coll. ("Antidiscrimination Act")
- Labour Code No. 262/2006 Coll.
- Act 2004–435 on Employment

Title of legislation	The Act on Equal Treatment and Legal Remedies of Protection against Discrimination, No. 198/2009 Coll. ("Anti-Discrimination Act")

Under the *Anti-Discrimination Act*, effective September 1, 2009, *sexual harassment* is considered to be discrimination and is prohibited. (Definitions—Article 2)

Sexual harassment means:

> ...any unwanted conduct of a sexual nature taking place with the purpose or effect of diminishing the dignity of a person and creating an intimidating, hostile, degrading, humiliating or offensive environment, or which could be legitimately perceived as a precondition for a decision affecting the exercise of rights and obligations following from legal relations.

A person may go to Court to request that sexual harassment be refrained from, that consequences of the discriminatory act be remedied and that (s)he be provided with appropriate compensation. Should a remedy not appear sufficient, particularly due to the fact that a person's reputation or dignity or respect in society has been harmed, the person shall also have the right to monetary compensation for non-material damage. The amount of the compensation shall be assessed by the court taking into account the seriousness of the damage and the circumstances under which the right was violated. (Section 10)

Title of legislation Labour Code, No. 262/2006 Coll.

In the *Labour Code*, No. 251/2005 Coll, effective January 1, 2007, Chapter IV Equal Treatment and Prohibition of Discrimination states that any form of discrimination in labor relations is prohibited, including *sexual harassment*, and refers to its regulation in the Anti-Discrimination Act.

Title of legislation Act 2004-435 on Employment, as amended

Act 2004–435 on Employment, as amended, prohibits discrimination in employment based on sex, among other grounds, but does not specifically mention sexual harassment (Article 4). It requires the employer to organize, manage, and control the performance of work to assure the observance of the principle of non-discrimination. Any form of discrimination of persons exercising their right to employment is prohibited in accordance with the Anti-Discrimination Act.

BIBLIOGRAPHY

Labour Office, Czech Republic, 2004. Act 2004–435 on Employment. Available at: https://portal.mpsv.cz/sz/obecne/prav_predpisy/akt_zneni/act_no._435_2004_coll._1.1.2018.pdf. Accessed March 7, 2019

Ministry of Labour and Social Affairs, 2006. Labour Code. Available at: https://www.mpsv.cz/files/clanky/3221/Labour_Code_2012.pdf. Accessed March 7, 2019

Ombudsman, 2008. Anti-Discrimination Act. Available at: https://www.legislationline.org/topics/country/35/topic/84. Accessed on March 7, 2019

FRANCE

2018 law reinforces employer's obligation to prevent sexual harassment: Law No. 2018–771 of 5 September 2018, as amended, for the freedom to choose one's professional future, effective January 1, 2019, strengthened the fight against sexual and gender-based violence and reinforced employers' obligations to prevent sexual harassment in France. The law requires that in any enterprise employing at least 250 employees, a reference person is appointed to guide, inform, and accompany employees in the fight against sexual harassment and sexist behavior. The law amended the Labour Code, discussed in the next section.

Additionally, Law No. 2018–703 of 3 August 2018 reinforced the fight against sexual and gender-based violence. In it, "Title II: provisions relating to the crimes of sexual harassment and moral harassment" broadens the scope of the criminal offense of sexual harassment, taking into account sexist behaviors.

Legislation

- Labour Code, 2008, as amended by Law No. 2018–771 of 5 September 2018
- Penal Code

Title of legislation	Labour Code, 2008 as amended by Law No. 2018-771 of September 5, 2018

The *Labour Code/Code du travail* 2008, as amended, applies to private and public employers and requires that the employer make all necessary arrangements to prevent, stop and punish acts of *sexual harassment.* (Article L1153–5 Modified by Law n ° 2018–771 of 5 September 2018—Article 105 (V))

Chapter III addresses *sexual harassment* under Article L1153–1 Article 7, which states:

No employee shall suffer facts:

1 Either sexual harassment, consisting of repeated sexual remarks or behavior that offend his dignity because of their degrading or humiliating nature, or create an intimidating situation against him; hostile or offensive;

2 Be assimilated to sexual harassment, consisting of any form of serious pressure, even if not repeated, exercised for the real or apparent purpose of obtaining an act of a sexual nature, whether it is sought for the benefit of the perpetrator or for the benefit of a third party.

Article 7 further states:

> No employee, no person in training or internship, no candidate for a recruitment, an internship or a training in company can not be sanctioned, dismissed or to be the object of a discriminatory measure, direct or indirect, in particular in matter remuneration, training, reclassification, assignment, qualification, classification, professional promotion, transfer or renewal of contract for having suffered or refused to suffer sexual harassment as defined in Article L. 1153–1, including, in the case mentioned in 1 ° of the same article, if the remarks or behaviors were not repeated.

Any employee who has committed acts of sexual harassment is liable to disciplinary action.

Law No. 2018–771 of 5 September 2018, as amended, for the freedom to choose one's professional future, Chapter IV Equal pay for women and men and the fight against sexual violence and sexist behavior at work, Article 104, effective January 1, 2019, amended the Labour Code by introducing new obligations for companies in the fight against sexual harassment and sexists behaviors. Article 105 requires that companies employing at least 250 employees appoint a referent responsible for orienting, informing, and accompanying employees in matters of sexual harassment and sexist behavior. The referent's stated role are to guide, inform, and accompany employees in the fight against sexual harassment and sexist behavior. The referent can be a member of the direction of the human resources or an employee in charge of the prevention of the psycho–social risks.

Similarly, Article L. 2314–1 was amended by the same 2018 law as follows:

> A referent in the fight against sexual harassment and the sexist acts is designated by the social and economic committee among its members, in the form of a resolution adopted according to the modalities defined in article L. 2315–32, for a period which ends with that of the mandate of the members elected members of the committee.

Article L1153–5 requires that the employer post in the workplaces and premises where the hiring is done, the civil and criminal consequences of sexual harassment, as well as the contact details of the authorities and competent services. The employer must also inform employees about sexual harassment and its consequences as stated in Article 222–33 of the Penal Code.

Title of legislation Penal Code

Article 222–33 of the Penal Code addresses *sexual harassment* as follows:

Sexual harassment is the act of repeatedly imposing on a person sexually or sexist-related words or behavior that are offensive to his or her dignity because of their degrading or humiliating character, or create against him or her an intimidating, hostile or offensive situation.

The offense also occurs as follows:

1. When these words or behaviors are imposed on the same victim by several persons, in a concerted manner or at the instigation of one of them, even though each of these persons has not acted repeatedly;
2. When these words or behaviors are imposed on the same victim, successively, by several persons who, even in the absence of consultation, know that these remarks or behaviors characterize a repetition.

Sexual harassment may be punishable by two years' imprisonment and a 30,000 EUR fine.

These penalties are increased to three years' imprisonment and a fine of 45,000 EUR when the acts are committed:

- By a person who abuses the authority conferred on him or her by his or her functions;
- On a minor of fifteen years;
- A person whose particular vulnerability, due to age, illness, infirmity, physical or mental disability or pregnancy, is apparent or known to the perpetrator;
- On a person whose particular vulnerability or dependence resulting from the precariousness of his economic or social situation is apparent or known to the author;
- By several persons acting as author or accomplice;

- By the use of a communication service to the public online or by means of a digital or electronic medium;
- While a minor was present and attended;
- By an ascendant or by any other person having a de jure or de facto authority over the victim.

Legal persons held criminally liable, under the conditions provided for in Article 121–2, for the offenses defined in Articles 222–22 to 222–31 incur, in addition to the fine in the manner provided for in Article 131–38, the penalties provided for in Article 131–3.

BIBLIOGRAPHY

Legifrance, 2019. Labour Code. Available at: https://www.legifrance.gouv.fr/affichCode.do?cidTexte=LEGITEXT000006072050. Accessed March 17, 2019

Labour Code (Sexual Harassment Provisions), 2019. Available at https://www.legifrance.gouv.fr/affichCode.do;jsessionid=5E0638EDA50BC8666384428A41571DE7.tplgfr41s_1?idSectionTA=LEGISCTA000006177846&cidTexte=LEGITEXT000006072050&dateTexte=20190228. Accessed March 17, 2019 and https://www.legifrance.gouv.fr/affichCode.do;jsessionid=0766CB9A4343288CE449B639D6985CCC.tplgfr41s_1?cidTexte=LEGITEXT000006072050&dateTexte=20191231. Accessed March 19, 2019

Legifrance, 2019. ION 2016–1088 of August 8, 2016 on Work, the Modernization of Social Dialogue and Career Security. Available at: https://www.legifrance.gouv.fr/affichTexte.do?cidTexte=JORFTEXT000032983213&categorieLien=id. Accessed March 17, 2019

Legifrance, 2019. Penal Code. Available at https://www.legifrance.gouv.fr/affichCodeArticle.do?cidTexte=LEGITEXT000006070719&idArticle=LEGIARTI000006417706&dateTexte=&categorieLien=cid. Accessed May 31, 2019

Legifrance, 2019. Law No. 2018-771 of September 5, 2018 for the Freedom to Choose One's Professional Future. Available at: https://www.legifrance.gouv.fr/affichTexte.do;jsessionid=50A262A390B4043BEC30B376CF377396.tplgfr41s_1?idSectionTA=JORFSCTA000037367679&cidTexte=JORFTEXT000037367660&dateTexte=20180906. Accessed May 31, 2019

Legifrance, 2018. Loi "Avenir Professionnel" of September 5, 2018, No.s 2018–771. Available at: https://www.legifrance.gouv.fr/affichTexte.do?cidTexte=JORFTEXT000037367660&categorieLien=id. Accessed July 25, 2019

Legifrance, 2019. Law 2018-703 of 3 August 2018 Reinforcing the Fight against Sexual and Gender-Based Violence. Available at: https://www.legifrance.gouv.fr/affichTexte.do?cidTexte=JORFTEXT000037284450&categorieLien=id#JORFSCTA000037284452. Accessed August 28, 2019

GERMANY

Although sexual harassment at work is prohibited, employers and employees do not appear well informed of their duties and rights.

The director of the German Federal Anti-Discrimination Agency has stated that many victims do not dare to make sexual harassment public. "They are afraid to lose their job, of receiving the blame themselves and being accused of damaging the reputation of a colleague or boss," she told DW. "We also found out in a survey that many employees are poorly informed about their rights. Eight out of 10 do not know that their employer is required to protect them from sexual harassment in the workplace, and many employers do not seem to be aware of this duty either" (Source: Deutsche Welle (DW), February 11, 2017. "You too? Sexual harassment in the German workplace," by Arthur Sullivan).

Germany's Federal Anti-Discrimination Agency 2015 survey, "Sexual harassment in the workplace," a representative survey of employees, included the following findings: when directly asked about sexual harassment, 17 percent of female employees and 7 percent of their male colleagues report that they have already been sexually harassed at work. Yet, when asked about the individual offences described in the legislation, approximately 50 percent of each group, women and men, state that they have already experienced this kind of situations once. Almost half of the respondents (46 percent) do not know about any measures of protection against sexual harassment which would have been initiated by their company or their agency. Only almost one-third of them (29 percent) know about a contact person at the workplace. Even a large part of the senior executives and staff representatives at public and private enterprises (60 percent) is not able to cite any protective measures at their institutions. However, only 25 percent of personnel managers and works council members were aware of the employers' duties of protection and care towards employees regulated by law (Source: Federal Anti-discrimination Agency, 2015. "Sexual harassment in the workplace: results of a representative survey of employees in Germany").

In 2016, Germany's Federal Anti-discrimination Agency published guidelines on preventing and tackling sexual harassment in the workplace. The Guidelines include causes and consequences, legal rights and duties, and best practices by major companies.

In a 2017 decision concerning the severe sexual harassment of a male temporary worker by a male member of the permanent staff, the Federal Labour Court made a landmark decision upon sexual harassment at the workplace in general. The court concluded that sexual harassment does not require sexual intentions, and that the intentional touching of primary or secondary sexual organs constitutes a severe sexual harassment, regardless of the perpetrator's sexual orientation or preferences. The court stated that sexual harassment at the workplace is very often an expression of hierarchies and the exercise of power rather than sexually determined pleasure. Its decision also confirmed that one severe assault is sufficient to constitute sexual harassment. (Sources: European Commission, European network of legal experts in gender equality and nondiscrimination. "Country Report, Gender Equality, Germany 2018," by Ulrike Lembke and Federal Labor Court judgment of 29.6.2017, 2 AZR 302/16)

Legislation

- General Act on Equal Treatment (AGG), 2006, as amended

Title of legislation	General Act on Equal Treatment (AGG) 2006 as amended

The *General Act on Equal Treatment (AGG)*, 2006, as amended, defines sexual harassment as discrimination and prohibits *sexual harassment* at work.

Sexual harassment:

> ...shall be deemed to be discrimination in relation to Section 2(1) Nos 1 to 4, when an unwanted conduct of a sexual nature, including unwanted sexual acts and requests to carry out sexual acts, physical contact of a sexual nature, comments of a sexual nature, as well as the unwanted showing or public exhibition of pornographic images, takes place with the purpose or effect of violating the dignity of the person concerned, in particular where it creates an intimidating, hostile, degrading, humiliating or offensive environment. (Article 3(4))

In the words of the law, Article 3 (4), a *sexual harassment* is a disadvantage:

> ...if an undesirable, sexually determined behavior, including unwanted sexual acts and prompts to these, sexually determined physical touches, comments sexual content as well unwanted pointing and visible attachment of pornographic images are, are

intended or intended to be detrimental to the dignity of the person concerned, in particular where an environment of intimidation, hostility, humiliation, humiliation or insults is created.

Under Section 12, the employer must take the necessary measures to protect against sexual harassment, including preventive measures such as appropriate training for preventing discrimination; taking the appropriate, necessary and appropriate measures to prevent discrimination such as warning, implementation, transfer or termination in individual cases if employees violate the prohibition of discrimination under § 7 (1); and taking the appropriate, necessary and appropriate measures to protect the employees in the individual case. Section 14 states that where the employer takes no or takes obviously unsuitable measures to stop the harassment or sexual harassment in the workplace, the affected employees shall have the right to refuse performance without loss of pay insofar as this is necessary for their protection.

This Act and Section 61b of the Labor Court Act as well as information on the authorities who are responsible for the handling of complaints in accordance with Section 13 must be made public in the company or at the office. The notice may be posted or interpreted at a suitable place or by using the usual information and communication technology at the establishment or department.

BIBLIOGRAPHY

Deutsche Welle (DW) You too? Sexual Harassment in the German Workplace, February 11, 2017 by Arthur Sullivan. Available at: https://www.dw.com/en/you-too-sexual-harassment-in-the-german-workplace/a-41215231. Accessed: June 23, 2019

Federal Anti-Discrimination Agency, 2016. Prevention and Action Options in Dealing with Sexual Harassment in the Workplace. Available at: http://www.antidiskriminierungsstelle.de/SharedDocs/Aktuelles/DE/2016/20160620_Fachtag_sexuelle_Belaestigung.html. Accessed March 13, 2019

European Commission, Published January 14, 2019. European Network of Legal Experts in Gender Equality and Nondiscrimination, Country Report, Gender Equality, Germany 2018, by Ulrike Lembke. Available at: https://www.equalitylaw.eu/downloads/4800-germany-country-report-gender-equality-2018-pdf-1-65-mb.

Federal Ministry of Justice and Consumer Protection, 2006. General Equal Treatment Act (AGG). Available at: http://www.gesetze-im-internet.de/agg/BJNR189710006.html#BJNR189710006BJNG000100000. Accessed February 27, 2019

Federal Ministry of Justice and Consumer Protection, 2002, German Civil Code, BGB. Available at: http://www.gesetze-im-internet.de/englisch_bgb/. Accessed March 21, 2019

Federal Anti-Discrimination Agency, 2015. Sexual Harassment in the Workplace Results of a Representative Survey of Employees in Germany Carried Out by SUZ – Sozialwissenschaftliches Umfragezentrum GmbH Duisburg on behalf of the Federal Anti-Discrimination Agency. Available at: http://www.antidiskriminierungsstelle.de/SharedDocs/Downloads/DE/publikationen/Umfragen/Handout_en_Umfrage_sex_Belaestigung_am_ArbPlatz_Beschaeftigte.pdf?__blob=publicationFile&v=6. Accessed March 21, 2019

Federal Anti-Discrimination Agency, 2016. Guide to the Equal Treatment Act. Available at: http://www.antidiskriminierungsstelle.de/SharedDocs/Downloads/EN/publikationen/guide_to_the_general_act.pdf?__blob=publicationFile&v=1. Accessed March 21, 2019

Federal Labor Court, 2017. Judgment of 29.6.2017, 2 AZR 302/16. Available at: https://juris.bundesarbeitsgericht.de/cgi-bin/rechtsprechung/document.py?Gericht=bag&Art=en&Datum=2017-6-29&nr=19424&pos=0&anz=19. Accessed March 21, 2019

HUNGARY

> In Hungarian law, sexual harassment is primarily covered by the general definitions of harassment stipulated by the Act CXXV of 2003 on Equal Treatment.

The #MeToo campaign in Hungary has received some notice. Seven women accused a renowned director and iconic figure of the theatre scene of sexual assault. He subsequently released an apology in October 2017 (Source: The Budapest Beacon, October 20, 2017. "László Marton apologizes over sexual assault allegations").

Legislation

- Act CXXV on Equal Treatment and Promotion of Equal Opportunities No. 125/2003
- Labour Code, 2012

Title of legislation	Act CXXV on Equal Treatment and Promotion of Equal Opportunities, 2003

Act CXXV of 2003 on Equal Treatment and Opportunity ("Act on Equal Treatment") No. 125/2003 prohibits sex discrimination and harassment, which are seen as a breach of the principle of equal treatment. The equal treatment principle is violated if the employer inflicts direct or indirect negative discrimination upon an employee, in working conditions or conditions of employment, terminates employment, or in relation to training, but not if the discrimination is proportional, justified by the characteristics or nature of the work, arising directly from a religious or other ideological conviction or national or ethnic origin fundamentally determining the nature of the organization, and proportional and justified by the nature of the employment activity.

Harassment is defined in Article 10 as "conduct violating human dignity related to the relevant person's characteristic defined in Article 8 with the purpose or effect of creating an intimidating, hostile, degrading, humiliating or offensive environment around a particular person." The Act does not explicitly mention sexual harassment.

Title of legislation	Labour Code, 2012

The Hungarian *Labour Code*, entitled Act I of 2012 on the Labour Code, prohibits direct discrimination and refers to discrimination on sexual grounds. An employer must ensure conditions for healthy and safe work: wrongful exercise of rights is prohibited. This section states:

> For the purposes of this Act "wrongful exercise of rights" means, in particular, any act that is intended for or leads to the injury of the legitimate interests of others, restrictions on the enforcement of their interests, harassment, or the suppression of their opinion. (Section 7)

There is no legal definition of the actions that constitute sexual harassment.

BIBLIOGRAPHY

The Budapest Beacon, October 20, 2017, László Marton Apologizes Over Sexual Assault Allegations. Available at: https://budapestbeacon.com/laszlo-marton-apologizes-sexual-assault-allegations/. Accessed August 28, 2019

Equal Treatment Authority, 2003. Act CXXV of 2003 on Equal Treatment and Promotion of Equal Opportunities. Available at: https://www2.ohchr.org/english/bodies/cescr/docs/e.c.12.hun.3-annex3.pdf. Accessed April 20, 2019

International Labour Organization, 2012. Act I of 2012 on the Labor Code. Available at: http://www.ilo.org/wcmsp5/groups/public/---ed_protect/---protrav/---ilo_aids/documents/legaldocument/wcms_186075.pdf. Accessed April 20, 2019

IRELAND

> Sexual harassment issues in the workplace appear to have surged by 200 percent since the start of the #MeToo movement.

The article reports on how sexual harassment issues in the workplace have surged by 200 percent in recent years, according to one of Ireland's leading law firms (Source: Independent.ie, December 9, 2018. "Sexual harassment issues in the workplace have surged by 200 percent—leading law firm," by Niamh Horan).

Ireland's Code of Practice discusses sexual harassment as follows: an excerpt from Part 1, "Forward on the impact of sexual harassment and harassment," states that sexual harassment works to:

> ...pollute the working environment and can have a devastating effect on the health, confidence, morale and performance of those affected by it. The anxiety and stress produced by sexual harassment...may lead to those subjected to it taking time off work due to sickness and stress, being less efficient at work or leaving their job to seek work elsewhere...

It further states that sexual harassment:

> ...may also have a damaging impact on employees not themselves the object of unwanted behaviour but who are witness to it or have a knowledge of the unwanted behaviour. There are also adverse consequences arising from sexual harassment...for employers. It has a direct impact on the profitability of the enterprise where staff take sick leave or resign their posts because of sexual harassment...It can also have an impact on the economic efficiency of the enterprise where employees' productivity is reduced by having to work in a climate in which the individual's integrity is not respected.
>
> *(Source: Employment Equality Act 1998 (Code Of Practice) (Harassment) Order 2012)*

Note: A Code of Practice is non-binding and designed to provide guidelines on arrangements, procedures, and general guidance.

Legislation

- Employment Equality Acts, 1998–2015, as amended

Title of legislation Employment Equality Acts, 1998-2015

The *Employment Equality Acts 1998–2015* ban *sexual harassment* in the workplace.

Under the Act, *sexual harassment* constitutes discrimination by the victim's employer in relation to the victim's conditions of employment.

Sexual harassment occurs:

> ...where an employee (referred to as "the victim") is sexually harassed either at the workplace or otherwise in the course of his or her employment by a person who is—

(i) employed at that place or by the same employer,
(ii) the victim's employer, or
(iii) a client, customer or other business contact of the victim's employer and the circumstances of the harassment are such that the employer ought reasonably to have taken steps to prevent it, or
  (i) such harassment has occurred, and
  (ii) either—
    (I) the victim is treated differently in the workplace or otherwise in the course of his or her employment by reason of rejecting or accepting the harassment, or
    it could reasonably be anticipated that he or she would be so treated. the harassment or sexual harassment constitutes discrimination by the victim's employer in relation to the victim's conditions of employment. (Article 14A)

References to sexual harassment are to any form of unwanted verbal, non-verbal or physical conduct of a sexual nature, being conduct which in either case has the purpose or effect of violating a person's dignity and creating an intimidating, hostile, degrading, humiliating or offensive environment for the person.

Employers are legally responsible for the *sexual harassment* directed at employees carried out by co-employees or clients, customers or other business contacts of the employer. It is a defense for the employer to prove that the employer took such steps as are reasonably practicable to prevent the person from sexually harassing the victim or any class of persons which includes the victim. However, a person's rejection of, or submission to, sexual harassment may not be used by an employer as a basis for a decision affecting that person.

Employer liability in general is addressed in Article 15: anything done by a person in the course of his or her employment shall, in any proceedings brought under this Act, be treated for the purposes of this Act as done also by that person's employer, whether or not it was done with the employer's knowledge or approval. It is a defense for the employer to prove that he or she took such steps as were reasonably practical to prevent the person from doing the act complained of. (Liability of employers and principals.)

Section 23, "Sexual harassment in the workplace," lays out helpful examples of sexual harassment which may occur in the workplace.

S.I. No. 208/2012—Employment Equality Act 1998 (Code of Practice) (Harassment) Order 2012 is applicable to all adaptation of the Code, employments, employment agencies and trade unions, employer bodies and professional bodies that are covered by the Employment Equality Act. A Code of Practice is non-binding and designed to provide guidelines on arrangements, procedures, and general guidance. The code seeks to promote the development and implementation of policies and procedures which establish working environments free of sexual harassment and harassment and in which the dignity of everyone is respected. The provisions of the code are admissible in evidence and if relevant may be taken into account in any criminal or other proceedings before a court.

The Code states that:

> ...employers should adopt, implement and monitor a comprehensive, effective and accessible policy on sexual harassment and harassment. The policy should be devised in consultation with employees and trade unions and should set out what constitutes sexual harassment and harassment; who is responsible for implementing the policy; and how complaints will be dealt with.

BIBLIOGRAPHY

Independent.Ie., December 9, 2018. Sexual Harassment Issues in the Workplace Have Surged by 200pc - Leading Law Firm, by Niamh Horan. Available at: https://www.independent.ie/irish-news/sexual-harassment-issues-in-the-workplace-have-surged-by-200pc-leading-law-firm-37608116.html Accessed June 18, 2019 and http://www.irishstatutebook.ie/eli/1998/act/21/section/23/enacted/en/html#sec23 Accessed May 17, 2019

Equality Act 2004, Irish Statute Book, 2004. Available at: http://www.irishstatutebo ok.ie/eli/2004/act/24/enacted/en/print.html. Accessed February 28, 2019

Law Reform Commission. Employment Equality Acts, 1998–2015 amended. Available at: http://revisedacts.lawreform.ie/eli/1998/act/21/front/revised/en/html. Accessed May 6, 2019

electronic Irish Statute Book (eISB), 2012. S.I. No. 208/2012 - Employment Equality Act 1998 (Code of Practice) (Harassment) Order 2012. Available at http://www.irishstatutebook.ie/eli/2012/si/208/made/en/print. Accessed February 28, 2019

S.I. No. 208/2012 - Employment Equality Act 1998 (Code of Practice) (Harassment) Order 2012. Available at: http://www.irishstatutebook.ie/eli/2012/si/208/made/en/pdf. Accessed February 28, 2019

ITALY

Liability fund for strictly verbal sexual harassment: in April 2018, a court awarded a woman who for years was sexually harassed by her boss more than 100,000 EUR in damages. The decision appeared to be the first time damages were awarded for strictly *verbal workplace sexual harassment*. Under Italian law, workplace harassment also includes unwanted touching to non-erogenous zones.

In 2012, the Italian Court of Cassation clarified that sexual harassment is illegal regardless of whether or not the offender was seeking sexual gratification when he or she made the comments in question. Until now, though, most judges have dismissed such behavior as jokes that "didn't really damage" the victims. News of the decision was cheered in a country that has lagged behind the rest of Western Europe in the #MeToo era (Source: ilFattoQuotidiano.it, April 12, 2018. "Como, entrepreneur convicted of verbal harassment. The employee 105 thousand euros in compensation").

Legislation

- Decree No. 198 of 6 April 2006 enacting the Act on Equal Opportunities between Men and Women 2006, as amended
- Civil Code
- Criminal Code

Title of legislation	Legislative Decree No. 198 of 11 April 2006

Legislative Decree No. 198 of 11 April 2006 characterizes *sexual harassment* as a form of discrimination as follows:

> Sexual harassment is also considered discrimination or rather those undesirable behaviors with sexual connotations, expressed in form physical, verbal or non-verbal, having the purpose or effect of violating the dignity of a worker or a worker and to create an intimidating, hostile climate, degrading, humiliating or offensive.

Further, the denial of sexual harassment by the person concerned or its submission cannot constitute a foundation for a decision affecting that person. (Article 26)

Title of legislation Civil Code

Under Article 2087 of the *Civil Code* the employer is obliged to do what it can to prevent harassment (including sexual harassment) in the workplace. Even if the employer does not perpetrate the harassment, he or she may still face liability due to the general obligation to ensure the health and safety of all employees under Article 2087 (in conjunction with Article 2103) which requires the employer to take appropriate steps to avoid risks both inherent and external to the work environment.

Title of legislation Criminal Code

Italy's *Criminal Code* states that, in cases of sexual harassment, employers can be punished pursuant to Article 660. The alleged harasser can be held personally liable for damages pursuant to tort law.

BIBLIOGRAPHY

ilFattoQuotidiano.it. Como, Entrepreneur Convicted of Verbal Harassment. The Employee 105 Thousand Euros in Compensation. April 12, 2018. Available at: https://www.ilfattoquotidiano.it/2018/04/12/como-imprenditore-condannato-per-molestie-verbali-alla-dipendente-105mila-euro-di-risarcimento/4287902/. Accessed May 17, 2019

Ministry of Labour and Social Policies, 2006. D.Lgs. 11 aprile 2006, No. 198. Available at: https://www.cliclavoro.gov.it/Normative/Decreto_Legislativo_11_aprile_2006_n.198.pdf. Accessed March 15, 2019

LUXEMBOURG

Sexual harassment is considered to be discrimination based on sex in Luxembourg.

Legislation

- Labour Code, 2006, as amended
- Act of 13 May 2008 on Equal Treatment for Men and Women

Title of legislation Labour Code, 2006, as amended

The *Labour Code,* as amended, prohibits *sexual harassment,* defined as any behavior with sexual overtones or any behavior grounded on sex from a person who knows or ought to know that it affects the dignity of the person at work when one of the three conditions is met:

- The behavior is misplaced, excessive and hurtful for the person who is the object of it;
- The fact that someone refuses or accepts such behavior from his employer, a worker, a client or a supplier, is used explicitly or implicitly as a ground for a decision affecting the rights of this person as regards vocational training, employment, employment maintenance, promotion, remuneration or any other decision related to employment; or
- Such behavior created a climate of intimidation, hostility or mortification for the person who was the object of it.

Sexual harassment is considered to be discrimination based on sex. The behavior may be physical, verbal or non-verbal. Any behavior enjoining someone else to discriminate or harass someone on the ground of gender is considered to be discrimination.

A 2018 Omnibus Law amended provisions of the Labor Code, including adding an article to the Labor Code specifying that if an employee initiates but subsequently withdraws certain legal claims, the employee is then required to reimburse the Employment Fund for any unemployment benefits received. This applies to claims brought (but then withdrawn) relating to:

(1) a dismissal for serious reasons,
(2) a resignation motivated by an act of *sexual harassment*, or
(3) an employer's serious act or fault. If an employee withdraws a legal claim because he or she has entered into a settlement agreement with his or her employer, then the employee is required to reimburse half of the unemployment benefits he or she has received, and the employer is required to reimburse the other half.

Title of legislation	Act of 13 May 2008 on Equal Treatment for Men and Women

The *Act of 13 May 2008 on Equal Treatment for Men and Women* transposes the EU Directive on the implementation of the principle of equal treatment between men and women as regards access to employment, training and promotion, and working conditions. The Act provides definitions of direct or indirect discrimination and harassment based on gender from EU Directives. *Sexual harassment* is defined as it is in the Labour Code. The Act covers conditions of access to employment, and conditions of employment and work, including the conditions of dismissal as well as remuneration.

BIBLIOGRAPHY

(Journal Officiel, 2018) Labour Code. Available at: http://legilux.public.lu/eli/etat/leg/loi/2018/04/08/a242/jo. Accessed March 7, 2019

Journal Officiel, 2008. Act of 13 May 2008 on Equal Treatment for Men and Women. Available at: http://www.legilux.public.lu/leg/a/archives/2008/0070/2008A0962A.html

MALTA

Legislation

- Gender-Based Violence and Domestic Violence Act of 2018, as amended
- Chapter 452 Employment and Industrial Relations Act 29, 2002, as amended
- Equality Act, 2015
- Equal Treatment in Employment Regulations, 2004

Title of legislation	Gender-Based Violence and Domestic Violence Act of 2018, as amended

Parties shall take the necessary legislative or other measures to ensure that any form of unwanted verbal, non-verbal or physical conduct of a sexual nature with the purpose or effect of violating the dignity of a person, in particular when creating an intimidating, hostile, degrading, humiliating or offensive environment, is subject to criminal or other legal sanction. (Article 40—Sexual harassment)

Title of legislation	Chapter 452 Employment and Industrial Relations Act 29, 2002

Chapter 452 Employment and Industrial Relations Act 29, 2002, as amended, protects against *sexual harassment* in employment. It is unlawful:

> ...for an employer or an employee to sexually harass another employee or the employer (hereinafter in this article referred to as "the victim") by: (a) subjecting the victim to an act of physical intimacy; or (b) requesting sexual favours from the victim; or (c) subjecting the victim to any act or conduct with sexual connotations, including spoken words, gestures or the production, display or circulation of written words, pictures or other material where—(i) the act, request or conduct is unwelcome to the victim and could reasonably be regarded as offensive, humiliating or intimidating to the victim; (ii) the victim is treated differently, or it could reasonably be anticipated that the victim could be so

treated, by reason of the victim's rejection of or submission to the act, request or conduct. (Article 29(2))

Title of legislation	Equality Act, 2015

Under the *Equality Act, 2015, sexual harassment* occurs where any form of unwanted verbal, non-verbal or physical conduct of a sexual nature occurs, with the purpose or effect of violating the dignity of a person, in particular when creating an intimidating, hostile, degrading, humiliating or offensive environment.

Under Article 19, persons responsible for any workplace, or for any establishment at which goods, services or accommodation facilities are offered to the public, shall not permit other persons who have a right to be present in, or to avail themselves of, any facility, goods or service provided at that place, to suffer sexual harassment at that place. It shall be a defense for the employer or responsible person to prove that he or she took such steps as are reasonably practicable to prevent such sexual harassment.

The failure by any person responsible for any establishment and/or entity to fulfil his or her obligation to suppress harassment shall constitute discrimination.

Under Article 22, the duties of the employer or organization to whom the provisions of this Act apply include taking effective measures to prevent all forms of discrimination, in particular sexual harassment in the workplace, in access to employment, vocational training, and promotion. It shall also be the duty of the employer or any person to use appropriate means to bring the provisions of this Act as well as of any measure taken to further the aim of these regulations to the attention of his or her employees, or of the organization's members, or to any other persons who may be affected by the actions of the employer or the organization concerned.

Title of legislation	Equal Treatment in Employment Regulations, 2004, as amended

The *Equal Treatment in Employment Regulations*, 461 of 2004, as amended, states that discriminatory treatment includes *sexual harassment.*

It further states that:

(5) No person shall sexually harass another person by subjecting him to any form of unwanted verbal, non-verbal or physical conduct or request of a sexual nature, when such conductor request takes place with the purpose, or which has the effect of violating the dignity of the person who is so subjected, in particular when creating an intimidating, hostile, degrading, humiliating or offensive environment for the person who is so subjected.

It goes on:

12A. It shall be the duty of the employer to take effective measures to prevent all forms of discrimination on grounds of sex, in particular harassment and sexual harassment in the workplace, in access to employment, vocational training and promotion.

An employer or person or organization to whom these regulations apply shall also be considered to have discriminated against a person by instructing any person to discriminate against another person; or neglecting an obligation to suppress any form of harassment at his or her workplace or within his or her organization.

BIBLIOGRAPHY

Ministry for European Affairs and Equality, 2015. Equality Act. Available at: https://meae.gov.mt/en/Public_Consultations/MSDC/Documents/2015%20HREC%20Final/Bill%20-%20Equality%20Act.pdf. Accessed March 7, 2019

http://www.justiceservices.gov.mt. Employment and Industrial Relations c. 452. 2002, as amended. Available at: http://www.justiceservices.gov.mt/DownloadDocument.aspx?app=lom&itemid=8918. Accessed March 7, 2019

http://www.justiceservices.gov.mt. Equal Treatment in Employment Regulations, 2004. Subsidiary Legislation 452.95 Equal Treatment in Employment Regulations. Available at: http://www.justiceservices.gov.mt/DownloadDocument.aspx?app=lom&itemid=11229. Accessed March 7, 2019

Laws of Malta website, 2019. Chapter 581 Gender-Based Violence and Domestic Violence Act, 2018, as amended. Available at: http://www.justiceservices.gov.mt/DownloadDocument.aspx?app=lom&itemid=12830&l=1 Accessed May 31, 2019

THE NETHERLANDS

> Sexual harassment in the Netherlands falls under psychosocial workload.

The Netherlands Inspectorate SZW, the agency that determines whether employers and employees comply with employment laws, states that how an employee feels in the workplace does not only affect performance, but also health. If operating conditions, including psychological pressure and getting along with others, are not good, stress can arise. This is also called psychosocial workload (PSA). Factors that influence PSA and hence possibly also can cause stress include *sexual harassment* (Source: Netherlands Inspectorate SZW. "Work Stress and psychosocial stress").

The Arbo portal, an initiative of the Ministry of Social Affairs and Employment, states:

> ...sexual harassment at work is any form of sexual approach, requests for sexual favors or other sexually explicit verbal, non-verbal or physical behavior in the work environment, which are experienced as undesirable. Employers are obliged to prevent all forms of sexual harassment, and if that is not possible, at least to limit as much as possible.
>
> *(Source: Ministry of Social Affairs and Employment)*

The Netherlands SZW Inspectorate states the following: *sexual harassment* involves comments, gestures and acts that are sexually oriented and that employees experience as undesirable. This can be verbal and non-verbal behavior and physical contact. It is quite possible that the perpetrator is unaware that he is guilty of sexual harassment. A comment may be intended as a joke. That makes it no less serious than "conscious" unwanted sexual harassment.

Close to 30 percent of doctors, medical students, and medical interns, the majority of them women, have faced *sexual harassment* during their work, according to a #MeToo survey by Medisch Contact and Arts in Spe. Based on 3,098 doctors and 440 medical students and interns being surveyed, it was found that approximately 75 percent of the sexual harassment incidents involved jokes and comments about the victim, that 60 percent who experienced sexual harassment also reported unwanted touches, and that texts and photos sent over email or social media appeared to be increasing. Situations such as inappropriate relationships or sex against one's will occurred less often. The survey also determined that the lower a person is in the workplace hierarchy, the greater the chance is that they will experience sexual harassment (Source: NLTimes.nl, June 6, 2018. "Nearly a third of Dutch doctors face sexual harassment," by Janene Pieters).

Legislation

- Working Conditions Act, 2007, as amended
- General Equal Treatment Act, 1994
- Equal Treatment of Men and Women Act, 1980

Title of legislation	Working Conditions Act (WCA) 2007, as amended

The *Working Conditions Act* (WCA) contains an obligation for employers to prevent harassment from occurring at the workplace. If the employer fails to do so, administrative fines can be given and the employer can be held liable for damages resulting from discriminating behavior of the employer.

The WCA defines psychosocial workload (PSW) as including *sexual harassment.* The PSW policy obligation in the Working Conditions Act requires the policy to be aimed at preventing PSW.

Employment-related psychosocial pressure is defined as the direct or indirect factors in the employment situation, including sexual intimidation, aggression and violence, aggravation, and work pressure, that cause stress. (Article 2)

An employer must establish a policy to prevent *sexual harassment* at work as part of a policy aimed at preventing employment-related psychosocial pressure, or limiting it if prevention is not possible, as part of the general working conditions policy. (Article 3)

The employer shall conduct a risk assessment with regard to psychosocial pressures in the workplace and adopt an action plan. (Article 5)

The Netherlands SZW Inspectorate states that the policy against sexual harassment based on the Risk Inventory & Evaluation (RI & E) may include the following measures:

- Identify the risks in the organization.
- Appoint a confidential adviser and complaints committee.
- Inform employees about sexual harassment.

- Where necessary, have further research carried out, whereby anonymity remains guaranteed.
- Draft a code of conduct and a complaints procedure.
- Consider guidance and aftercare of victims of sexual harassment and treatment of the perpetrator(s) of sexual harassment.
- Evaluate whether measures taken have the desired effect.

Title of legislation	General Equal Treatment Act, 1994, as amended

Chapter 1 of the *General Equal Treatment Act*, entitled "Equal treatment of persons irrespective of their religion, belief, political affiliation, race, gender, nationality, heterosexual or homosexual orientation or marital status," states that the prohibition of discrimination includes a prohibition of *sexual harassment*.

Sexual harassment in this Act is understood to mean any form of verbal, non-verbal or physical behavior with a sexual connotation that has the purpose or effect of compromising the dignity of the person, in particular when threatening, hostile, abusive, degrading or hurting environment is created. It is prohibited in job offers and placement, working conditions, and training.

Title of legislation	Equal Treatment of Men and Women Act, 1980, as amended

The *Equal Treatment of Men and Women Act, 1980*, as amended, prohibits *sexual harassment* under Article 1a as follows:

- The prohibition of direct discrimination also includes a prohibition of intimidation and a prohibition of *sexual harassment*. Intimidation means behavior that is related to the sex of a person and that has the purpose or consequence that the dignity of the person is affected and that a threatening, hostile, offensive, humiliating or hurtful environment is being created.
- Sexual harassment also means any form of verbal, non-verbal or physical behavior with a sexual connotation that has as its object or effect that the dignity of the person is affected, in particular when

a threatening, hostile, abusive, humiliating or hurtful situation is created.

- The fact that a person rejects or endures the above conduct must not be the basis for a decision affecting that person.

BIBLIOGRAPHY

Ministry of Social Affairs and Employment, n.d. Available at: https://www.arboportaal.nl/onderwerpen/seksuele-intimidatie. Accessed May 17, 2019

Netherlands Inspectorate SZW, Work Stress and Psychosocial Stress. n.d. Available at: https://www.inspectieszw.nl/onderwerpen/algemeen-werkstress-en-psychosociale-belasting. Accessed August 23, 2019

NLTimes.nl, June 6, 2018. Nearly a Third of Dutch Doctors Face Sexual Harassment, by Janene Pieters. Available at: https://nltimes.nl/2018/06/06/nearly-third-dutch-doctors-face-sexual-harassment. Accessed August 23, 2019

Netherlands Focal Point. The Working Conditions Act, 2017. European Agency for Safety and Health and Work. Available at: https://www.arboineuropa.nl/en/legislation/wetgeving-in-het-engels. Accessed February 28, 2019

(overheid.nl), 1980, as amended. Equal Treatment of Men and Women Act. Available at: https://wetten.overheid.nl/BWBR0003299/2015-07-01. Accessed February 28, 2019

Equal Rights Trust. General Equal Treatment Act, 1994, as amended. Available at: https://www.equalrightstrust.org/sites/default/files/ertdocs//Microsoft%20Word%20-%20Equal_Treatment_Act_1994.pdf. Accessed May 31, 2019

Netherlands Focal Point. The Working Conditions Act, 2017. European Agency for Safety and Health and Work. Available at: https://www.arboineuropa.nl/en/legislation/wetgeving-in-het-engels. Accessed May 17, 2019

POLAND

A 2016 report on sexual abuse titled "Breaking Tabu," by Fundacja STER, revealed 87.6 percent of women in Poland had experienced sexual harassment at work and in public places: nearly half of them (49.6 percent) were touched against their will. Over 40 percent got improper sexual proposals (also in electronic communication) and 7.5 percent were exposed to forced sexual contacts by threats at the workplace or school. (Sources: Fundacja STER, 2016. "Breaking Tabu"; and Press Service Monitoring Mediów, October 31, 2017. "The Wall Of Shame Has Fallen. Over 35,000 #Metoo #Jateż Publications In Polish Media")

Legislation

- The Labour Code, 1974, as amended

Title of legislation	The Labour Code, 1974 as amended

The Labour Code, 1974, as amended, includes the definition and prohibition of *sexual harassment,* and applies with respect to fixed-term or open-ended or full- or part-time employment status. *Sexual harassment* is treated as a manifestation of discrimination, as behavior aimed at or resulting in violation of dignity or humiliation or abuse of an employee. The Code states that sexual harassment includes any unacceptable sexual behavior or any behavior related to the employees' sex aimed at or resulting in violation of dignity or humiliation or abuse of an employee. Such behavior may be manifested by physical, verbal or non-verbal elements (sexual harassment).

BIBLIOGRAPHY

Press Service Monitoring Mediów, October 31, 2017. The Wall of Shame Has Fallen. Over 35,000 #Metoo #Jateż Publications in Polish Media. Available at: https://psmm.pl/en/informacja-prasowa/wall-shame-has-fallen-over-35000-metoo-jatez-publications-polish-media. Accessed August 15, 2019

Breaking Tabu, by Fundacja STER, 2016. Available at: http://www.fundacjaster.org.pl/upload/Raport-STERu-do-netu.pdf. Accessed August 15, 2019.

Chancellery of the Sejm. 1974. Labour Code. Available at (in Polish): http://www.ilo.org/dyn/natlex/docs/ELECTRONIC/45181/91756/F1305793969/POL45181%20Pol.pdf. Accessed May 31, 2019

PORTUGAL

In Portugal, the effect of #MeToo has not been as visible as in other countries.

Legislation

- Labour Code, 2012, as amended

Title of legislation	Labour Code, 2012, as amended

The *Portuguese Labour Code* ("Code") includes provisions on *sexual harassment* at the workplace, with sections on prohibition of harassment and non-discrimination based on sex. The Code states that the employer and worker have the right to physical and moral integrity.

Division II Harassment Ban: this ban prohibits harassment by unwanted behavior, and in particular based on discrimination, with the purpose or effect of hindering or embarrassing the person, affecting their dignity, or creating an intimidating, hostile, degrading, humiliating or offensive environment. It includes sexual harassment, unwanted conduct of a sexual nature, verbally, non-verbally or physically, with the purpose or effect referred to here (Article 29). Updated with Law No. 73/2017, dated August 16, 2017, which strengthened the legislative framework for the prevention of harassment.

Article 29 prohibits harassment. Harassment is considered as unwelcome behavior, such as discrimination based on access to employment, work or vocational training, with the aim or the effect of disrupting or embarrassing the person, affecting his or her dignity, or creating an intimidating, hostile, degrading, degrading or humiliating environment.

Sexual harassment constitutes unwanted sexual behavior, verbally, non-verbally or physically, with the purpose or effect referred to under the harassment definition.

Harassment gives the victim the right to compensation. Those who complain of harassment or have a role as witnesses cannot be retaliated against. The practice of harassment constitutes a very serious offense, without prejudice to the criminal liability under the law. (Note: the Penal Code, Article 170 on sexual harassment, states that anyone who harasses another person, practicing before him or her exhibitionist acts, formulating proposals of sexual content or forcing a contact of a sexual nature, is punished with imprisonment up to one year or with a fine of up to 120 euros.)

BIBLIOGRAPHY

Commission for Equality in Labour and Employment, 2012 updated to May 2018. Available (translated to English). Labour Code. Available at: http://www.cite.gov.pt/pt/legis/CodTrab_indice.html. Accessed January 24, 2019

RUSSIA

Russia does not have a law against sexual harassment at work.

Following the dismissal of sexual harassment allegations by three female journalists against a senior member of the Russian State Duma, Denis Krivosheev, Amnesty International's Deputy Director for Eastern Europe and Central Asia, stated:

> Russian legislation desperately needs to be reformed so that it complies with international human rights standards and effectively combats all forms of sexual violence, including sexual harassment and assault in the workplace, at home and elsewhere. Right now, Russian law completely fails to protect victims of sexual harassment and many victims of sexual assault.
>
> *(Source: Amnesty International, March 8, 2018. "Russia: Mockery of sexual harassment claims against MP prompts protest on International Women's Day")*

BIBLIOGRAPHY

Amnesty International, March 8, 2108. Russia: Mockery of Sexual Harassment Claims against MP Prompts Protest on International Women's Day. Available at: https://www.amnesty.org/en/latest/news/2018/03/russia-mockery-of-sexual-harassment-claims-against-mp-prompts-protest-on-international-womens-day/. Accessed May 29, 2109

SLOVAKIA

Legislation

- Act on Equal Treatment in Certain Areas and Protection against Discrimination, No. 365/2004, as amended
- Occupational Safety and Health Protection Act, Collection of Laws 2006–2011

Title of legislation	Act on Equal Treatment in Certain Areas and Protection against Discrimination, No. 365/2004, as amended

The *Act on Equal Treatment in Certain Areas and Protection against Discrimination, No. 365/2004* ("Antidiscrimination Act"), as amended, includes *sexual harassment* in its definition of discrimination, which is prohibited in employment relations.

Sexual harassment shall mean verbal, non-verbal or physical conduct of a sexual nature whose intention or consequence is or may be a violation of person's dignity and which creates an intimidating, degrading, disrespectful, hostile or offensive environment. The burden of proof is on the alleged harasser to prove that he or she is not guilty.

Title of legislation	Labour Code, 2002, as amended

The Labour Code, 2002, as amended by the Antidiscrimination Act in 2013, forbids discrimination on the grounds of sex. (Article 1)

An employee who assumes that his or her rights or interests protected by law were aggrieved by failure to comply with the principle of equal treatment or by failure to comply with the conditions stated may have recourse to a court and claim of legal protection stipulated by the Antidiscrimination Act. (Article 13 (5))

BIBLIOGRAPHY

Ministry of Labour, Social Affairs and Family of the Slovak Republic, 2013. Available at: https://www.employment.gov.sk/files/praca-zamestnanost/

vztah-zamestnanca-zamestnavatela/zakonnik-prace/zakonnik-prace-anglick a-verzia-labour-code-full-wording-2012.pdf. Accessed March 15, 2019

International Labour Organization, 2004. 365 Act of 20 May 2004 on Equal Treatment in Certain Areas and Protection against Discrimination, amending and supplementing Certain Other Laws (Antidiscrimination Act). Available at: http://www.ilo.org/dyn/natlex/docs/ELECTRONIC/68611/77169/F1638461182/SVK68611.pdf. Accessed March 15, 2019

SPAIN

Union and hotel chain sign 2019 agreement on preventing sexual harassment in the workplace, a first in the global hospitality sector: IUF, the global union for the hospitality sector, signed a landmark agreement with Meliá Hotels International, a Spanish hotel chain, on preventing sexual harassment in the workplace. The agreement incorporates the ILO definition of sexual harassment, affirms a policy of "zero tolerance," and commits both parties to develop appropriate local implementation procedures based on a shared recognition of the need "to protect the dignity of everyone who works for Meliá, as well as their rights relating to their physical and moral integrity and non-discrimination." Progress in implementation will be jointly evaluated on a regular basis. The IUF general secretary welcomed Meliá's lead, stating, "Our members have reported that as many as 85 percent of employees in the hospitality industry have experienced sexual harassment on the job." Meliá is the largest hotel chain in Spain and has operations in 41 countries (Source: iuf.org, January 24, 2019. "IUF and Meliá agreement on preventing sexual harassment in the workplace, a first in the global hospitality sector").

Although a 2018 survey, conducted by the pollster Metroscopia, showed that one out of every four women has been groped, or attempts at groping were made at least once, statistics were not found specifically on sexual harassment in the workplace. There is barely any statistical data in Spain to help understand the real magnitude of sexual harassment (Source: El Pais, March 6, 2018. "One in three Spanish women has felt sexually harassed, new poll finds," by Silvia Blanco).

Legislation

- Constitutional Act 3/2007 of 22 March for Effective Equality Between Women and Men
- The Workers Statute, 1995
- Royal Legislative Decree 5/2000 of 4 August
- Spanish Penal Code, Organic Law 5/2010 of 22 June

Title of legislation Constitutional Act 3/2007 of 22 March

The *Constitutional Act 3/2007 of 22 March for Effective Equality Between Women and Men* ("Equality Law") transposes 2002/73/EC. The Act defines the basic legal concepts and categories relating to equality, direct and indirect discrimination, *sexual harassment, harassment on the grounds of sex* and positive action. It includes, among the labor rights of workers and workers, protection against sexual harassment and harassment based on sex.

The Act establishes the employer's legal obligation to prevent *sexual harassment and harassment related to sex* and determines specific procedures to channel complaints or claims about these matters.

Sexual harassment is defined as "any behavior, verbal or physical, of a sexual nature that has the purpose or effect of violating the dignity of a person, in particular when an intimidating, degrading or offensive environment is created." Harassment on the grounds of sex is "any behavior depending on the sex of a person, with the purpose or effect of violating their dignity and creating an intimidating, degrading or offensive environment." (Article 7, Sections 7.1 and 7.2)

Under Article 7, sexual harassment and harassment based on sex are considered discriminatory in all cases. Further, "the conditioning of a right or an expectation of right to the acceptance of a situation constituting sexual harassment or harassment based on sex will also be considered an act of discrimination based on sex."

Businesses should encourage working conditions that prevent *sexual harassment* and harassment based on sex, arbitrate specific procedures for prevention, and channel complaints or claims of those who have experienced harassment or sexual harassment. (Article 48)

Article 48 addresses specific measures to prevent sexual harassment and harassment based on sex at work as follows:

- Companies should promote working conditions that avoid sexual harassment and harassment based on sex and arbitrate specific procedures for their prevention and to channel the complaints or claims that may be made by those who have been subject to it. With this purpose, it will be possible to establish measures that must be negotiated with workers' representatives, such as the preparation and dissemination of codes of good practice, the carrying out of information campaigns or training actions.
- Workers' representatives should contribute to prevent sexual harassment and harassment based on sex at work by raising awareness among workers about the same and informing the company management of the behaviors or behaviors of workers that they had knowledge and that they could propitiate it.

Title of legislation The Workers Statute, 2015

The Workers Statute, as amended, prohibits discrimination on the grounds of sex. Workers' rights include protection against *sexual harassment and harassment on the grounds of sex.*

Article 4 of Labour Rights states that in labor relations, workers' rights include respect for their privacy and consideration for their dignity, including sexual and sexist harassment.

A breach of contract shall be considered for reasons including *sexual harassment.* In this case, the employment contract may be terminated. (Article 54)

Title of legislation	Spanish Penal Code, Organic Law 5/2010 of 22 June, as amended 2015

Article 184 of the *Spanish Penal Code, Organic Law 5/2010 of 22 June*, as amended, discusses *sexual harassment*, stating in relevant part: whoever solicits favours of a sexual nature, for himself or for a third party, within the setting of a continuous or usual work relation, and by such conduct causes the victim a situation that is objective and seriously intimidating, hostile or humiliating, shall convicted of sexual harassment and punished with a sentence of imprisonment of three to five months or a fine from six to ten months.

BIBLIOGRAPHY

iuf.org, January 24, 2019. IUF and Meliá Agreement on Preventing Sexual Harassment in the Workplace, a First in the Global Hospitality Sector. Available at: http://www.iuf.org/w/?q=node/6692. Accessed August 26, 2019

El Pais, March 6, 2018. One in Three Spanish Women Has Felt Sexually Harassed, New Poll Finds, by Silvia Blanco. Available at: https://elpais.com/elpais/2018/03/06/inenglish/1520325751_504683.html. Accessed March 1, 2019

Government of Spain, 2007. Organic Law 3/2007 of 22 March for Effective Equality of Women and Men. Available at: http://www.boe.es/buscar/doc.php?id=BOE-A-2007-6115. Accessed February 2, 2019

Ministry of Labour and Social Security, 1995. Workers Statute. Available at: http://www.juntadeandalucia.es/empleo/anexos/estatico/1_571_0.pdf. Accessed February 2, 2019

Ministry of Justice, 1995. Spanish Penal Code, Organic Law 5/2010 of 22 June, by Which Modifies the Organic Law 10/1995 of 23 November, of the Penal Code. Available at: http://www.sanchezcerveraabogados.com/en/files/2012/06/Criminal_Code_C%C3%B3digo_Penal.pdf. Accessed February 2, 2019

SWITZERLAND

Statistics: in a survey of media professionals in Switzerland, over half of female respondents and a tenth of males reported being the victims of harassment during their work. Other, more representative surveys, carried about by bodies such as the State Secretariat for Economic Affairs and Amnesty International, have shown that around 30 percent of women overall have reported being harassed in the workplace (Source: Swissinfo.ch, June 9, 2019. "Survey sheds light on harassment in the Swiss media industry").

A 2008 government-commissioned study found that 28% of women in Switzerland experience sexual harassment over the course of their professional lives (Source: State Secretariat for Economic Affairs. "Risk and extent of sexual harassment in the workplace," by Silvia Strub: Bureau of Labor and Social Policy Studies BASS, Berne; Marianne Schär Moser: Forschung und Beratung, Bern, 2008).

Legislation

- Federal Act on Gender Equality, ("Gender Equality Act" or GEA) 1995, as amended
- Code of Obligations 1911, as amended
- Swiss Criminal Code of 21 December 1937

Title of legislation	Federal Act on Gender Equality ("Gender Equality Act" or GEA) 1995, as amended

The *Federal Act on Gender Equality* ("Gender Equality Act" or GEA) of 24 March 1995 applies to employment relationships under the Swiss Code of Obligations. it defines *sexual harassment* as discrimination in Article 4, as follows:

> Any harassing behaviour of a sexual nature or other behaviour related to the person's sex that adversely affects the dignity of women or men in the workplace is discriminatory. Such behaviour includes in particular threats, the promise of advantages, the use of coercion and the exertion of pressure in order to obtain favours of a sexual nature.

A victim of discrimination may apply to the court or to the administrative authority for an order for the following: prohibiting or stopping threatened discrimination; requiring existing discrimination to cease; confirming that discrimination is taking place if it is continuing to have a disruptive effect; or for the payment of any salary due. In case of discrimination through *sexual harassment,* the court or the administrative authority may also award compensation, unless the employer proves that it took measures that have been proven in practice to be necessary and adequate to prevent sexual harassment and which it could reasonably have been expected to take. Compensation in the case of sexual harassment must not exceed an amount equivalent to six months' salary. (Article 5)

Switzerland's Federal Office for Gender Equality issued "Sexual harassment in the workplace: information for employers and for employees" on its website in 2017.

Title of legislation Swiss Code of Obligations, 1911 as amended

The *Swiss Code of Obligations*, 1911, as amended, states:

> Within the employment relationship, the employer must acknowledge and safeguard the employee's personality rights, have due regard for his health and ensure that proper moral standards are maintained. In particular, he must ensure that employees are not sexually harassed and that any victim of *sexual harassment* suffers no further adverse consequences. In order to safeguard the personal safety, health and integrity of his or her employees, the employer must take all measures that are shown by experience to be necessary. (Article 328)

Title of legislation Swiss Criminal Code of 21 December 1937

Though not mentioning the workplace, Article 198 of the *Swiss Criminal Code* states:

> Any person who causes offence by performing a sexual act in the presence of another who does not expect it, any person who

sexually harasses another physically or through the use of indecent language shall on complaint be liable to a fine.

BIBLIOGRAPHY

Swissinfo. ch. Survey Sheds Light on Harassment in the Swiss Media Industry, June 9, 2019. Available at: https://www.swissinfo.ch/eng/sexual-molestation_survey-sheds-light-on-harassment-in-the-swiss-media-industry/45019792. Accessed August 20, 2019

State Secretariat for Economic Affairs, 2008. Risk and Extent of Sexual Harassment in the Workplace, by Silvia Strub: Bureau of Labor and Social Policy Studies BASS, Berne; Marianne Schär Moser: Forschung und Beratung, Bern. Available at: https://www.seco.admin.ch/seco/fr/home/Publikationen_Dienstleistungen/Publikationen_und_Formulare/Arbeit/Arbeitsbedingungen/Studien_und_Berichte/risiko-und-verbreitung-sexueller-belaestigung-am-arbeitsplatz.html. Accessed August 22, 2019

Switzerland's Federal Office for Gender Equality, 2017. Sexual Harassment in the Workplace: Information for Employers. Available at: https://www.ebg.admin.ch/ebg/en/home/topics/work/sexual-harassment-in-the-workplace.html. Accessed May 29, 2019

Federal Council, 2011. Federal Act on Gender Equality (Gender Equality Act, GEA) of 24 March 1995, as amended. Available at: https://www.admin.ch/opc/en/classified-compilation/19950082/201701010000/151.1.pdf. Accessed May 29, 2019

Federal Council, 2015. Federal Act on the Amendment of the Swiss Civil Code (Part Five: The Code of Obligations), 1911 as amended. Available at: https://www.admin.ch/opc/en/classified-compilation/19110009/201507010000/220.pdf. Accessed February 3, 2019

https://www.admin.ch. Swiss Criminal Code. Available at: https://www.admin.ch/opc/en/classified-compilation/19370083/201903010000/311.0.pdf. Accessed June 18, 2019

UKRAINE

Although Ukraine criminalizes sexual harassment in the workplace or any environment, the International Labor Organization found the legal definition of sexual harassment "does not cover situations where conduct of a sexual nature creates a hostile working environment, irrespective of whether there is a relation of subordination between the harasser and the victim" (Source: Center on Human Rights Education, April 27, 2017, by Jessica Ruch).

Legislation

- Law of Ukraine on Equal Rights and Opportunities for Women and Men, 2006

Title of legislation	Law of Ukraine on Equal Rights and Opportunities for Women and Men, 2006, as amended

The objective of the *Law of Ukraine on Equal Rights and Opportunities for Women and Men,* effective January 1, 2006, defines *sexual harassment* as "verbally expressed sexual actions (threats, intimidation, scurrilities) or physical actions (touching, patting) which humiliate or offend persons in the state of work, service, material or other subordination." (Article 1)

The employer is obliged to take measures to prevent cases of sexual harassment. (Article 17)

A person who believes he or she was the object of sexual harassment has the right to submit a complaint to the state authorities, authorities of the Autonomous Republic of Crimea, local self-government authorities and their officials, the Ukrainian Parliament Commissioner for Human Rights and/or to the court according to the procedure provided by law. (Article 22)

A person also has the right to compensation for material loss and moral damage caused in the result of sexual harassment. The procedure of compensation for material loss and moral damage, caused by sexual harassment, is defined by the Civil Code of Ukraine (435–15) and other laws. (Article 23)

BIBLIOGRAPHY

Center on Human Rights Education, April 27, 2017. By Jessica Ruch. Available at: https://www.centeronhumanrightseducation.org/pervasive-gender-based-violence-ukraine/. Accessed March 1, 2019

International Labour Organization, 2007. Law of Ukraine on Ensuring Equal Rights and Equal Opportunities of Women and Men. Available at: http://www.ilo.org/wcmsp5/groups/public/---ed_protect/---protrav/---ilo_aids/documents/legaldocument/wcms_127500.pdf. Accessed March 1, 2019

UNITED KINGDOM

> The #MeToo movement and telling statistics lead to government action in the United Kingdom.

A 2018 survey by the trade union Prospect found that more than a third (35 percent) of women in the UK had experienced sexual harassment at work (Source: Prospect, June 11, 2018. "A third of women say they have faced sexual harassment at work"). Further statistics on sexual harassment in the workplace from a 2017 survey of UK adults, "Sexual harassment in the work place," on behalf of the BBC, revealed the following:

- 40 percent of women have experienced some form of sexual harassment in the workplace; and
- Women aged 18–34 are most at risk of sexual harassment at work, with 43 percent having experienced it.

(Source: BBC, 2017. "Sexual harassment in the work place")

> After widespread reports of women's experiences of sexual harassment at work, the government's Women and Equalities Committee opened an inquiry into what actions government and employers can take to change workplace culture.

July 2018: the Women and Equalities Committee published a report on the results of its six-month-long inquiry into sexual harassment in the workplace. The report's summary stated, in part:

> Sexual harassment in the workplace is widespread and commonplace. It is shameful that unwanted sexual behaviours such as sexual comments, touching, groping and assault are seen as an everyday occurrence and part of the culture in workplaces. A BBC survey in November 2017 found that 40 percent of women and 18 percent of men had experienced unwanted sexual behaviour in the workplace. These behaviours are unlawful, but the government, regulators and employers have failed to tackle them, despite their responsibilities to do so under UK and international law. As a result these legal protections are often not available to workers in practice. The #MeToo movement has put sexual harassment in the spotlight, but it is not a new phenomenon. Employers and regulators have ignored their responsibilities for too long. It is time for the government to put sexual harassment at the top of the

> agenda. Currently, there is little incentive for employers and regulators to take robust action to tackle and prevent unwanted sexual behaviours in the workplace.

The report calls on the government to focus on five priorities to put sexual harassment at the top of the agenda for employers, as follows:

- Introduce a new duty on employers to prevent harassment, supported by a statutory code of practice outlining the steps they can take to do this; and ensuring that interns, volunteers and those harassed by third parties have access to the same legal protections and remedies as their workplace colleagues;
- Require regulators to take a more active role, starting by setting out the actions they will take to help tackle this problem, including the enforcement action they will take; and making it clear to those they regulate that sexual harassment is a breach of professional standards and a reportable offence with sanctions;
- Make enforcement processes work better for employees by setting out in the statutory code of practice what employers should do to tackle sexual harassment; and reducing barriers to taking forward tribunal cases, including by extending the time limit for submitting a claim, introducing punitive damages for employers and reducing cost risks for employees;
- Clean up the use of non-disclosure agreements (NDAs), including by requiring the use of standard, plain English confidentiality clauses, which set out the meaning, limit and effect of the clause, and making it an offence to misuse such clauses; and extending whistleblowing protections so that disclosures to the police and regulators such as the EHRC are protected;
- Collect robust data on the extent of sexual harassment in the workplace and on the number of employment tribunal claims involving complaints of harassment of a sexual nature.

December 2018: in response to the report, on December 18, 2018, the government announced a new Code of Practice to tackle sexual harassment at work. The code aims to help employers better understand their legal responsibilities to protect their staff as part of a package of commitments to tackle sexual harassment at work. Additionally, 12 government announcements were launched to tackle sexual harassment at work, including consultations on non-disclosure agreements and on strengthening and clarifying the laws on third party harassment in the workplace.

The UK subsequently consulted on "Confidentiality clauses: measures to prevent misuse in situations of workplace harassment or discrimination, seeking views on proposals to improve the regulation of confidentiality clauses, also known as non-disclosure agreements or NDAs." The consultation sought comments by April 29, 2019 on both general provisions in employment contracts and specific clauses in settlement agreements. Its stated purpose was to better understand how confidentiality clauses and the legal framework around them work in practice; and to assess what changes are required to ensure individuals are appropriately protected from their misuse.

July 2019: most recently, the UK published a consultation on harassment in the workplace in response to concerns raised by the Women and Equalities Select Committee in their 2018 report. The consultation acknowledges that sexual harassment in the workplace persists at "a startling rate." The consultation ran from July 11 until October 2, 2019 and sought comments on the following:

- The evidence for the introduction of a mandatory duty on employers to protect workers from harassment in the workplace;
- How to strengthen and clarify the laws relating to third party harassment; and
- Evidence to extend Employment Tribunal time limits in the Equality Act from three months.

Legislation

- The Equality Act 2010, as amended
- Protection from Harassment Act 1997

Title of legislation The Equality Act 2010

Sexual harassment is unlawful under the *Equality Act.* Three types of harassment are defined for the purposes of the Act, including sexual harassment, which in turn includes sexual harassment which is unwanted conduct of a sexual nature where this has the same purpose or effect as the first type of harassment, and treating someone less favorably because they have either submitted to or rejected sexual harassment.

The Equality Act 2010 defines sexual harassment as "unwanted conduct of a sexual nature" which has the purpose or effect of violating dignity or "creating an intimidating, hostile, degrading, humiliating or offensive environment." A wide range of behaviour can come under this definition: sexual jokes or comments, remarks about someone's body or appearance, displays of pornographic material, cat calls or wolf-whistling, flashing, sexual advances, groping, sexual assault, or rape. The common factors are the effect that the conduct has on the victim, and that it is unwanted. Some forms of workplace sexual harassment can constitute a criminal offence, for example under the Protection from Harassment Act 1997 (harassment and stalking), the Sexual Offences Act 2003 (sexual assault and voyeurism) or the Criminal Justice and Courts Act 2015 ("revenge porn").

Under the Equality Act, Person A harasses Person B if (a) A engages in unwanted conduct related to a relevant protected characteristic, and (b) the conduct has the purpose or effect of (i) violating B's dignity, or (ii) creating an intimidating, hostile, degrading, humiliating or offensive environment for B. A also harasses B if (a) A engages in unwanted conduct of a sexual nature, and (b) the conduct has the purpose or effect referred to in subsection (1) (b).

The Equality Act protects and applies equally to people who are discriminated against because they are subjected to comments and behavior regarding sex which they find offensive.

More information for employers and workers may be found in the Equality Act Guidance, available at https://www.equalityhumanrights.com/en/advice-and-guidance/equality-act-guidance.

Title of legislation Protection from Harassment Act 1997

Under the *Protection from Harassment Act 1997* victims of harassment can go before a Court to seek civil injunctions against behavior which causes distress. The purpose of the Act is to make provision for protecting persons from harassment and similar conduct.

The Act does not expressly define sexual harassment but does prohibit harassment in the following terms:

- A person must not pursue a course of conduct which amounts to harassment of another, and which he knows or ought to know amounts to harassment of the other.
- A person must not pursue a course of conduct which involves harassment of two or more persons, and which he knows or ought to know involves harassment of those persons, and by which he intends to

persuade any person (whether or not one of those mentioned above) (i) not to do something that he is entitled or required to do, or (ii) to do something that he is not under any obligation to do.

A person who pursues a course of conduct in breach of the above is guilty of an offence. A person guilty of an offence under this section is liable on summary conviction to imprisonment for a term not exceeding six months, or a fine not exceeding level 5 on the standard scale, or both.

This does not apply to a course of conduct if the person who pursued it shows that:

- It was pursued for the purpose of preventing or detecting crime,
- It was pursued under any enactment or rule of law or to comply with any condition or requirement imposed by any person under any enactment, or
- In the particular circumstances the pursuit of the course of conduct was reasonable.

Section 3, "Civil Remedy," creates a statutory tort based on the same acts as the criminal offence, stating that an actual or apprehended breach of Section 1 may be the subject of a claim in civil proceedings by the person who is or may be the victim of the course of conduct in question. On such a claim, damages may be awarded for (among other things) any anxiety caused by the harassment and any financial loss resulting from the harassment.

Application of Protection from Harassment Act 1997 in an employment context: in the 2005 case of Majrowski v Guy's and St Thomas's NHS Trust, 2005 EWCA Civ 251, the Court found that an employer may be civilly vicariously liable under the *Protection from Harassment Act* for harassment in breach of the Act committed by an employee in the course of his or her employment (Source: William Majrowski and Guy's and St Thomas's NHS Trust, 2005. England and Wales Court of Appeal (Civil Division) Decisions).

BIBLIOGRAPHY

Prospect, June 11, 2018. A Third of Women Say They Have Faced Sexual Harassment at Work. Available at: https://www.prospect.org.uk/news/id/2018/June/11/A-third-women-say-they-have-faced-sexual-harassment-at-work. Accessed August 28, 2019 legislation. gov. uk, 2010. Equality Act 2010. Available at: https://www.legislation.gov.uk/ukpga/2010/15/contents. Accessed March 1, 2019

BBC, Sexual Harassment in the Work Place, 2017. Available at https://www.comresglobal.com/polls/bbc-sexual-harassment-in-the-work-place-2017/ and https://www.comresglobal.com/wp-content/uploads/2017/12/BBC-sexual-harassment_FINAL_v3.pdf. Accessed August 26, 2019

Equality and Human Rights Commission. What Is the Equality Act? Available at: https://www.equalityhumanrights.com/en/equality-act-2010/what-equality-act. Accessed March 1, 2019

Equality and Human Rights Commission. Equality Act Guidance. Available at https://www.equalityhumanrights.com/en/advice-and-guidance/equality-act-guidance. Accessed March 1, 2019

Legislation.gov.uk, 1997. Protection from Harassment Act 1997. Available at: http://www.legislation.gov.uk/ukpga/1997/40/contents. Accessed March 1, 2019

Majrowski and Guy's and St Thomas's NHS Trust, 2005. England and Wales Court of Appeal (Civil Division) Decisions. Available at: http://www.bailii.org/ew/cases/EWCA/Civ/2005/251.html. Accessed March 1, 2019

House of Commons, Women and Equalities Committee, 2018. Sexual Harassment in the Workplace Fifth Report of Session 2017–19.

Report, July 18, 2018. Available at https://publications.parliament.uk/pa/cm201719/cmselect/cmwomeq/725/725.pdf. Accessed May 31, 2019

Gov.UK, 2019. Government Announces New Code of Practice to Tackle Sexual Harassment at Work. Available at: https://www.gov.uk/government/news/government-announces-new-code-of-practice-to-tackle-sexual-harassment-at-work. Accessed May 31, 2019

Gov.UK, 4 March 2019. Confidentiality Clauses: Measures to Prevent Misuse in Situations of Workplace Harassment or Discrimination. Available at: https://www.gov.uk/government/consultations/confidentiality-clauses-measures-to-prevent-misuse-in-situations-of-workplace-harassment-or-discrimination. Accessed April 15, 2019

www.parliament.uk, July 25, 2018. Five-Point Plan to Tackle Sexual Harassment in the Workplace. Available at: https://www.parliament.uk/business/committees/committees-a-z/commons-select/women-and-equalities-committee/news-parliament-2017/sexual-harassment-workplace-report-published-17-19/. Accessed August 28, 2019

4 Sexual harassment laws in the Asia-Pacific region

"How #MeToo is taking on a life of its own in Asia," Time Magazine's cover story on October 9, 2018 by Suyin Haynes and Aria Hangyu Chen, stated, "The reckoning over sexual assault in the U.S. has helped reignite long-simmering movements in South Korea, China and beyond. But speaking out comes with huge risks." It reported that "daring to speak out in some of these deeply patriarchal societies comes with enormous risks." The article also noted:

> In Asia, #MeToo isn't just synonymous with sexual harassment and assault. As women across the region turn their anger into action, its manifestations have become a broader feminist rallying cry. In Japan, #WithYou has been used to express solidarity with survivors of workplace harassment; in Thailand, women voiced their frustration at being slut-shamed with #DontTellMeHowToDress; and in the Philippines, women have flooded social media and the streets in protest against President Rodrigo Duterte's sexist comments, under the hashtag #BabaeAko (I Am Woman).

BIBLIOGRAPHY

Time Magazine, October 9, 2018. How #MeToo Is Taking on a Life of Its Own in Asia, by Suyin Haynes and Aria Hangyu Chen. Available at: http://time.com/longform/me-too-asia-china-south-korea/. Accessed June 27, 2019

AUSTRALIA

> Sexual harassment is any unwanted or unwelcome sexual behaviour, which makes a person feel offended, humiliated or intimidated. It is not interaction, flirtation or friendship which is mutual or consensual.
>
> *(Source: Australia Human Rights Commission)*

Sexual harassment is a type of sex discrimination. It can be committed by an employer, workmate, or other person in a working relationship with the victim.

Sexual harassment continues to be a major problem in Australian workplaces: the fourth national survey on sexual harassment in Australian workplaces (2018) conducted by Roy Morgan Research surveyed 10,000 people. It showed that sexual harassment continues to affect both men and women, finding that 39 percent of Australian women and 26 percent of Australian men have been sexually harassed at work in the past five years. Formal reporting of workplace sexual harassment was low, with only 17 percent of people making a report or complaint (Source: Australian Human Rights Commission, September 21, 2018. "Everyone's Business: 2018 Sexual Harassment Survey").

According to the survey, the three most common forms of sexual harassment at work are:

- Offensive, sexually suggestive comments or jokes;
- Inappropriate physical contact; and
- Unwelcome touching, hugging, cornering or kissing.

The survey results led to the Australian Human Rights Commission's (AHRC) National Inquiry into sexual harassment in Australian workplaces, announced on June 20, 2018 by Australia's Sex Discrimination Commissioner. The year-long inquiry accepted public submissions until the end of January 2019, followed by a public consultation process. The focus of the National Inquiry is on the nature and prevalence of sexual harassment in Australian workplaces, the drivers of this harassment, and measures to address sexual harassment in Australian workplaces.

Legislation

- Sex Discrimination Act 1984 (SDA) as amended
- Workplace Gender Equality Act, 2012

Title of legislation	The Sex Discrimination Act 1984 as amended

The *Sex Discrimination Act 1984* (SDA) No. 4, 1984, as amended, protects individuals across Australia from *sexual harassment*. The Act makes it unlawful for a person to sexually harass another person in a number of areas, including employment.

Under the Act, a person sexually harasses another person if:

- The person makes an unwelcome sexual advance, or an unwelcome request for sexual favors, to the person harassed; or
- Engages in other unwelcome conduct of a sexual nature in relation to the person harassed;

in circumstances in which a reasonable person, having regard to all the circumstances, would have anticipated the possibility that the person harassed would be offended, humiliated or intimidated.

The circumstances to be taken into account include, but are not limited to, the following:

- The sex, age, sexual orientation, gender identity, intersex status, marital or relationship status, religious belief, race, colour, or national or ethnic origin, of the person harassed;
- The relationship between the person harassed and the person who made the advance or request or who engaged in the conduct;
- Any disability of the person harassed; and
- Any other relevant circumstance.

Conduct of a sexual nature also includes making a statement of a sexual nature to a person, or in the presence of a person, whether the statement is made orally or in writing.

Title of legislation	Workplace Gender Equality Act 2012 No. 91, 1986

The principal objects of the *Workplace Gender Equality Act 2012* No. 91, 1986 include promoting, amongst employers, the elimination of discrimination on the basis of gender in relation to employment matters, including arrangements for dealing with sex-based harassment of employees in the workplace. However, no specific provisions on sexual harassment measures are contained in this Act.

BIBLIOGRAPHY

Australian Government, Federal Register of Legislation, 1984. Sex Discrimination Act 1984, No. 4, 1984 as Amended. This Is a Compilation of the Sex Discrimination Act 1984 That Shows the Text of the Law as Amended and in Force on December 9, 2018 (The Compilation Date). Available at: https://www.legislation.gov.au/Details/C2018C00499. Accessed March 20, 2019

Australian Government, Federal Register of Legislation, 2012. Gender Equality Act. Available at: https://www.legislation.gov.au/Details/C2016C00895. Accessed March 20, 2019

Australian Human Rights Commission, December 20, 2018. National Inquiry into Sexual Harassment in Australian Workplaces. Available at: https://www.humanrights.gov.au/our-work/sex-discrimination/projects/national-inquiry-sexual-harassment-australian-workplaces. Accessed August 27, 2019

Australian Human Rights Commission, September 21, 2018. Everyone's Business: 2018 Sexual Harassment Survey. Available at: https://www.humanrights.gov.au/news/stories/everyone-s-business-2018-sexual-harassment-survey. Accessed August 27, 2019

Australian Human Rights Commission, May 21, 2014. "Ending Workplace Sexual Harassment: A Resource for Small, Medium and Large Employers." Available at: https://www.humanrights.gov.au/our-work/sex-discrimination/publications/ending-workplace-sexual-harassment-resource-small-medium. Accessed June 27, 2019

AUSTRALIAN STATES

> Each Australian State has its own legislation. The majority of States regulate sexual harassment under Anti-Discrimination Acts, with a few addressing it under Equality Acts.

Commonwealth laws and state/territory laws generally cover the same grounds and areas of discrimination, although there are some gaps in the protection offered between different states and territories and at a Commonwealth level. In addition, there are circumstances where only the Commonwealth law would apply or where only the state law would apply.

AUSTRALIAN CAPITAL TERRITORY

Legislation

- Discrimination Act, 1991

Title of legislation	Discrimination Act, 1991

The *Discrimination Act, 1991* was republished in 2015. Objects of the Act include eliminating, so far as possible, *sexual harassment* in areas which include the workplace.

The meaning of sexual harassment in Part 5 of the Act is as follows:

> A person subjects someone else to sexual harassment if the person makes an unwelcome sexual advance, or an unwelcome request for sexual favors, to the other person or engages in other unwelcome conduct of a sexual nature in circumstances in which the other person reasonably feels offended, humiliated or intimidated. Conduct of a sexual nature includes the making of a statement of a sexual nature to, or in the presence of, a person, whether the statement is made orally or in writing.

Under the law, the following are unlawful:

- For an employer to subject an employee, or a person seeking employment, to sexual harassment.

- For an employee to subject a fellow employee, or a person seeking employment with the same employer, to sexual harassment.
- For a principal to subject a commission agent or contract worker, or a person seeking to become his or her commission agent or contract worker, to sexual harassment.
- For a commission agent or contract worker to subject a fellow employee, or a person seeking employment with the same employer, to sexual harassment.
- For a partner in a partnership to subject another partner in the partnership, or a person seeking to become a partner in the partnership, to sexual harassment.
- For a workplace participant to subject another workplace participant to sexual harassment at a place that is a workplace, or potential workplace, as the case requires, of both of those people. Retaliation is prohibited.

BIBLIOGRAPHY

Australian Capital Territory, 1991. Discrimination Act 1991, A1991-81, Republication No. 42, Effective: November 7, 2015. Available at: https://www.legislation.act.gov.au/a/1991-81. Accessed March 20, 2019

NEW SOUTH WALES

Legislation

- Anti-Discrimination Act, 1977

Title of legislation	Anti-Discrimination Act 1977

Under the New South Wales *Anti-Discrimination Act 1977*, grounds of unlawful discrimination include *sexual harassment.*

Part 2A covers *Prohibition of Sexual Harassment*, and contains the following relevant provisions:

A person sexually harasses another person if:

- The person makes an unwelcome sexual advance, or an unwelcome request for sexual favors, to the other person, or
- The person engages in other unwelcome conduct of a sexual nature in relation to the other person,

in circumstances in which a reasonable person, having regard to all the circumstances, would have anticipated that the other person would be offended, humiliated or intimidated.

The following are unlawful under the Act:

- For an employer to sexually harass an employee, or a person who is seeking employment with the employer.
- For a partner in a partnership to sexually harass another partner, or a person who is seeking to become a partner, in the same partnership.
- For a workplace participant to sexually harass another workplace participant at a place that is a workplace of both those persons.
- For a person to sexually harass another person in the course of receiving, or seeking to receive, goods or services from that other person, or providing, or offering to provide, goods or services to that other person.
- For a person to sexually harass another person in the course of providing, or offering to provide, (whether as principal or agent) accommodation to that other person.

BIBLIOGRAPHY

New South Wales, 1977. Anti-Discrimination Act 1977, as of June 2, 2016, Act 48 of 1977. Available at: https://www.legislation.nsw.gov.au/#/view/act/1977/48 and https://www.legislation.nsw.gov.au/#/view/act/1977/48/part2a. Accessed June 27, 2019

NORTHERN TERRITORY

Legislation

- Anti-Discrimination Act, 1996

Title of legislation	Anti-Discrimination Act, 1996

Prohibited conduct under the Northern Territory *Anti-Discrimination Act, 1996*, includes sexual harassment.

A person shall not *sexually harass* another person.

Sexual harassment takes place if a person:

- Subjects another person to an unwelcome act of physical intimacy; or
- Makes an unwelcome demand or request (whether directly or by implication) for sexual favors from the other person; or

- Makes an unwelcome remark with sexual connotations; or
- Engages in any other unwelcome conduct of a sexual nature, and that person does so:
  - (i) with the intention of offending, humiliating or intimidating the other person; or
  - (ii) in circumstances where a reasonable person would have anticipated the possibility that the other person would be offended, humiliated or intimidated by the conduct. (Circumstances that are relevant in determining whether a reasonable person would have anticipated the possibility that the other person would be offended, humiliated or intimidated by the conduct include the sex, age or race of the other person; and any impairment that the other person has; and the relationship between the other person and the person engaging in the conduct; and any other circumstance of the other person); or
- That other person is, or reasonably believes that he or she is likely to be, subjected to some detriment if he or she objects to the act, demand, request, remark or conduct.

BIBLIOGRAPHY

Northern Territory Government, 1996. Northern Territory Anti-Discrimination Act. Available at: https://legislation.nt.gov.au/Legislation/ANTIDISCRIMINATION-ACT-1992. Accessed March 20, 2019

QUEENSLAND

Legislation

- Queensland Anti-Discrimination Act 1991

Title of legislation	Queensland Anti-Discrimination Act, 1991

Sexual harassment is prohibited by the Anti-Discrimination Act under Chapter 3, Sections 117–120, which state that:

Sexual harassment happens if a person—

(a) subjects another person to an unsolicited act of physical intimacy; or
(b) makes an unsolicited demand or request (whether directly or by implication); or
(c) makes a remark with sexual connotations relating to the other person; or
(d) engages in any other unwelcome conduct of a sexual nature in relation to the other person;

and the person engaging in the conduct described in paragraphs (a), (b), (c) or (d) does so—

(e) with the intention of offending, humiliating or intimidating the other person; or
(f) in circumstances where a reasonable person would have anticipated the possibility that the other person would be offended, humiliated or intimidated by the conduct.

Examples for paragraph (a)—

Physical contact such as patting, pinching or touching in a sexual way, unnecessary familiarity such as deliberately brushing against a person

Example for paragraph (b)—Sexual propositions

Examples for paragraph (c)—Unwelcome and uncalled for remarks or insinuations about a person's sex or private life, suggestive comments about a person's appearance or body

Examples for paragraph (d)—offensive telephone calls, indecent exposure

Section 120 of the Act lists the circumstances that are relevant when determining whether conduct is likely to be offensive, humiliating, or intimidating. These include the age, sex, race and any impairment the other person (i.e. the victim) has, any other circumstances and the relationship they have with the person.

BIBLIOGRAPHY

Anti Discrimination Commission Queensland. Sexual Harassment, last updated July 2019. Available at: https://www.adcq.qld.gov.au/complaints/sexual-harassment. Accessed May 14, 2019

Queensland Government, 1991. Queensland Anti-Discrimination Act, 1991. Available at: https://www.legislation.qld.gov.au/view/html/inforce/2018-03-30/act-1991-085, Accessed March 30, 2019

SOUTH AUSTRALIA

Legislation

- South Australia Equal Opportunity Act, 1984, as amended

Title of legislation	South Australia Equal Opportunity Act, 1984, as amended

The *South Australia Equal Opportunity Act, 1984, as amended*, covers *sexual harassment.*

The Act states that a person sexually harasses another if—

(i) the person makes an unwelcome sexual advance, or an unwelcome request for sexual favours, to the person harassed; or

(ii) engages in other unwelcome conduct of a sexual nature in relation to the person harassed, in circumstances in which a reasonable person, having regard to all the circumstances, would have anticipated that the person harassed would be offended, humiliated or intimidated; and

The Act states that

(a) a persons sexually harasses another if-

(b) conduct of a sexual nature includes making a statement of a sexual nature to a person, or in the presence of a person, whether the statement is made orally or in writing.

Section 87—Sexual harassment states the following:

(1) It is unlawful for a person to subject to sexual harassment—(a) a person with whom he or she works; or (b) a person who is seeking to become a fellow worker, while in attendance at a place that is a workplace of both the persons or in circumstances where the person was, or ought reasonably to have been, aware that the other person was a fellow worker or seeking to become a fellow worker.

(6aa) It is unlawful for a person to whom goods, services to which this Act applies or accommodation are being offered, supplied, performed or provided by another person to subject that other person to sexual harassment.

(7) If an employee reports to his or her employer specific circumstances in which the employee was subjected, in the course of his or her employment, to sexual harassment by a person other than a fellow worker, and it is reasonable in all the circumstances to expect that further sexual harassment of the employee by the same person is likely to occur, it is unlawful for the employer to fail to take reasonable steps to prevent the further sexual harassment.

BIBLIOGRAPHY

Government of South Australia, Attorney General's Department, 1984. Equal Opportunity Act 1984. Available at: https://www.legislation.sa.gov.au/LZ/C/A/EQUAL%20OPPORTUNITY%20ACT%201984/CURRENT/1984.95.AUTH.PDF. Accessed March 30, 2019

TASMANIA

Legislation

- Tasmania Anti-Discrimination Act, 1998

Title of legislation	Tasmania Anti-Discrimination Act, 1998

Under the *Tasmania Anti-Discrimination Act 1998,* a person must not sexually harass another person.

Sexual harassment takes place if a person does the following:

- Subjects another person to an unsolicited act of physical contact of a sexual nature; or
- Makes an unwelcome sexual advance or an unwelcome request for sexual favours to another person; or
- Makes an unwelcome remark or statement with sexual connotations to another person or about another person in that person's presence; or
- Makes any unwelcome gesture, action or comment of a sexual nature; or
- Engages in conduct of a sexual nature in relation to another person that is offensive to that person, in circumstances in which a reasonable person, having regard to all the circumstances, would have anticipated that the other person would be offended, humiliated, intimidated, insulted or ridiculed.

BIBLIOGRAPHY

Tasmanian Government. Anti-Discrimination Act 1998 (TAS). Available at: https://www.legislation.tas.gov.au/view/html/inforce/current/act-1998-046. Accessed March 20, 2019

VICTORIA

Legislation

- Victoria Equality Opportunity Act, 2010
- Sex Discrimination Act, 1984

Title of legislation Victoria Equality Opportunity Act, 2010

The *Victoria Equality Opportunity Act, 2010,* No. 16 of 2010, effective August 1, 2011, protects against *sexual harassment.*

The Act imposes a *Duty to Eliminate Sexual Harassment* (Part 3) with the following requirements:

- Employers must take reasonable and proportionate measures to eliminate sexual harassment as far as possible;
- Contravention of this obligation can be the subject of an investigation or public inquiry by the Commission;
- In determining what is "reasonable and proportionate" the following factors must be considered: the size of the employer's business or operations, the nature and circumstances of the employer's business or operations, the employer's business and operational priorities and the practicability and the cost of the measures.

A person *sexually harasses* another person if he or she makes an unwelcome sexual advance, or an unwelcome request for sexual favors, to the other person; or engages in any other unwelcome conduct of a sexual nature in relation to the other person, in circumstances in which a reasonable person, having regard to all the circumstances, would have anticipated that the other person would be offended, humiliated or intimidated. (Article 92)

An employer must not sexually harass a person seeking employment with that employer; or an employee of that employer. (Article 93)

A person must not sexually harass another person at a place that is a workplace of both of them. It is irrelevant whether each person is an employer, an employee or neither; and if they are employees, whether their employers are the same or different. A workplace means any place where a person attends for the purpose of carrying out any functions in relation to his or her employment, occupation, business, trade or profession and need not be a person's principal place of business or employment. (Article 4)

An employer may be vicariously liable under Article 109. (Vicarious liability of employers and principals)

BIBLIOGRAPHY

Victorian Legislation and Parliamentary Documents, 2011. Equal Opportunity Act 2010, No. 16 of 2010, as Amended. Available at: http://www.legislation.vic.gov.au/domino/Web_Notes/LDMS/LTObject_Store/LTObjSt6.nsf/DDE300B846EED9C7CA257616000A3571/6A457BE6293E797DCA25796D0014F920/$FILE/10-16aa011%20authorised.pdf. Accessed March 30, 2019

WESTERN AUSTRALIA

Legislation

- Western Australia Equal Opportunity Act 1984 (WA)

Title of legislation	Equal Opportunity Act 1984

The Western Australia *Equal Opportunity Act 1984* includes the following: to eliminate, so far as is possible, *sexual harassment* in the workplace.

Under Division 4—Discrimination involving sexual harassment, 24. Sexual harassment in employment: (1) It is unlawful for a person to harass sexually an employee of that or any other person; or a person who is seeking employment by that or any other person.

In the words of the law: (3) A person shall be taken to harass sexually another person if the first-mentioned person makes an unwelcome sexual advance, or an unwelcome request for sexual favours, to the other person, or engages in other unwelcome conduct of a sexual nature in relation to the other person, and—

(a) the other person has reasonable grounds for believing that a rejection of the advance, a refusal of the request or the taking of objection to the conduct would disadvantage the other person in any way in connection with the other person's employment or work or possible employment or possible work; or
(b) as a result of the other person's rejection of the advance, refusal of the request or taking of objection to the conduct, the other person

is disadvantaged in any way in connection with the other person's employment or work or possible employment or possible work.

(4) A reference in subsection (3) to conduct of a sexual nature in relation to a person includes a reference to the making, to or in the presence of, a person, of a statement of a sexual nature concerning that person, whether the statement is made orally or in writing.

BIBLIOGRAPHY

Department of the Premier and Cabinet, Western Australia, 1984. Equal Opportunity Act 1984. Available at: https://www.legislation.wa.gov.au/legislation/prod/filestore.nsf/FileURL/mrdoc_41630.pdf/$FILE/Equal%20Opportunity%20Act%201984%20-%20%5B07-f0-02%5D.pdf?OpenElement. Accessed March 30, 2019

CHINA

> The Chinese Civil Code is expected to be fully drafted and adopted in 2020. Its drafters have taken note of the #MeToo movement.

China presently has two sexual harassment laws—the Law on the Protection of the Rights and Interests of Women and the Special Rules on the Labour Protection of Female Employees. Although these laws ban *sexual harassment* against women in the workplace, legislation on sexual harassment in China lacks a clear definition of *sexual harassment* and there are no national regulations on how to handle such cases in workplaces. This makes it difficult for victims to seek redress; very few *sexual harassment* cases have been brought by female employees. However, change may be coming. In August 2018, China submitted a civil code draft introducing measures to address sexual harassment in the workplace to the National People's Congress (NPC) Standing Committee. The measures would require employers to take reasonable measures to prevent and handle sexual harassment complaints and would hold an employer responsible for not combating sexual harassment in the workplace.

The Chinese Civil Code ("Code") *is expected to be fully drafted and adopted in 2020. The drafters of the Code have taken note of the #MeToo movement*: a September 2018 draft of the Code submitted to the National People's Congress (NPC) Standing Committee would impose increased obligations on Chinese employers and provide more protections to employees against sexual harassment. This includes implementing a process for reporting and investigating sexual harassment claims.

The measures would require employers to take reasonable measures to prevent, stop, and deal with complaints about sexual harassment. They would hold an employer responsible for not combating sexual harassment in the workplace; however, the employer can take reasonable measures to stop and deal with complaints about sexual harassment. In addition, it would permit victims to hold perpetrators liable for sexual harassment. Victims also could extend civil liability to employers who fail to properly investigate sexual harassment claims.

The draft defines sexual harassment as "sexual advances against other's will by languages or actions or utilizing the subordination relationship." This is particularly important as it is the first time in history where sexual harassment is defined in a national law. This definition also extends the protection to men—the existing law only considers sexual harassment against women. The draft places additional responsibilities on employers to take reasonable measures for prevention, internal reporting and settlement of sexual harassment cases in the workplace (Source: Reuters, August 27, 2018. "China considers measures to curb workplace harassment: Xinhua").

#MeToo in the Chinese workplace: while the global #MeToo movement has encouraged some Chinese women who have experienced sexual harassment in the workplace to speak out, those who have experienced sexual harassment in the workplace have mostly stayed silent, as they are worried about their career as well as the response they will receive (Source: South China Morning Post, April 21, 2018. "Why Chinese women don't speak out about sexual harassment in the workplace," by Mandy Zuo).

Legislation

- Women's Right to Protection, 1992 as amended 2005
- Special Provisions on Labor Protection for Female Employees, 2012
- Criminal Law of the People's Republic of China

Title of legislation	Law of the People's Republic of China on the Protection of Rights and Interests of Women, 1992, as amended

The *Law of the People's Republic of China on the Protection of Rights and Interests of Women, 1992, as amended,* ("Women's Right to Protection") was amended in 2005 to prohibit *sexual harassment of women.* The Law prohibits sex discrimination and sexual harassment.

- Sexual harassment against women is prohibited. Female victims have the right to file complaints with the units and departments where they work. (Article 40)
- Article 58 states that although sexual harassment was written into the amendment of the national law on the protection of women's rights in 2005, it does not provide a clear definition of sexual harassment.

Title of legislation	Special Provisions on Labor Protection for Female Employees, 2012

The *Special Provisions on Labor Protection for Female Employees*, issued by the China State Council, took effect on April 28, 2012. Article XI provides that in the workplace, the employer shall prevent and stop *sexual harassment* against female employees. However, no definition is provided and no further reference to sexual harassment is made in this law. Under the regulations, an employer who fails to comply with the law's requirements, including the obligation to prevent sexual harassment, will be liable for compensating the employee for her damages arising therefrom. Additionally, actions or omissions of an employer or management constitute a crime, and criminal liabilities may apply.

Title of legislation	Criminal Law of the People's Republic of China

The *Criminal Law of the People's Republic of China*, Article 237, states that:

> Whoever, by violence, coercion or other means, forces, molests, or humiliates a woman is to be sentenced to not more than five years of fixed-term imprisonment or criminal detention.
>
> Whoever assembles a crowd to commit the crimes described in the preceding paragraph, or commits such crimes in the public is to be sentenced to not less than five years of fixed-term imprisonment.

BIBLIOGRAPHY

China Daily, 2007. Shanghai Passes China's First Sexual Harassment Law. Available at: http://www.chinadaily.com.cn/china/2007-04/27/content_862173.htm. Accessed September 8, 2018

China Daily, Wenfang, Li and Wang Huazhong, May 28, 2010. Law Lists Specifics of Sexual Harassment. Available at: http://www.chinadaily.com.cn/china/2010-05/28/content_9901810.htm. Accessed September 8, 2018

Entrepreneur Asia Pacific Komal Nathani, August 28, 2018. China Considers Law against Sexual Harassment at Workplace. Available at: https://www.entrepreneur.com/article/319146. Accessed September 8, 2018

Legal Daily News, July 13, 2018. Silent Culture: Workplace Sexual Harassment Litigation. Available at: http://www.cclpp.com/newsshow.php?cid=5&id=4800. Accessed September 8, 2018

Reuters, August 27, 2018, China Considers Measures to Curb Workplace Harassment: Xinhua. Available at: https://www.reuters.com/article/us-china

-harassment/china-considers-measures-to-curb-workplace-harassment-xinhua-idUSKCN1LC1W6?il=0. Accessed September 8, 2018

South China Morning Post, April 21, 2018. Why Chinese Women Don't Speak Out about Sexual Harassment in the Workplace, by Mandy Zuo. Available at: https://www.scmp.com/news/china/society/article/2142703/why-chinese-women-dont-speak-out-about-sexual-harassment. Accessed August 23, 2019

The National People's Congress of the People's Republic of China, 1992. Law of the People's Republic of China on the Protection of Rights and Interests of Women, 1992. Available at: www.china.org.cn/english/government/207405.htm. Accessed September 8, 2018

www.gov.cn, 2012. Female Workers Special Labor Protection Provisions. Available at (in Chinese): http://www.gov.cn/zwgk/2012-05/07/content_2131567.htm. Accessed September 8, 2018

www.fmprc.gov.cn, 1997. Criminal Law of the People's Republic of China. Available at: https://www.fmprc.gov.cn/ce/cgvienna/eng/dbtyw/jdwt/crimelaw/t209043.htm. Accessed August 28, 2019

www.gov.cn, 2012. Special Provisions on Labor Protection for Female Employees. Available at: http://www.gov.cn/zwgk/2012-05/07/content_2131567.htm

CHINA PROVINCES

A number of China provinces have enacted sexual harassment laws: such provinces define sexual harassment as actions against a woman by means of language, words, images, electronic information, or bodily actions related to sex or containing sexual content against her will. Under all of these local rules, sexual harassment conducted only by males against females is prohibited.

The Shanghai City Council enacted China's first local law clearly defining sexual harassment in 2007. The law states "sexual harassment of women in the form of spoken and written language, images, electronic information and bodily gestures is prohibited." The law states that harassment can include abuse conveyed verbally, in writing, or by pictures or cell phone text messaging, as well as actual physical contact. Women victims have the right to complain to their employer or relevant departments and such departments and employers must take necessary measures to prevent and stop sexual harassment toward those complaining. (China Daily, April 24, 2007. "Shanghai passes China's first sexual harassment law")

In Shenzhen, a municipality in Guangdong Province, the definition includes "utilizing one's position, employment or other advantage as a condition to exchange interests in relation to hiring, promotion, salary, award, etc." Employers must prohibit and address:

> any sexual harassment, whether explicit or implicit, by means of actions, language, characters, images, electronic information related to sex or containing sexual content, committed against another's will by utilizing one's position, employment or other advantages as a condition to exchange interests in relation to hiring, promotion, salary, award, etc.

Guangzhou, Guangdong implemented special rules for female workers labor protection in 2016. The city of Guangzhou had introduced specifications on the protection of women's rights and interests in June 2010, to assist in enforcement of the 2005 Law on the Protection of Women's Rights. The specifications allow women to request that employers write in stipulations preventing sexual harassment to their employment contracts.

The *Shandong Women Workers Labor Protection Measures, 2019,* became effective on March 1, 2019. Article 19 requires that the employer ensure that sexual harassment of female employees in the workplace is prevented. If a female employee has been sexually harassed in the workplace and subsequently reported the harassment to the employer, the employer must promptly and properly handle this report. The employer must also ensure that, when dealing with sexual harassment of female employees, their personal privacy is protected, according to law (Source: Linyi Municipal Resources and Social Security Bureau, 2019. "Measures for Labor Protection of Female Workers in Shandong Province," Provincial Government Order No. 322).

Jiangsu amended its law to define sexual harassment in 2008. The revised Jiangsu Provincial Measures for Implementing China's Law on Protection of Women's Rights states that "sexual harassment of women in the form of spoken and written language, images, electronic information and bodily gestures is prohibited." The measures permit those alleging harassment to report such cases to employers, authorities, and the police, who must prevent or stop such behavior. Women can also sue those they contend have harassed them (Source: Ministry of Justice, 2008; China Daily, 2008. "Jiangsu amends law to define sexual harassment").

The *Special Regulations on Labor Protection of Female Employees of Jiangsu Province in China* took effect on July 1, 2018, providing, for the first time in China, requirements for employers to establish internal policies and systems against sexual harassment.

Article 19 requires employers to do the following:

- Establish rules and regulations against workplace sexual harassment;
- Offer workplace education and training to prevent sexual harassment;
- Promote a general working environment free from sexual harassment;
- Create an effective complaint channel that is handled effectively and appropriately; and
- Take all other measures needed to prohibit and prevent sexual harassment of female employees.

BIBLIOGRAPHY

China Daily, 2007. Shanghai Passes China's First Sexual Harassment Law, April 24, 2007. Available at: http://www.chinadaily.com.cn/china/2007-04/27/content_862173.htm. Accessed March 30, 2019

China Daily, 2008. Jiangsu Amends Law to Define Sexual Harassment. Available at: http://www.chinadaily.com.cn/china/2008-01/21/content_6409254.htm. Accessed August 27, 2019

China Daily, Wenfang, Li and Wang huazhong, Contributors, May 28, 2010. Law Lists Specifics of Sexual Harassment. Available at: http://www.chinadaily.com.cn/china/2010-05/28/content_9901810.htm. Accessed March 30, 2019

Linyi Municipal Resources and Social Security Bureau, 2019. Measures for Labor Protection of Female Workers in Shandong Province (Provincial Government Order No. 322). Available at: http://rsj.linyi.gov.cn/info/1207/15767.htm. Accessed July 1, 2019

The National People's Congress of the People's Republic of China, 1992. Law of the People's Republic of China on the Protection of Rights and Interests of Women, 1992. Available at: www.china.org.cn/english/government/207405.htm. Accessed March 30, 2019

Wuxi City Federation of Trade Unions, 2018. Special Provisions on Labor Protection of Female Workers in Jiangsu Province. Available at: http://zgh.wuxi.gov.cn/doc/2018/05/14/1828865.shtml. Accessed May 21, 2019

www.gov.cn, 2012. Special Provisions on Labor Protection for Female Employees. Available at (in Chinese): http://www.gov.cn/zwgk/2012-05/07/content_2131567.htm. Accessed March 30, 2019

HONG KONG

The Discrimination Legislation (Miscellaneous Amendments) Bill 2018, published in the Hong Kong Government Gazette in November 2018, aims to increase protection against discrimination and harassment in Hong Kong. The Bill amends a number of Hong Kong's anti-discrimination laws, including the Sex Discrimination Ordinance (SDO). Protections from sexual harassment would include workplace participants working in a common workplace, or, in the words of the law, "at a workplace of them both" would be added to the SDO. Workplace and workplace participant are defined in the new Section 23 A (2). The Bill was tabled before the Legislative Council on December 14, 2018 and is expected to come into force in 2019.

A 2018, "A study on knowledge of sexual harassment and experience of being sexually harassed in the service industries: comparing recent female Mainland Chinese immigrants with locally-born women" showed that 12.1 percent of the survey respondents had experienced sexual harassed in the service workplace (14.6 percent of locally born women and 9.6 percent of recent female Mainland Chinese immigrants). Among respondents who had experienced sexual harassed at work, 45.5 percent of the women born locally and 24.1 percent of recent female Mainland Chinese immigrants took no action. (This study and other sexual harassment surveys may be found on the Equal Opportunities Commission website.)

Legislation

- The Sex Discrimination Ordinance, as amended, and Code of Practice on Employment under the Sex Discrimination Ordinance, 1995

Title of legislation	Sex Discrimination Ordinance, 1995, as amended and Code of Practice

The *Sex Discrimination Ordinance, 1995*, as amended in 2018, makes sexual harassment illegal and provides for its elimination by employers and other institutions in the employment field. The Ordinance covers not only employees but also job applicants, contract workers, trainees, and people using employment services. It applies to all employers in Hong Kong except where their employees work wholly or mainly outside Hong Kong.

Sexual harassment is defined as follows: a person is a sexual harasser if he or she makes unwelcome sexual advances or unwelcome request for sexual favors, or he or she makes other unwelcome conduct of a sexual nature in which a reasonable person would anticipate that the subject of attention would be offended, humiliated or intimidated.

Two forms of sexual harassment are addressed: any unwelcome sexual behavior or conduct which is offensive, humiliating or intimidating; and a hostile working environment due to actions, languages or pictures that are of a sexual nature.

It is unlawful for a person, in relation to employment by him at an establishment in Hong Kong, to sexually harass a woman who is seeking to be employed by the person. It is unlawful for a person, in the case of a woman employed by him at an establishment in Hong Kong, to sexually harass her. (Section 23)

Employers may be held vicariously liable under the Sex Discrimination Ordinance for sexual harassment perpetrated by an employee: an act done by a person in the course of his or her employment may render both that person and his or her employer liable. Similarly, an act done by a person as agent for another may render both the agent and principal liable. Employers are legally responsible for the actions of their employees, done in the course of their employment, whether or not these were done with the employer's knowledge or approval.

The *Code of Practice on Employment under the Sex Discrimination Ordinance* is voluntary. The employer is encouraged to follow the guidelines and the recommended good practices in this Code, unless there are justifiable grounds for not doing so. Article 6 Sexual harassment in employment sets forth examples of sexual harassment.

BIBLIOGRAPHY

Equal Opportunities Commission, 1995. Code of Practice on Employment under the Sex Discrimination Ordinance. Available at: http://www.eoc.org.hk/eoc/graphicsfolder/showcontent.aspx?content=cops_sdo. Accessed December 4, 2018

Equal Opportunities Commission, 1995. Sex Discrimination Ordinance. Available at: http://www.eoc.org.hk/eoc/graphicsfolder/showcontent.aspx?content=sex%20discrimination%20ordinance%20and%20i. Accessed December 4, 2018

Equal Opportunities Commission, 2018. A Study on Knowledge of Sexual Harassment and Experience of Being Sexually Harassed in the Service Industries: Comparing Recent Female Mainland Chinese. Available at: http://www.eoc.org.hk/eoc/graphicsfolder/inforcenter/research/default.aspx. Accessed May 20, 2019

Government of Hong Kong Gazette. Discrimination Legislation (Miscellaneous Amendments) Bill 2018. Available at: https://www.gld.gov.hk/egazette/pdf/20182248/es32018224825.pdf. Accessed May 20, 2019

The Discrimination Legislation (Miscellaneous Amendments) Bill 2018. Available at: https://www.gld.gov.hk/egazette/pdf/20182248/es32018224825.pdf. Accessed August 23, 2019

INDIA

> Although India has in place the Sexual Harassment of Women at Workplace (Prevention, Prohibition and Redressal) Act, the #MeToo campaign revealed that many victims of sexual harassment could not speak up.
>
> *(Source: Economic Times, October 24, 2018. "GoM set up to strengthen safety laws for women at workplaces")*

Sexual harassment allegations in India emerged in allegations against the Bollywood entertainment industry, followed by female journalists coming out with stories of harassment by their male colleagues in the news media (Source: Quartz India, October 7, 2018. "It took a year, but #MeToo is finally roiling Bollywood and Indian media," by Kuwar Singh).

India's #MeToo wave, with 1.2 million #MeToo tweets since September 2018 and a number of public figures leaving their positions after allegations of sexual misconduct and abuse, culminated in internal investigations and firings or resignations. Consequently, in October 2018 India's government constituted a group of ministers (GoM) to strengthen the legal and institutional frameworks to prevent and deal with sexual harassment of women in workplaces. The GoM will examine the existing provisions for dealing with sexual harassment of women in offices (Source: Telegraph India, December 19, 2018. "#MeToo in India: Crucial lessons from the US experience," by Nityanjali Thummalachetty and Abby DiCarlo).

SHe-BoxOnline Complaint Management System: India's Ministry of Women & Child Development launched an electronic complaint box to allow women to submit their complaints of sexual harassment committed against them, regardless of their work status. The box is known as the SHe-Box.

Telangana's and Maharashtra's Sexual Harassment Electronic Box (T-she box): the Indian state Telangana's Women Development and Child Welfare Department, Government of Telangana issued on July 1, 2019 a general notice requiring establishments in Telangana employing 10 or more employees to register their IC with the State SHe-Box portal by July 15, 2019. Once a complaint is submitted to the "T-she box," it will be directly sent to the concerned authority with jurisdiction to take action into the matter.

Additionally, Maharashtra's Women Development and Child Development Department, Government of Maharashtra issued a general letter requiring all establishments in Maharashtra to register their

IC constituted pursuant to the Sexual Harassment of Women at the Workplace (Prevention, Prohibition and Redressal) Act. Employers were required to file details of their IC in the prescribed form and submit it with the Sub-Divisional Magistrate by July 20, 2019.

Legislation

- Sexual Harassment of Women at the Workplace (Prevention, Prohibition and Redressal) Act, 2013
- The Criminal Law (Amendment) Act, 2013

Title of legislation	Sexual Harassment of Women at the Workplace (Prevention, Prohibition and Redressal) Act, 2013

The *Sexual Harassment of Women at the Workplace (Prevention, Prohibition and Redressal) Act, 2013* states that no woman shall be subjected to *sexual harassment* at any workplace.

The following circumstances may amount to *sexual harassment*:

- Implied or explicit promise of preferential treatment in her employment;
- Implied or explicit threat of detrimental treatment in her employment;
- Implied or explicit threat about her present or future employment status;
- Interferes with her work or creating an intimidating or offensive or hostile
- Work environment for her; or
- Humiliating treatment likely to affect her health or safety.

The law requires that an employer with more than 10 employees shall, by an order in writing, constitute a Committee to be known as the "Internal Complaints Committee" (provided that where the offices or administrative units of the workplace are located at different places or divisional or sub-divisional level, the Internal Committee shall be constituted at all administrative units or offices). Any aggrieved woman may make, in writing, a complaint of sexual harassment at workplace to the Internal Committee, or the Local Committee, within a period of three months from the date of incident, or if a series of incidents, within three months from the date of the last incident.

The employer's responsibilities include the following:

- Provide a safe working environment at the workplace, including safety from the persons coming into contact at the workplace;
- Display the penal consequences of sexual harassment at a visible place in the workplace;
- Regularly organize workshops for informing employees concerning the Act;
- Provide necessary facilities to the Internal Committee or the Local Committee for dealing with a sexual harassment complaint and conducting an inquiry, and assist in securing the attendance of respondent and witnesses before the Internal Committee or the Local Committee;
- Provide assistance to the woman if she chooses to file a complaint in relation to the offence under the Indian Penal Code or any other law for the time being in force;
- Initiate action, under the Indian Penal Code or other relevant law, against the perpetrator, or if the aggrieved woman desires, where the perpetrator is not an employee, in the workplace at which the incident of sexual harassment took place;
- Treat sexual harassment as misconduct under the service rules and initiate action for such misconduct; and
- Monitor the timely submission of reports by the Internal Committee.

Title of legislation Criminal Law (Amendment) Act, 2013

The *Criminal Law (Amendment) Act, 2013* to the Indian Penal Code added provisions treating *sexual harassment* as a criminal offence, as the new offense of sexual harassment was inserted as section 354A of the Indian Penal Code (Amendment Act § 7).

The Criminal Law (Amendment) Ordinance, 2013, Section 354A, protecting women, states that a man committing any of the following acts shall be guilty of sexual harassment:

- Physical contact and advances involving unwelcome and explicit sexual overtures;
- A demand or request for sexual favors;

- Making sexually colored remarks; or
- Forcibly showing pornography.

Other sections (Sections 354B, 354C, and 354D) protect women from stalking and voyeurism. The offences added by the amendment are punishable with imprisonment of a term extending up to three years, a fine, or both. In case of sexually colored remarks the punishment can extend up to an imprisonment of one year, a fine, or both.

BIBLIOGRAPHY

Economic Times, October 24, 2018. GoM Set Up to Strengthen Safety Laws for Women at Workplaces. Available at: https://economictimes.indiatimes.com/news/politics-and-nation/government-sets-up-gom-to-look-into-sexual-harassment-at-work-place/articleshow/66347515.cms?utm_source=contentofinterest&utm_medium=text&utm_campaign=cppst. Accessed May 20, 2019

Government of India, Ministry of Women and Child Development, November 2015. Handbook on Sexual Harassment of Women at Workplace (Prevention, Prohibition and Redressal) Act. Available at: http://wcd.nic.in/sites/default/files/Handbook%20on%20Sexual%20Harassment%20of%20Women%20at%20Workplace.pdf. Accessed March 30, 2019

Quartz India, October 7, 2018. It Took a Year, but #MeToo Is Finally Roiling Bollywood and Indian Media, by Kuwar Singh. Available at: https://qz.com/india/1416009/metoo-finally-hits-bollywood-and-indian-media/. Accessed May 16, 2019

Ministry of Women & Child Development, Government of India, 2017.

SHe-BoxOnline Complaint Management System If You are Facing Sexual Harassment at Workplace. Available at: http://www.shebox.nic.in/. Accessed June 4, 2019

TelegraphIndia, December 19, 2018. #MeToo in India: Crucial Lessons from the US Experience, By Nityanjali Thummalachetty and Abby DiCarlo. Available at: https://www.telegraphindia.com/opinion/metoo-in-india-crucial-lessons-from-the-us-experience/cid/1679235. Accessed May 20, 2019

The Gazette of India, Ministry of Law and Justice, 2013. Criminal Law (Amendment) Act 2013. Available at: http://www.pib.nic.in/newsite/erelease.aspx?relid=91979. Accessed May 14, 2019

The Gazette of India, Ministry of Law and Justice, 2013. Sexual Harassment of Women at Workplace (Prevention, Prohibition and Redressal) Act, 2013. Available at: http://www.iitbbs.ac.in/notice/sexual-harrassment-of-women-act-and-rules-2013.pdf. Accessed March 30, 2019

Women Development & Child Welfare, 2019. Welcome To T-she Box. Available at: https://tshebox.tgwdcw.in/. Accessed July 12, 2019

INDONESIA

> Indonesia's version of #MeToo, #SayaJuga, has met with limited success.

Indonesia currently has no law to protect women from such uncomfortable and sometimes even violent cases, which means many Indonesian companies do not have sexual harassment policies or standards of procedure. A draft law on the Elimination of Sexual Violence has been sitting in Parliament since 2014 (Source: Tempo.com, January 1, 2019. "Indonesia's law fails victims of sexual harassment in workplace," by Aoife Scales, Chelsea Cosgrave, Aurelia Michelle R and Benedictus Billy Briliandditya).

The draft law defines forms of sexual violence that are not covered under existing legislation, such as sexual harassment, sexual exploitation, and forced prostitution. The proposed legislation has been under development since 2014, led by the National Commission for the Elimination of Violence against Women (Komnas Perempuan) in consultation with legal experts, women's groups, academics, and government ministries (Source: aljazeera.com, February 8, 2019. "Indonesia sexual violence bill sparks conservative opposition," by Kate Walton).

Indonesian feminist Tunggal Pawestri coined #SayaJuga—a direct translation of #MeToo—to encourage more public discussion of sexual assault. Still, in Indonesia, #MeToo remains limited to the social media savvy and middle-upper class women (Source: The Conversation, March 8, 2019. "#MeToo has skipped Indonesia—here's why").

However, one case has become a "Me Too" movement-like moment for Indonesia: a teacher, Ms. Nuril, began receiving telephone calls from the headmaster describing his sexual relationship with another woman. He also insisted Ms. Nuril accompany him and his sexual partner on trips. She was afraid to report the headmaster but recorded one of the calls and later played it to colleagues to dispel rumors she was having an affair with him, maintaining that she had recorded conversations to gather evidence and protect herself from sexual harassment. However, she was charged under Indonesia's Electronic Information and Transactions (ITE) law for circulating indecent content and defamation. Although Ms. Nuril was initially found not guilty in 2017, she was convicted in Indonesia's Supreme Court last year and lost her appeal in July 2019. She had been facing six months in jail for recording of the sexual harassment until July 2019, when Indonesia's government approved a pardon for her (Sources: The Guardian, July 25, 2019. "Indonesia jails teacher who documented sexual harassment;" and BBC, November 15, 2018. "Indonesia pardons woman jailed after reporting sexual harassment").

A 2017 survey by Perempuan Mahardika revealed that 56.5 percent of the 773 women garment laborers in a Jakarta industrial complex were sexually harassed. Most of them, however, did not report it to their supervisors.

The *Guidelines on Sexual Harassment Prevention at the Workplace,* issued by the Circular Note of the Minister of Manpower and Transmigration, No. SE.03/MEN/IV/2011, April 2011, are not legally binding but provide guidance to employers and workers on preventing and effectively responding to sexual harassment.

Sexual harassment is defined as:

> any unwanted conduct of a sexual nature, request for sexual favours, verbal or physical conduct or gesture of a sexual nature; or other behaviour of a sexual nature that makes the recipient feels humiliated, offended and/or intimidated, where such reaction is reasonable in the situation and condition; or made into working requirement or create an intimidating, hostile or inappropriate working environment.

In other words, sexual harassment is:

1. misuse of sexual behaviour
2. request for sexual favour, and
3. verbal statement or physical action or gestures that describe a sexual act, or
4. unwanted action of a sexual nature
    a. the recipient has made it clear that the behaviour is unwanted;
    b. the recipient feels humiliated, offended and/or intimidated by the conduct; or
    c. the perpetrator should have reasonably anticipated that the other person would be offended, humiliated and/or intimidated by the conduct.

BIBLIOGRAPHY

aljazeera.com, February 8, 2019. Indonesia Sexual Violence Bill Sparks Conservative Opposition, by Kate Walton. Available at: https://www.aljazeera.com/news/2019/02/indonesia-sexual-violence-bill-sparks-conservative-opposition-190208062416667.html. Accessed August 26, 2019

BBC, July 25, 2019. Indonesia Pardons Woman Jailed after Reporting Sexual Harassment. Available at: https://www.bbc.com/news/world-asia-49110578. Accessed August 26, 2019

Circular Note of the Minister of Manpower and Transmigration, April 2011. Guidelines on Sexual Harassment Prevention at the Workplace No. SE.03/MEN/IV/2011. Available at: https://www.ilo.org/wcmsp5/groups/public/---asia/---ro-bangkok/---ilo-jakarta/documents/publication/wcms_171329.pdf. Accessed May 20, 2019

Tempo.com, January 1, 2019. Indonesia's Law Fails Victims of Sexual Harassment in Workplace, by Aoife Scales, Chelsea Cosgrave, Aurelia Michelle R and Benedictus Billy Brilianditya. Available at: https://en.tempo.co/read/1160639/indonesias-law-fails-victims-of-sexual-harassment-in-workplace?page_num=3. Accessed August 26, 2019

The Conversation, March 8, 2019. #MeToo Has Skipped Indonesia — Here's Why. Available at: http://theconversation.com/metoo-has-skipped-indonesia-heres-why-112530. Accessed August 26, 2019

The Guardian, November 15, 2018. Indonesia Jails Teacher Who Documented Sexual Harassment. Available at: https://www.theguardian.com/world/2018/nov/15/indonesia-jails-teacher-who-documented-sexual-harassment. Accessed August 26, 2019

JAPAN

> Japan's socially conservative society has been slow to join the worldwide #MeToo movement, known in Japan as #WithYou.

#MeToo arose in Japan over a female reporter's sexual harassment claims: a Japanese female reporter from TV Asahi alleged that she was sexually harassed by a former top Finance Ministry bureaucrat; he subsequently resigned over the alleged harassment and maintained his innocence (Source: BBC, April 19, 2018. "#MeToo hits Japan as Junichi Fukuda quits over harassment claims").

According to Japan's health ministry, 30 percent of Japanese women report unwanted sexual attention at work (Source: The Guardian, March 2, 2016. "Nearly a third of Japan's women 'sexually harassed at work'," by Justin McCurry).

Legislation

- Act on Securing, Etc. of Equal Opportunity and Treatment between Men and Women in Employment, No. 113/1972, as amended
- Industrial Safety and Health Law, 1972, as amended
- Labour Standards Law, 1947, as amended

Title of legislation	Act on Securing, Etc. of Equal Opportunity and Treatment between Men and Women in Employment, No. 113/1972, as amended

Japan's *Act on Securing, Etc. of Equal Opportunity and Treatment between Men and Women in Employment* (Act No. 113 of July 1, 1972, as amended), ("Equal Employment Opportunity Law") provides that both women and men shall be protected from *sexual harassment* and requires employers to take workplace measures to address it. Companies contravening these provisions will be publicly denounced, with detrimental effects on their image.

Employers are required to establish measures in employees' working environments in order that they do not suffer sexual harassment. Specifically, Article 11 requires that employers establish necessary measures to provide advice to their workers, and take other necessary measures in order that these workers do not suffer any disadvantage in working conditions due to their responses to sexual harassment in the workplace, or in their working environments do not suffer any harm due to such sexual harassment.

Japan's law requires employers to prevent sexual harassment through the following steps:

- Clarify and disseminate policies against sexual harassment and educate employees through measures such as handbooks and seminars.
- Set up an objective system to address complaints and grievances.
- Respond promptly to sexual harassment claims, and they should investigate and implement disciplinary actions.
- The guidelines also request employers to protect the privacy of employees who file sexual harassment complaints and to adopt anti-retaliation policies.

The *Amendment of the Ordinance for Enforcement of the Act on the Securing, Etc. of Equal Opportunity and Treatment of Men and Women in Employment,* effective July 1, 2014, requires that the employer establish measures to treat the victim employee who has been sexually harassed properly, such as by providing consulting with the supervisor or occupational health staff and/or mediation by an independent institution.

Title of legislation	Labour Standards Act No. 49/1947, as amended

The *Labour Standards Law* applies to every business where one or more workers are employed. It states that an employer shall not force workers to work against their will by means of violence, intimidation, imprisonment, or any other unfair restraint on the mental or physical freedom of the workers. (Article 5)

BIBLIOGRAPHY

BBC, April 19, 2018. #MeToo Hits Japan as Junichi Fukuda Quits over Harassment Claims. Available at: https://www.bbc.com/news/world-asia-43819001. Accessed May 16, 2019

Japanese Law Translation Database System, Ministry of Justice, Translation date 2013. Labour Standards Act, 1947, as Amended. Available at: http://www.japaneselawtranslation.go.jp/law/detail/?id=2236. Accessed March 30, 2109

Ministry of Health, Labour and Welfare, 1972. Act on Securing, Etc. of Equal Opportunity and Treatment between Men and Women in Employment, No.

113/ 1972 as Amended 2007. Available at: https://www.mhlw.go.jp/general/seido/koyou/danjokintou/dl/kt-e.pdf. Accessed March 20, 2019

The Guardian, March 2, 2016. Nearly a Third of Japan's Women 'Sexually Harassed at Work', by Justin McCurry. Available at: https://www.theguardian.com/world/2016/mar/02/japan-women-sexually-harassed-at-work-report-finds. Accessed August 20, 2019

MALAYSIA

> Malaysia prohibits sexual harassment under the Employment Act, which may punish an employer's failure to act upon a sexual harassment complaint promptly as an offence subject to a fine.

A 2016 Federal Court ruling in Mohd Ridzwan Bin Abdul Razak vs. Asmah Binti Mohd Nor; Case No: (246–16A) introduced the law of tort and sexual harassment in Malaysia, and permitted employees who are sexually harassed at work to file a civil suit to claim damages against the perpetrators. The Court noted that what constituted sexual harassment was undefined under Malaysian law and looked to the non-binding 1999 Code of Practice, discussed in the next paragraph. The Court decided that it was timely to import the tort of harassment into the legal and judicial system, with sexual harassment being part of it, and did so (Source: Federal Court of Malaysia, Mohd Ridzwan Bin Abdul Razak vs. Asmah Binti Mohd Nor; Case No: (246–16A)).

Code of Practice on the Prevention and Eradication of Sexual Harassment in the Workplace: the Code of Practice on the Prevention and Eradication of Sexual Harassment in the Workplace, 1999, by the Ministry of Human Resources, applies to the private sector in Malaysia, and is non-binding. It provides guidelines to employers on the establishment of in-house mechanisms at the enterprise level to prevent and eradicate sexual harassment in the workplace, aims to ensure that sexual harassment in the workplace does not occur and, if it does occur, adequate procedures are available to deal with the problem and prevent its recurrence. For the purpose of the Code, *sexual harassment* means:

> Any unwanted conduct of a sexual nature having the effect of verbal, non-verbal, visual, psychological or physical harassment: that might, on reasonable grounds, be perceived by the recipient as placing a condition of a sexual nature on her/his employment; or that might, on reasonable grounds, be perceived by the recipient as an offence or humiliation, or a threat to his/her well-being, but has no direct link to her/his employment.
>
> *(Source: International Labour Organization, 1999)*

Legislation

- Employment (Amendment) Act, 2012

Title of legislation Employment (Amendment) Act, 2012

The *Employment (Amendment) Act, 2012* ("Amendment Act") came into force on April 1, 2012, amending the Employment Act 1995. The Amendment Act introduced *sexual harassment*-specific criminal offences in the workplace as well as personal liability of directors and other officers for offences committed by a body corporate. Sexual harassment complaints are defined broadly to encompass complaints by an employee against another employee; by an employee against any employer; or by an employer against an employee.

The Amendment Act defines sexual harassment as any unwanted conduct of a sexual nature, whether verbal, non-verbal, visual, gestural or physical, directed at a person which is offensive or humiliating or is a threat to his well-being, arising out of and in the course of his employment.

Part XVa, titled Sexual Harassment, imposes a duty on the employer to adequately deal with sexual harassment complaints at the workplace. It addresses the employer's inquiry into a complaint of sexual harassment and provides that an employer who refuses to inquire into a complaint of sexual harassment in circumstances required under the Act commits an offense, and on conviction, may be liable to a fine not exceeding ten thousand ringgit.

Note: This Act is copyright protected.

BIBLIOGRAPHY

Federal Court of Malaysia. Mohd Ridzwan Bin Abdul Razak vs. Asmah Binti Mohd Nor; Case No: (246–16A). Available at: http://www.foongchengleong.com/judgements/Mohd%20Ridzwan%20bin%20Abdul%20Razak%20v%20Asmah%20Binti%20Hj%20Mohd%20Nor%20(FC).pdf. Accessed May 16, 2019

International Labour Organization, 1999. Code of Practice on the Prevention and Eradication of Sexual Harassment in the Workplace, 1999. Available at: http://www.ilo.org/dyn/travail/docs/1627/CODE%20OF%20PRACTICE%20ON%20THE%20PREVENTION%20AND%20ERADICATION%20OF%20SEXUAL%20HARASSMENT%20IN%20THE%20WORKPLACE.pdf. Accessed March 21, 2019

Laws of Malaysia, 2012. Employment (Amendment) Act 2012. Available at: http://www.mkma.org/Notice%20Board/2012/EmploymentAmendedAct2012.pdf. Accessed March 21, 2019

NEW ZEALAND

> Employees are protected from sexual harassment in the workplace under the Employment Relations Act 2000 and the Human Rights Act 1993.

Almost 90 percent of lawyers have either experienced or witnessed harassment, including sexual, or bullying in the legal workplace, a survey reveals. The Criminal Bar Association of NZ (CBA) conducted a voluntary survey with those practising at the criminal bar about harassment, including sexual, and bullying in the legal workplace. Three hundred people responded, just under two-thirds were women. Eighty-eight percent said they had personally experienced or witnessed harassment or bullying behaviour in the last four years (Source: nzherald.co.nz, March 23, 2108. "Survey reveals 'high level' of harassment and bullying in the legal workplace").

New Zealand's Ministry of Business, Innovation and Employment (MBIE) Began Collecting Workplace Sexual Harassment Data on July 2, 2018. It had been collecting data on harassment and bullying, but not on sexual harassment specifically. A separate register is kept all such claims, so as to better understand the scale of the problem. All information gathered is confidential and any personal identifying features removed from the incident reports. Sixty-eight reports of workplace sexual harassment were made to the MBIE service centre between July 2 and September 30, 2018, the first three months MBIE had ever collected that data specifically (Source: Stuff.co.nz, October 16, 2018. "One year on from #metoo, the fight against sexual misconduct is far from over," by Leith Huffadine).

Legislation

- The Human Rights Act, 1993
- Employment Relations Act, 2000

Title of legislation The Human Rights Act 1993

The *Human Rights Act 1993* prohibits *sexual harassment* in employment. Part 62: Sexual harassment states that it shall be unlawful for any person to make a request of any other person for sexual intercourse, sexual contact, or other form of sexual activity which contains an implied or overt promise of preferential treatment or an implied or overt threat of detrimental treatment; or, by the use of language (whether written or spoken) of a sexual nature, or of visual material of a sexual nature, or by physical behaviour of a sexual nature, to subject any other person to behaviour that is unwelcome or offensive to that person (whether or not that is conveyed to the first-mentioned person); and is either repeated, or of such a significant nature, that it has a detrimental effect on that person.

Where a person complains of sexual harassment, no account shall be taken of any evidence of the person's sexual experience or reputation.

The *Harmful Digital Communication Act (HDCA)*, which aims to deter, prevent and mitigate harm caused to individuals by digital communications, amended the Human Rights Act in 2015.

Title of legislation Employment Relations Act, 2000

The *Employment Relations Act 2000* (the ER Act) prohibits discrimination on the grounds listed in the *Human Rights Act 1993*. It refers to procedures to be followed for complaints of *sexual harassment*.

Personal grievances include that the employee has been sexually harassed in the employee's employment. (Section 103)

An employee is *sexually harassed* in employment if the employer or a representative of that employer:

Directly or indirectly makes a request of that employee for sexual intercourse, sexual contact, or other form of sexual activity that contains—

(i) an implied or overt promise of preferential treatment in that employee's employment; or
(ii) an implied or overt threat of detrimental treatment in that employee's employment; or
(iii) an implied or overt threat about the present or future employment status of that employee; or

By—

(i) the use of language (whether written or spoken) of a sexual nature; or
(ii) the use of visual material of a sexual nature; or
(iii) physical behavior of a sexual nature,

> directly or indirectly subjects the employee to behavior that is unwelcome or offensive to that employee (whether or not that is conveyed to the employer or representative) and that, either by its nature or through repetition, has a detrimental effect on that employee's employment, job performance, or job satisfaction.
>
> *(Section 108)*

An employee may also be sexually harassed by a co-employee or by a client or customer of the employer, depending on the circumstances which have occurred. (Section 108)

Where a personal grievance involves allegations of sexual harassment, no account may be taken of any evidence of the complainant's sexual experience or reputation. (Article 116, special provision where sexual harassment has been alleged)

Where the Authority or the court determines that an employee has a personal grievance, it may, in settling the grievance, provide for any one or more of the following remedies:

- If the Authority or the court finds an employee to have been sexually harassed in his or her employment, recommendations to the employer concerning the action the employer should take in respect of the person who made the request or was guilty of the harassing behavior, which action may include the transfer of that person, the taking of disciplinary action against that person, or the taking of rehabilitative action in respect of that person, or about any other action that it is necessary for the employer to take to prevent further harassment of the employee concerned or any other employee. (Section 123: Remedies)

BIBLIOGRAPHY

nzherald.co.nz, March 23, 2108. Survey Reveals 'High Level' of Harassment and Bullying in the Legal Workplace. Available at: https://www.nzherald.co.nz/nz/news/article.cfm?c_id=1&objectid=12018553. Accessed August 28, 2019

Parliamentary Counsel Office, 1993. Human Rights Act. Available at: http://www.legislation.govt.nz/act/public/1993/0082/60.0/DLM304212.html. Accessed March 20, 2019

Parliamentary Counsel Office, 2000, reprint April 4, 2016. Employment Relations Act, 2000. Available at: http://www.legislation.govt.nz/act/public/2000/0024/112.0/DLM58317.html. Accessed March 20, 2019

Parliamentary Counsel Office, 2015. Harmful Digital Communications Act 2015. Available at: http://www.legislation.govt.nz/act/public/2015/0063/latest/whole.html. Accessed March 21, 2019

Stuff.co.nz, October 16, 2018. One Year on from #Metoo, the Fight against Sexual Misconduct Is Far from over, by Leith Huffadine. Available at: https://www.stuff.co.nz/national/107823335/one-year-on-from-metoo-the-fight-against-sexual-misconduct-is-far-from-over. Accessed August 28, 2019

PHILIPPINES

An expanded Anti-Sexual Harassment Act—House Bill No. 8244—was passed by the House of Representatives in November 2018; as of August 15, 2019, no further action appears to have been taken. If enacted, it would replace the Anti-Sexual Harassment Act of 1995.

(Source: Republic of Philippines, House of Representatives. Bill 8244, September 13, 2018)

Reporter and news anchor became one of first news personalities to speak up against sexual harassment in the media. In October 2018, reporter Gretchen Fullido filed a sexual harassment complaint against a former executive of her station and a segment producer alleging that they sent her text messages "filled with sexual innuendos and even requested sexual favors" and "made it difficult" for her to work as a reporter and anchor of the network's nightly news show when she rejected them. In June 2019, the Quezon City prosecutor's office indicted a former official of ABS–CBN and a segment producer for the network on a charge of sexual harassment over Fullido's complaint, finding that elements of the crime under Republic Act 7877 or the Anti-Sexual Harassment Act existed in the case.

Legislation

- Anti-Sexual Harassment Act of 1995

Title of legislation The Anti-Sexual Harassment Act of 1995

The Anti-Sexual Harassment Act of 1995, Republic Act No. 7877, was enacted in relevant part to protect and respect the dignity of workers, employees, and applicants for employment. Under it, all forms of *sexual harassment* in employment are unlawful (Section 2). The Act provides for a clear definition of work-related sexual harassment and specifies the acts constituting sexual harassment. It also provides for the duties and liabilities of the employer in cases of sexual harassment and sets penalties for violations of its provisions.

Work or training-related *sexual harassment* is committed by an employer, employee, manager, supervisor, agent of the employer, or any other person who, having authority, influence or moral ascendancy over another in a work or training or education environment, demands, requests, or otherwise requires any sexual favor from the other, regardless of whether the demand, request, or requirement for submission is accepted by the object of said Act. (Section 3)

In a work-related or employment environment, sexual harassment is committed when:

- The sexual favor is made as a condition in the hiring or in the employment, re-employment or continued employment of said individual, or in granting said individual favorable compensation, terms of conditions, promotions, or privileges; or the refusal to grant the sexual favor results in limiting, segregating or classifying the employee which in any way would discriminate, deprive or diminish employment opportunities or otherwise adversely affect said employee;
- The above acts would impair the employee's rights or privileges under existing labor laws or;
- The above acts would result in an intimidating, hostile, or offensive environment for the employee. (Section 3)

Any person who directs or induces another to commit any act of sexual harassment as herein defined, or who cooperates in the commission thereof by another without which it would not have been committed, shall also be held liable under this Act. (Section 3)

An employer shall prevent or deter the commission of acts of sexual harassment and provide procedures for the resolution, settlement, or prosecution of acts of sexual harassment. Toward this end, the employer shall:

- Promulgate appropriate rules and regulations in consultation with and jointly approved by the employees through their duly designated representatives, prescribing the procedure for the investigation of sexual harassment cases and the administrative sanctions.
- Administrative sanctions shall not be a bar to prosecution in the proper courts for unlawful acts of sexual harassment.
- The rules and regulations issued pursuant to the Act shall include, among others, guidelines on proper decorum in the workplace and educational or training institutions.

A committee shall be created on decorum and investigation of cases on sexual harassment. The committee shall conduct meetings with officers and employees to increase understanding and prevent incidents of sexual harassment and shall also conduct the investigation of alleged cases constituting sexual harassment. The committee shall be composed of at least one representative each from the management, the union, if any, the employees from the supervisory rank, and from the rank and file employees. (Section 4)

The employer shall disseminate or post a copy of this Act for the information of all concerned. (Section 4)

The employer shall be solely liable for damages arising from the acts of sexual harassment committed in the workplace if the employer is informed of such acts by the offended party and no immediate action is taken. (Section 5)

A victim of sexual harassment is not barred from filing a separate and independent action for damages and other relief aside from filing the charge for sexual harassment. (Section 6)

Sanctions range from imprisonment of not less than one month or more than six months, or a fine of not less than P10,000 or more than P20,000, or both, such fine and imprisonment being at the discretion of the court.

Note: The law does not specifically address the issue of hostile environment resulting from sexual harassment between peers or co-workers. Coverage of the law, however, is quite limited. Cases where both the harasser and the harassed party are peers or have the same rank or status, or when the offended party is a superior position at work, are not covered by the law.

BIBLIOGRAPHY

Philippines House of Representatives, 2018. Bill 8244. Available at: http://congress.gov.ph/legisdocs/first_17/CR00863.pdf. Accessed June 27, 2019

Republic of Philippines, House of Representatives, September 13, 2018. Bill 8244. Available at: http://congress.gov.ph/legisdocs/first_17/CR00863.pdf. Accessed August 20, 2019.

Congress of the Philippines, 1995. Anti-Sexual Harassment Act of 1995. Available at: https://pcw.gov.ph/law/republic-act-7877. Accessed March 20, 2019

www.Philstar.com, June 6, 2019. Prosecutors Indict 2 in Gretchen Fullido Sexual Harassment Case. Available at: https://www.philstar.com/nation/2019/06/06/1924178/prosecutors-indict-2-gretchen-fullido-sexual-harassment-case. Accessed July 16, 2019

SINGAPORE

> On May 8, 2019, the Senior Parliamentary Secretary for Manpower and Education stated that over 960 companies employing close to 500,000 workers in Singapore have adopted a voluntary set of good practices to address workplace unhappiness, including sexual harassment complaints, as of January 1, 2019.

These good practices, introduced in October 2018, are voluntary for employers. The Tripartite Advisory for Managing Workplace Harassment includes a sample copy of a harassment prevention policy for companies to refer to, and also defines what constitutes workplace and sexual harassment (Source: The Straits Times, May 8, 2019. "Parliament: More than 960 Firms Adopt Standard to Handle Staff Grievances, Including Sexual Harassment," by Ng jun Sen).

Singapore's *Protection from Harassment Act* became effective in November 2014. The Act addresses a number of scenarios from online stalking to cyber bullying and sexual harassment and permits harassment victims to seek both criminal and civil remedies. As of 2018, there were 535 applications for protection orders filed under the Act, with 213 granted by the courts. The orders granted included victims of workplace harassment (Source: The Straits Times, March 4, 2019. "Parliament: 4 in 10 applications for protection orders granted by court since 2014, says Edwin Tong").

Legislation

- Protection from Harassment Act, 2014

Title of legislation	Protection from Harassment Act, 2014

The *Protection from Harassment Act, 2014* came into effect on November 15, 2014 to protect persons against *harassment*, cyberbullying, and unlawful stalking. Civil remedies and criminal recourse are provided through the State Courts.

The legislation criminalizes a "course of conduct" related to stalking, which has the effect of causing harassment, alarm or distress. The "course of conduct" includes acts which may in themselves be innocuous, but which when done repeatedly, and especially where unwanted, may cause victims harassment, alarm and distress.

Offenses include:

- Intentionally causing harassment, alarm or distress;
- Harassment, alarm or distress;
- Fear or provocation of violence;
- Threatening, abusing or insulting public servant or public service worker;
- Unlawful stalking.

Article 3–5 defines intentionally causing harassment, alarm or distress; harassment, alarm or distress; and fear or provocation of violence.

Any person who contravenes the above shall be guilty of an offence and, subject to section 8, shall be liable on conviction to a fine not exceeding $5,000 or to imprisonment for a term not exceeding 12 months or to both. It is a defense for the accused person to prove in respect of a contravention of subsection (1)(b), that he had no reason to believe that the words or behavior used, or the communication made, by him would be heard, seen or otherwise perceived by the victim; or (b)that his conduct was reasonable. (Article 5 (1))

At the time the Act came into effect, subsidiary legislation was also issued: Protection from Harassment (Exempt Class of Persons) Order 2014 ("Exempt Persons Order"); and Protection from Harassment (Public Service Worker) Order 2014 ("Public Service Worker Order").

Note: following passage of the Protection from Harassment Act, Singapore's Ministry of Manpower, National Trades Union Congress, and National Employers Federation, known as the Singapore Tripartism Forum (STF), issued on December 23, 2015 an advisory document encouraging employers to take the lead in combating workplace harassment. It includes a sample *sexual harassment* policy.

BIBLIOGRAPHY

Singapore Statutes Online, 2014. Protection from Harassment Act (Chapter 256A). Available at: https://sso.agc.gov.sg/Act/256A. Accessed March 21, 2019

Singapore Tripartism Forum, 2015. Tripartite Advisory on Managing Workplace Harassment. Available at: http://www.mom.gov.sg/~/media/mom/documents/employment-practices/guidelines/tripartite-advisory-on-managing-workplace-harassment.pdf?la=en. Accessed March 21, 2019

The Straits Times, March 4, 2019, Parliament: 4 in 10 Applications for Protection Orders Granted by Court Since 2014, Says Edwin Tong. Available at: https://www.straitstimes.com/politics/four-in-10-applications-for-protection-orders-granted-by-court-since-2014-edwin-tong. Accessed May 21, 2019

The Straits Times, May 8, 2019. Parliament: More Than 960 Firms Adopt Standard to Handle Staff Grievances, Including Sexual Harassment, by Ng Jun Sen. Available at: https://www.straitstimes.com/politics/parliament-more-than-960-firms-adopt-standard-to-handle-staff-grievances-including-sexual. Accessed August 1, 2019

SOUTH KOREA

South Korea in the Middle of its own #MeToo movement: the growing #MeToo movement in South Korea was sparked in January 2018 when a prosecutor appeared on a popular television program with a story of how a senior male colleague had groped her years earlier (Source: Washington Post, March 26, 2018. "South Korea is in the middle of its own #MeToo movement," by Sue Mi Terry and Lisa Collins).

Cabinet approves bill to strengthen employers' responsibility for sexual harassment at work: reported cases of workplace sexual harassment were 519 in 2014, 522 in 2015, 556 in 2016, and 532 as of October 2017. For this reason, the *Act on Equal Employment and Support for Work–Family Reconciliation* was amended to strengthen employers' responsibility for sexual harassment at work and measures to protect victims of workplace sexual harassment (Source: Ministry of Employment and Labour, November 21, 2017. "Cabinet approves three amendment bills, including bill to amend Labor Standards"). (See more in the following section.)

Legislation

- Act on Equal Employment and Support for Work–Family Reconciliation, 1987, as amended / Enforcement Decree of the Act on Equal Employment and Support for Work–Family Reconciliation (Presidential Decree No. 16189)

Title of legislation	Act on Equal Employment and Support for Work–Family Reconciliation, 1987, as amended/Enforcement Decree of the Act on Equal Employment and Support for Work–Family Reconciliation (Presidential Decree No. 16189)

The *Act on Equal Employment and Support for Work–Family Reconciliation, 1987*, as amended, and the Enforcement Decree of the Act on Equal Employment and Support for Work–Family Reconciliation (Presidential Decree No. 16189), as amended, and also referred to as the Gender Equal Employment Act ("EEO Act"), are applicable to all businesses or workplaces that employ workers. It includes obligations on prevention, education, and disciplinary measures placed on an employer against an employee who commits *sexual harassment.* The Act penalizes employers if they are found to not have carried out their duty in preventing and taking action against an alleged perpetrator.

The term "sexual harassment on the job" means that:

> an employer, a superior or a worker causes another worker to feel sexual humiliation or repulsion by sexual words or actions by utilizing a position in the workplace or in relation with duties, or providing any disadvantages in employment on account of disregard for sexual words or actions or any other demands, etc.
>
> *(Article 2 Definitions)*

Sexual harassment at work refers to a situation where an employer, a superior, or a worker causes another worker to feel sexually humiliated or offended by sexually charged words or actions by using their position in the workplace or in relation to work, or gives disadvantages in employment for disregarding sexual words or actions or any other demands, etc. (Article 2). No employer, superior, or worker shall engage in sexual harassment at work. (Article 12)

An employer shall conduct education in order to prevent sexual harassment at work and to create a safe working environment for workers at least once a year. An employer may conduct education to prevent sexual harassment by entrusting it to the institution designated by the Minister of Employment and Labor. (Article 13, 13–2)

Pursuant to a January 14, 2014 amendment, employers, as well as workers, must also receive sexual harassment prevention training. Prior to this amendment, those who could be classified as employers were not included. The law requires that all businesses in South Korea provide sexual harassment awareness and prevention education to their employees at least once a year.

An employer shall take without delay disciplinary measures or any other equivalent actions against the sexual harasser if an occurrence of sexual harassment at work has been verified. No employer shall dismiss or take any other disadvantageous measures against a worker who has been damaged with regard to sexual harassment at work or claimed damage occurred from sexual harassment. (Article 14)

If a person closely related to the duties, such as a client, etc., causes a worker to feel sexually humiliated or offended by sexual words, actions, etc., during the performance of duties, and such worker requests resolution of the grievances thereby, the employer shall make efforts to take all possible measures, such as the change of the place of work, relocation, etc. No employer shall dismiss or take any other disadvantageous measures against the worker on account of his or her claim for any damage or of disregard for sexual demands from clients, etc. (Article 14–2)

Effective May 29, 2018, amendments strengthened employers' obligations to take measures against sexual harassment at work as follows:

- In cases where sexual harassment occurs in the workplace, anyone will be allowed to report it to the employer and the employer will be obligated to conduct a fact-finding investigation and take protective measures for the victim, such as moving the victim to another place of work and granting him/her annual leave. (A person who violates this provision will be punished by a fine of not more than 5 million KRW.)
- The employer is prohibited from dismissing or unfavorably treating any worker or victim who reports workplace sexual harassment and imposes a higher fine for violating this prohibition (20 million KRW → 30 million KRW).
- In cases where sexual harassment by a client, etc., occurs, the employer will be obligated to take protective measures for the victim, such as reassigning or transferring the victim to another place of work and ordering him/her to take paid leave. (A person who violates this provision will be punished by a fine of not more than 3 million KRW.)

The employer must also do the following:

- Prepare sexual harassment prevention guidelines in accordance with Article 13(4) of the Act on Equal Employment and Support for Work–Family Reconciliation. (Article 5.2)
- Ensure all workers receive sexual harassment prevention education. The employer must ensure the education includes matters necessary for counseling and grievance handling at work; procedures for handling sexual harassment; victim protection procedures; disciplinary procedures; and other matters necessary for the prevention of sexual harassment at work. The employer may conduct sexual harassment prevention education by entrusting it to an institution designated by the Minister of Employment and Labor. (Article 13.2)
- Take, without delay, disciplinary measures or any other equivalent actions against the sexual harasser if an occurrence of sexual harassment at work has been verified. (Article 14.1)
- Not dismiss or take any other disadvantageous measures against a worker who has been damaged with regard to sexual harassment at work or claimed damage occurred from sexual harassment. (Article 14.2)

- Make efforts to take all possible measures, such as the change of the place of work and relocation. If a person closely related to the duties, such as a client, causes a worker to feel sexually humiliated or offended by sexual words, actions, etc. during the performance of duties, and such worker requests resolution of the grievances thereby. (Article 14–2.1)
- Not dismiss or take any other disadvantageous measures against the worker on account of their claim for any damage under requirement 14–2.1 or of disregard for sexual demands from clients, etc. (Article 14–2.2)

BIBLIOGRAPHY

Ministry of Employment and Labour. Act on Equal Employment and Support for Work-Family Reconciliation, Act No. 3989, December 4, 1987 as Amended to February 29, 2016. Available at: http://www.moel.go.kr/english/poli/poliLaw:view.jsp?idx=224&tab=4. Accessed May 21, 2019

Ministry of Employment and Labour, November 21, 2017. Cabinet Approves Three Amendment Bills, Including Bill to Amend Labor Standards Act. Available at: http://www.moel.go.kr/english/poli/poliLaw:view.jsp?idx=1465. Accessed August 28, 2019

Ministry of Employment and Labour. Employment Policy, 2017. Available at: http://www.moel.go.kr/english/poli/poliLaw:view.jsp?idx=1465. Accessed May 21, 2019

Washington Post, March 26, 2018. South Korea Is in the Middle of Its Own #MeToo Movement, by Sue Mi Terry and Lisa Collins. Available at: https://www.washingtonpost.com/news/democracy-post/wp/2018/03/26/south-korea-is-in-the-middle-of-its-own-metoo-movement/?noredirect=on&utm_term=.8953218ccdd6. Accessed August 20, 2019. Read more at: https://www.channelnewsasia.com/news/asia/sexual-harassment-south-korea-exposes-hypocrisy-intimidation-10039994

TAIWAN

A 2017 Ministry of Labor (MOL) survey found that 3.5 percent of the female respondents have been sexually harassed at work, yet 80 percent of the incidents went unreported. 1.5 percent of sexual harassment came from clients, 1.4 percent from coworkers, and 0.8 percent from superiors. However, only 0.7 percent of those cases were reported. Most women who had been sexually harassed at work were either too embarrassed of the incident to admit it, or chose not to report the incident to avoid becoming the target of office gossip, while some decided to keep it a secret for fear of losing their jobs (Source: Taiwan News, March 8, 2017. "80 percent of women don't report workplace sexual harassment: survey," by Wendy Lee).

Legislation

- Gender Equality in Employment Act, 2002, as amended
- Regulations for Establishing Measures of Prevention, Correction, Complaint and Punishment of Sexual Harassment at Workplace, 2002, as amended
- Civil Code, 2015

Title of legislation	Gender Equality in Employment Act, 2002, as amended

The *Gender Equality in Employment Act*, 2002, as amended, in relevant part, aims to eliminate sex discrimination and prevent *sexual harassment.* The Act also applies to trainees (as defined in Article 3) who are sexually harassed during the duration of their training. (Article 2)

The Act states:

Sexual harassment referred to in the Act shall mean one of the following two circumstances:

- In the course of an employee executing his or her duties, any one makes a sexual request, uses verbal or physical conduct of a sexual nature or with an intent of gender discrimination, causes him or her a hostile, intimidating and offensive working environment leading to infringe on or interfere with his or her personal dignity, physical liberty or affects his or her job performance.

- An employer explicitly or implicitly makes a sexual request toward an employee or an applicant, uses verbal or physical conduct of a sexual nature or with an intent of gender discrimination as an exchange for the establishment, continuance, modification of a labor contract or as a condition to his or her placement, assignment, compensation, evaluation, promotion, demotion, award and discipline.

The determination of sexual harassment is based on the background of the incident, work environment, relationship between the parties, the actor's testimony and conduct, and the counterpart's perception. (Article 12)

Employers shall prevent sexual harassment from occurring and correct it when it does. Employers with over 30 employees shall establish measures for preventing, correcting sexual harassment, related complaint procedures and disciplinary measures. All these measures shall be openly displayed in the workplace. (Article 13)

When employers know of the occurrence of sexual harassment, immediate and effective correctional and remedial measures shall be implemented.

Title of legislation	Regulations for Establishing Measures of Prevention, Correction, Complaint and Punishment of Sexual Harassment at Workplace, 2002, as amended

Regulations for Establishing Measures of Prevention, Correction, Complaint and Punishment of Sexual Harassment at Workplace, 2002, as amended, require that an employer provide a work environment free of *sexual harassment* for his or her employees and applicants. The employer shall adopt appropriate measures to prevent, correct, punish and handle such conduct and protect the privacy of the parties involved. (Article 3)

Measures for preventing and correction of sexual harassment shall include:

- Implementing educational programs for preventing and correction of sexual harassment.
- Announcing and publicly presenting a written policy for the prohibition of sexual harassment in the workplace.
- Promulgating complaint procedures for handling sexual harassment incidents and designate specific personnel or organization in charge of these procedures.

- Handling these complaints in confidentiality and protect complainant from any retaliation or other adverse treatment.
- Establishing measures for punishing those who are proven to be perpetrators after formal investigation. (Article 4)

Employers shall identify the risks of sexual harassment in the work environment and provide necessary prevention measures for employees and thoroughly inform employees of such information beforehand. (Article 4–1)

An employer shall set up designated telephone, telex, special mail boxes or e-mail addresses to handle complaints concerning sexual harassment. The information shall be openly displayed at a noticeable place in the workplace. (Article 5)

A complaint of sexual harassment shall be filed orally or in writing. For orally filed complaints, the personnel or unit in charge of receiving these complaints shall put them in record. After clearly announcing them to the complainant or letting him or her read and ascertain the correctness of their contents, the complainant shall sign his or her name or imprint his or her seal on the record. (Article 6)

An employer who deals with a complaint concerning sexual harassment shall do so confidentially. To deal with the complaint, the employer and the employee representatives shall organize a committee for handling sexual harassment complaints, with attention paid to an appropriate proportion of committee members' gender. (Article 7)

Articles 8–14 refer to the complaint and investigation process: after the employer receives a complaint, he or she may proceed to conduct an investigation. The complaint shall be decided two months after it is filed, with a one-month extension if necessary. The right of privacy and other legal rights concerning personality of the parties involved shall be protected and respected. If sexual harassment is proven to have taken place, an employer shall make an appropriate punishment or render other corrective measures to the respondent of the complaint in accordance with the seriousness of the incident.

Title of legislation Civil Code, as amended 2015

The *Civil Code*, amended June 10, 2015, may possibly be applied in cases of *harassment*. The Civil Code provides that the employer is jointly liable to make compensation for any damage which the employee wrongfully causes to the rights of another person in the performance of his duties.

The employee must prove that the employer intentionally or negligently behaved in a discriminatory fashion in order to prove injury.

The employer is not liable for damages if it exercised reasonable care in the selection of the employee and in supervising his or her duties or if the damage would have been occasioned regardless of such reasonable care. An employer may defend himself or herself by demonstrating that the acts of discrimination were not committed during the performance of the alleged violator's duties or with the instructions and authorization of the company's top management. (Article 188)

BIBLIOGRAPHY

Laws & Regulations Database of the Republic of China, Ministry of Justice, 2015. Civil Code, as Amended 2015. Available at: http://law.moj.gov.tw/Eng/LawClass/LawAll.aspx?PCode=B0000001. Accessed July 10, 2019

Ministry of Labor, 2002. Gender Equality in Employment Act, 2002, as Amended. Available at: https://law.moj.gov.tw/ENG/LawClass/LawAll.aspx?pcode=N0030014. Accessed April 4, 2019

Ministry of Labor, 2002. Regulations for Establishing Measures of Prevention, Correction, Complaint and Punishment of Sexual Harassment at Workplace, 2002, as Amended 2015. Available at: https://law.moj.gov.tw/ENG/LawClass/LawAll.aspx?PCode=N0030019. Accessed April 4, 2019

Taiwan News, March 8, 2017. 80 Percent of Women Don't Report Workplace Sexual Harassment: Survey, by Wendy Lee. Available at: https://www.taiwannews.com.tw/en/news/3111739. Accessed May 14, 2019

THAILAND

Thailand lags significantly behind many countries in addressing sexual harassment in the workplace.

Legislation

- The Labour Protection Act B.E. 2541, 1998 as amended

Title of legislation	Labour Protection Act B.E. 2541, 1998 as amended

The *Labour Protection Act B.E. 2541, 1998, as amended*, section 16 prohibits an employer, a chief, a supervisor, or a work inspector from performing an act of *sexual harassment* against an employee. Thus, the harassment must be at the hands of a senior employee or employer towards someone junior to them. This is the only mention of sexual harassment in the Act.

The Labour Protection Act was amended in 2008; it previously only protected employees against sexual abuse, but the amendments extended its coverage to sexual harassment, including offensive sexual remarks. In addition, the former provisions only prohibited harassment directed towards female employees and minors, whereas the amended provisions prohibit harassment against all employees.

BIBLIOGRAPHY

Department of Labour Protection and Welfare, 1998. Labour Protection Act B.E. 2541, as Amended. Available at: https://www.labour.go.th/en/attachments/article/18/Labour_Protection_Act_BE2541.pdf. Accessed March 29, 2019

VIETNAM

Sexual harassment is defined as any behavior of a sexual nature that affects the dignity of women and men, which is considered as unwanted, unacceptable, inappropriate, and offensive to the recipient, and that creates an intimidating, hostile, unstable, or offensive work environment. Sexual harassment in the workplace can be physical, verbal, or non-verbal (Vietnam Industrial Relations Committee, 2015). The Code recommends the development, implementation, and monitoring of a workplace policy on sexual harassment, and includes suggested components of the policy. The policy is to be effectively communicated though measures including training all staff members, including managers, supervisors, and workers. Employers are advised to respond promptly to any accusation of sexual harassment, ensuring that alleged victims do not have fear of reprisals or feel that their grievances are being ignored or trivialized.

Following a Facebook post on April 19, 2018 by an intern at Vietnam's most prestigious newspaper that she had been raped by her supervising editor and attempted suicide, women from across the country began sharing stories about harassment and abuse they had experienced while working as reporters. They tagged their posts #toasoansach (clean newsroom), #ngungimlang (stop staying silent) and #MeToo (Source: The Diplomat. May 15, 2018. "Me Too, Vietnam," by Isabelle Taft).

A quotation from the *Guardian* reads:

> Despite the rising popularity of social media campaigns in Vietnam to raise awareness of sexual harassment, such as #MeToo and #ngungimlang (stop silence), most garment workers said they were too afraid to speak up, fearing the loss of their jobs or further harassment, according to the study.

Female factory workers producing clothing and shoes in Vietnam face systemic sexual harassment and violence at work. Close to 43 percent of 63 women interviewed in factories in three Vietnamese provinces said they had suffered at least one form of violence and/or harassment in the previous year, according to a study by the Fair Wear Foundation and Care International (Source: The Guardian, April 7, 2019. "Revealed: Women Making Clothes for West Face Sexual Abuse," by Kate Hodal).

Legislation

- Labour Code, 2013

Title of legislation	Labour Code, 2013

Vietnam's *Labour Code No. 10/2012/QH13* states that an employer has obligations to respect and honor the dignity of the employee, and behave properly toward the employee (Article 6). *Sexual harassment* at workplaces is prohibited (Article 8). However, sexual harassment is not defined nor are employers required to take preventive measures or to establish complaint procedures in the workplace (but see the *Vietnam Code of Conduct on Sexual Harassment in the Workplace* in the following paragraph).

The *Vietnam Code of Conduct on Sexual Harassment in the Workplace,* issued in 2015, prohibits sexual harassment and aims to help employers and workers to develop their own policy or regulation for preventing and addressing sexual harassment, and to promote healthy, safe, and productive workplaces. It is applicable to all companies, regardless of size. The Code's Introduction states:

> Sexual harassment in the workplace is a form of sex discrimination which negatively affects the working environment, undermines gender equality at work, creates unfair practices in employment, and adversely impacts the dignity and well-being of workers. It creates psychological anxiety and stress for victims and if ignored, can result in high costs for companies through loss of productivity, low worker morale, absenteeism, and staff turnover.

BIBLIOGRAPHY

Ministry of Labour, Invalids and Social Affairs and International Labour Organization, 2013. Report on Sexual Harassment at The Workplace in Vietnam: An Overview of the Legal Framework. Available at: http://www.ilo.org/wcmsp5/groups/public/---asia/---ro-bangkok/---ilo-hanoi/documents/publication/wcms_206106.pdf. Accessed March 29, 2019

National Assembly, Socialist Republic of Viet Nam, 2012. Law No. 10/2012/Qh13 Labor Code. Available at: http://ljip.vn/web/images/stories/labour-documents/luat%20lao%20dong%20English.pdf. Accessed March 29, 2019

The Diplomat, May 15, 2018. Me Too, Vietnam, by Isabelle Taft. Available at: https://thediplomat.com/2018/05/metoo-vietnam/. Accessed May 16, 2019

The Guardian, April 7, 2019. Revealed: Women Making Clothes for West Face Sexual Abuse, by Kate Hodal. Available at: https://www.theguardian.com/global-development/2019/apr/07/violence-sexual-abuse-vietnam-garment-factory. Accessed August 19, 2019

Vietnam Industrial Relations Committee, 2015. Code of Conduct on Sexual Harassment in the Workplace. Available at: http://www.ilo.org/wcmsp5/groups/public/---asia/---ro-bangkok/---ilo-hanoi/documents/publication/wcms_421220.pdf. Accessed March 29, 2019

5 Sexual harassment laws in the Americas region

LATIN AMERICA

> Numerous countries in Latin America have laws in place regulating sexual harassment. Some are specific stand-alone regulations, such as in Panama, or a part of the Labor Code, like in Chile, while Brazil classifies sexual harassment as a type of crime addressed in its penal code. Often, sexual harassment is addressed in one or more of a country's laws.

Definitions of sexual harassment vary from country to country, but most generally regard sexual harassment as any unwelcome sexual advance, request for sexual favors, verbal or physical conduct or gesture of a sexual nature, creating an intimidating, hostile, or offensive work environment.

Latin America lags behind on sexual harassment in the workplace: while the United States is having its "me too" moment regarding harassment principally in the workplace, Latin America lags several steps behind, with femicides from Mexico to Argentina periodically triggering protests from the *ni una más* ("not one more") and the more recent *ni una menos* movement in Peru (Source: NBC News, May 17, 2018. "While the U.S. has #MeToo, Latin America's 'Ni Una Menos' spotlights femicides, violence against women," by Simeon Tegel).

However, all of Latin America has signed the United Nations convention on the elimination of discrimination against women, and 31 countries had taken steps to outlaw sexual harassment by 2016, up from 24 in 2013 (Source: Bloomberg Opinion, December 28, 2017. "Latin America's #MeToo Moment," by Mac Margolis).

BIBLIOGRAPHY

Bloomberg Opinion, December 28, 2017. Latin America's #MeToo Moment, by Mac Margolis. Available at: https://www.bloomberg.com/opinion/articles/2017-12-28/latin-america-s-metoo-moment. Accessed August 23, 2019

NBC News, May 17, 2018. While the U.S. Has #MeToo, Latin America's 'Ni Una Menos' Spotlights Femicides, Violence against Women, by Simeon Tegel. Available at: https://www.nbcnews.com/news/latino/while-u-s-has-metoo-latin-america-s-ni-una-n875091. Accessed April 11, 2019

ARGENTINA

Labor relationships in Argentina are governed by the Argentine Constitution, international treaties and conventions, and, in most cases, by the Labour Contract Law (LCL) (Law No. 20,744). The Constitution establishes a number of workers' rights, including dignified and equitable working conditions.

There is no specific regulation for sexual harassment in the workplace, except for public sector employees, although Argentina has signed several international treaties, such as the Convention on elimination of all forms of discrimination against women (CEDAW) and the Convention to erase and punish all kinds of violence against women and the declaration of elimination of all violence against women, which was adopted by the General Assembly of the United Nations.

Although there is no specific statutory prohibition of sexual harassment at the workplace in the private sector, there is, more widely, a statutory prohibition of violence against women, which is defined as including sexual and psychological harassment. Additionally, there are several criminal and civil offences related to sexual, emotional, and physical abuse that may be considered to include forms of sexual harassment.

Sexual harassment is prohibited in Law No. 264.85, the Women's Global Protection Law, which addresses discrimination and violence against women generally throughout Argentina. While it is a gender protection act and is exclusively applicable to women, it does not expressly address sexual harassment situations in the workplace. However, as discrimination is the major offence, it is to be deduced that sexual harassment is a cause of discrimination (Law 26.485).

In the employment context, employers have a statutory duty to ensure their employees' health and safety at work. This implies a duty to prevent and eliminate sexual harassment. An employer is directly liable if he or she or a representative commits harassment, and is indirectly responsible if another employee commits harassment. In the latter case, in order to establish that the employer is responsible, the burden of proof is on the victim of harassment to prove that the employer had knowledge of the harasser's conduct but did nothing to prevent or stop it.

Legislation

- The Employment Contract Law, (Labor Contract Law)
- Anti-Discrimination Law No. 23, 592, 1988
- Executive Order, No. 2385/93 (public sector)

Title of legislation	Employment Contract Law No. 20, 744, 1974

The *Employment Contract Law*, No. 20.744, 1974, also known as the *Labor Contract Law*, sets forth the main conditions of employment that all employment contracts must comply with, and includes provisions prohibiting discrimination among employees. The law contains a general principle of non-discrimination on grounds including sex.

Title of legislation	Anti-Discrimination Law No. 23, 592, 1988, as amended

Anti-Discrimination Law No. 23, 592, enacted on August 23, 1988, as amended, prohibits any discrimination on grounds which include sex. It is not specified if this applies to the workplace, as it only references public places.

Title of legislation	Executive Order, No. 2385/93

Executive Order No. 2385/93 prohibits sexual harassment for public sector employees, defining sexual harassment in Section 1.

BIBLIOGRAPHY

Ministerio de Justicia y Derechos Humanos de la Nación, 1988, Anti-Discrimination Law No. 23, 592. Available at: http://servicios.infoleg.gob.ar/infolegInternet/anexos/20000-24999/20465/texact.htm. Accessed May 14, 2019

BRAZIL

> Brazil is behind many other countries in awareness of workplace sexual harassment, but has taken a few small steps recently. Sexual harassment is a crime in Brazil, but only in case of a superior's interactions with subordinates.

In Brazil, sexual harassment is considered a criminal offense as well as a violation of civil and constitutional rights and a breach of the employee's duties. The offender is subject to criminal prosecution, to a civil claim for damages, and to dismissal for cause. The law has been condemned as too narrow, particularly in a country where sexualized misbehavior is so widespread. More than four in 10 women in Brazil say they've been sexually harassed at work, on the street, on a bus, or at school, according to a poll conducted in 2017 by Datafolha. Brazil's public ministry of labor and the International Labour Organization tried to address the issue, publishing a new primer on how to identify and report sexual harassment at work. But it went far beyond what's established in the law, adding to the confusion about what's right and what's wrong (Source: Bloomberg Business Week, March 8, 2018. "This famously affectionate country has a serious #MeToo problem," by David Biller).

Legislation

- Federal Law 9029/95, as amended
- Penal Code, as amended by Law 10.224,2001
- Labour Code, 1943, as amended

Title of legislation	Federal Law 9029/95, as amended

Federal Law 9029/95, as amended, prohibits discrimination in the workplace on grounds which include sex. (Article 1)

Disruption of the employment relationship by a discriminatory act and the right to compensation for moral damage is provided for.

Title of legislation	Penal Code, as amended by Law No. 10.224, of 15 May 2001

Law 10.224, 2001, amended *Decree–Law No 2.848, of December 7, 1940—Penal Code.* It provides for the crime of *sexual harassment,* defining sexual harassment as coercing someone with the intention of obtaining sexual advantage or favor, whichever is the agent of his superior status or ancestry inherent in employment, position or function. The penalty is detention for one to two years.

Title of legislation Labour Code, 1943 as amended

The *Labour Code, Decree–Law No. 5,452, 1943,* as amended by Law No. 9799, of May 26, 1999, forbids discrimination in employment on grounds which include sex.

BIBLIOGRAPHY

Camara Dos Deputados, 1999. Lei No. 9.799, DE 26 DE MAIO DE 1999. Available at: http://www2.camara.leg.br/legin/fed/lei/1999/lei-9799-26-maio-1999-368710-publicacaooriginal-1-pl.html. Accessed August 28, 2019

Labour Code. Available at: http://www.planalto.gov.br/ccivil_03/decreto-lei/Del5452compilado.htm. Accessed December 18, 2018

Presidency of the Republic Civil House Subchefia for Legal Affairs, Law No. 9.029, of April 13, 1995. Available at: http://www.planalto.gov.br/ccivil_03/Leis/L9029.htm. Accessed August 28, 2019

Presidency of the Republic Civil House Subchefia for Legal Affairs, 2001. Law 10.224, 2001. Available at: http://www.planalto.gov.br/ccivil_03/Leis/LEIS_2001/L10224.htm. Accessed April 10, 2019

Presidency of the Republic Civil House Subchefia for Legal Affairs, 1943. Decree-Law No. 5,452, 1st May 1943, as Amended (Labour Code). Available at: http://www.planalto.gov.br/ccivil_03/Decreto-Lei/Del5452compilado.htm. Accessed August 28, 2019

Presidency of the Republic, Civil House, Deputy Head of Legal Affairs, Legislative Decree the 2.848 of 7, 1940. Penal Code, 1940, as Amended 2001. Available at: http://www.planalto.gov.br/ccivil_03/decreto-lei/Del2848compilado.htm. Accessed August 28, 2019

Source: Bloomberg Business Week, March 8, 2018. This Famously Affectionate Country Has a Serious #MeToo Problem, by David Biller. Available at: https://www.bloomberg.com/news/articles/2018-03-08/brazil-has-a-serious-metoo-problem. Accessed August 20, 2019

CHILE

> In Chile, sexual harassment is perceived as a conduct that is incompatible with an individual's dignity.

Bulletin 12257–13 modifies the Labor Code to require the employer to develop protocols for the prevention and protection of its workers against sexual harassment: a Bill in the Chamber of Deputies since November 2018 would modify the Labor Code to require employers to develop protocols for the prevention and protection of its workers against sexual harassment. Bulletin 12257–13 modifies the Labor Code to require the employer to develop protocols for the prevention and protection of its workers against sexual harassment. As of August 22, 2019, it remains in process (Source: Chamber of Deputies, November 21, 2018. "Modifies the Labor Code to require the employer to develop protocols for prevention and protection of their workers against sexual harassment").

Chile's Labor Directorate offers the following information on sexual harassment: the victim of sexual harassment must submit their complaint in writing to the address of the company, establishment or service in which they work or to the respective Labor Inspectorate. The employer may choose to directly conduct an internal investigation or, within five days of receiving the complaint, refer it to the Labor Inspectorate, which has 30 days to conduct the investigation. The internal investigation carried out by the employer must be carried out within 30 days. Once the investigation is completed, the results must be submitted to the Labor Inspectorate. If the complaint is made by the affected party—male or female—or referred by the employer to the Labor Inspectorate, it will conduct an investigation in the same terms described above. More information is available on the website.

Legislation

- Labour Code

Title of legislation Labour Code, 2003, as amended

The *Labour Code* 2003, as amended, applies to all workplace and governs labor relations between employers and workers. It prohibits discrimination on a number of grounds, workplace harassment, and *sexual harassment.*

According to Article 2 of the *Labour Code,* sexual bullying is understood as "a person acting inappropriately or making sexual advances, not consented to by the person who received such advances, and who threatened or harmed that person's place of work or their employment opportunities."

Article 2 provides for labor relations to be compatible with the dignity of the person, and states that discrimination and sexual harassment are contrary to this. Harassment is also contrary to the dignity of a person meaning conduct constituting aggression or repeated harassment exerted by the employer or by one or more workers against of one or more other workers, by any means, and that results for the or affected their impairment, abuse or humiliation, or that threatens or harms the situation employment or employment opportunities.

An amendment to the *Labour Code,* Act No. 20,005 of 8 March 2005 defined sexual harassment as "undue harassment by a person in any way, requirements of a sexual nature without the consent of the subject of those requirements that threaten or impair their job status or their employment opportunities." The amendment also states that the internal regulations of order, hygiene and safety must contain the "procedure to which they will be subjected and the measures of protection and sanctions that will be applied in case of complaints of sexual harassment."

- An employer must adopt measures to safeguard those involved after a sexual harassment complaint by separating workplaces and schedules and must launch internal investigations and report back to the Ministry of Labor. If the harassment is confirmed, the perpetrator is to be fired without compensation. If the perpetrator is the victim's boss, the victim can quit the company and receive the compensation normally paid when a worker resigns, plus an additional 80 percent. He or she also maintains the right to pursue legal action in the courts and demand additional compensation for moral and psychological damage. In the case of sexual harassment in the workplace, the affected person shall file a claim to the establishment.
- Upon receiving a sexual harassment claim, the employer must adopt the necessary safeguard measures to protect the affected parties.
- The employer must conduct an investigation within five days of the notification of sexual harassment, giving both parties the opportunity to be heard and reporting the results to the Inspectorate of

Work. Note: the employer may also have the investigation be completed by the Inspectorate of Work.

- Within 15 days of receiving the conclusions of an investigation of a sexual assault case conducted by the Inspectorate of Work, the employer shall apply the resulting measures or sanctions. *Labor Code*, 2002 (amended 2018), Article 211A, 211B, and 211C.

BIBLIOGRAPHY

Biblioteca del Congreso Nacional de Chile, 2003. Consolidated Labour Code, 2003, as of November 2018. Available at: https://www.leychile.cl/Navegar?idNorma=207436&idParte=. Accessed April 10, 2019

Chamber of Deputies, November 21, 2018. Modifies the Labor Code to Require the Employer to Develop Protocols for Prevention and Protection of Their Workers against Sexual Harassment. Available at: https://www.camara.cl/pley/pley_detalle.aspx?prmID=12780&prmBoletin=12257-13. Accessed August 26, 2019

Direccion del Trabajo. Law No. 20.005 on Sexual Harassment. Available at: https://www.dt.gob.cl/portal/1626/articles-80095_recurso_1.pdf. Accessed May 15, 2019

Labor Directorate, Query Center, Sexual Harassment, n.d. Available at: https://www.dt.gob.cl/portal/1628/w3-propertyvalue-22997.html. Accessed August 25, 2019

COLOMBIA

> In Colombia there is no specific labor regulation defining sexual harassment. However, Colombia, as part of the International Labor Organization, has used its definition, "a sex-based behavior that is unwelcome and offensive to its recipient. For sexual harassment to exist these two conditions must be present," as is illustrated in the court decision below.

In the January 31, 2018 decision of Luis Carlos Cajamarca Barragán v. Pimpollo S.A., the Labor Chamber of the Supreme Court of Justice upheld the decision of the regional labor tribunal of an employee who had been dismissed due his undesired and implicit sexual insinuations and behaviors toward three female subordinates. In its decision, the Court referred to the International Labor Organization's (ILO) guidelines, reasoning that in order to consider behavior as sexual harassment, the conduct should be not desired, be offensive to the individual, and have a sexual connotation. It also noted that sexual harassment could take place on a quid pro quo basis or through the harasser generating a hostile work environment for the victim. The Court identified and characterized the circumstances in which sexual harassment might take place, indicating that it could be physical (which is not limited to explicit sexual contact), verbal, or nonverbal. It also stated that sexual harassment was not limited to explicit physical contact and could also include "any action that may represent an undue sexual requirement that can be made by any means; verbal proposals, e-mails, letters, phone calls, etc." (Supreme Court of Justice Decision, *Luis Carlos Cajamarca Barragán v. Pimpollo S.A*, SL648–2018)

Legislation

- Work Harassment Law 1010 of 2006
- Penal Code

Title of legislation The Work Harassment Law 1010 of 2006

The Work Harassment Law 1010 of 2006 protects against harassment, defined as any persistent and demonstrable conduct taken against an employee by a supervisor or co-worker with the intent of causing the employee intimidation or fear, or inducing the employee to resign.

Harassment includes conduct which offends or threatens an employee's dignity or sexual freedom (Article 2). *Sexual harassment* is only briefly mentioned as a category of labor harassment but does not include specifics on which acts and/or behaviors may constitute sexual harassment.

Article 2, "Definition And Modalities Of Labor Harassment," states that:

> For the purposes of this law, harassment at work means any persistent and demonstrable behavior, exercised on an employee, worker by an employer, a boss or superior immediate or mediate, a co-worker or a subordinate, aimed at instilling fear, intimidation, terror and anguish, to cause work injury, generate demotivation at work, or induce the resignation of the same.

The law includes labor abuse as physical, psychological, and verbal abuse for part of the employer. Any act of violence against the physical or moral integrity, physical or sexual freedom and property of one who serves as employee or worker; any abusive or outrageous verbal expression that damages the moral integrity or injures the rights to privacy and good name of those involved in an employment relationship or job type, all behavior tending to undermine the self-esteem and dignity of one who participates in a working relationship job type.

The law sets out behaviors that do and do not constitute harassment at work. An employee may commence administrative or judicial labor actions for unlawful harassment. Employers found liable for harassment can be fined pursuant to Colombia's Disciplinary Code.

Title of legislation Penal Code as amended

Article 210 of the *Penal Code* states that *sexual harassment* is an offense punishable by imprisonment of one to three years. The Code states that the nature of sexual harassment as an offense is applicable to sexual harassment that occurs both at work and anywhere outside it, and whether or not there is an employment relationship.

BIBLIOGRAPHY

Official Gazette No. 46160 of January 23, 2006, Lei 1010 of 2006. Available at: http://www.secretariasenado.gov.co/senado/basedoc/ley_1010_2006.html. Accessed May 6, 2019

Penal Code (Law No. 599 of July 24, 2000, as Amended Up to Law No. 1773 of January 6, 2016). Available at: https://www.refworld.org/docid/3dbd1fd94.html%20. Accessed June 19, 2019

Supreme Court of Justice Decision, Luis Carlos Cajamarca Barragán v. Pimpollo S.A, SL648-2018. Available at: http://www.cortesuprema.gov.co/corte/wp-content/uploads/relatorias/la/bmar2018/SL648-2018.pdf. Accessed May 6, 2019.

MEXICO

> On May 1, 2019, Mexico published a decree amending Mexico's Federal Labor Law. In relevant part, the decree requires that a company must implement, in agreement with its employees, an internal protocol to address sexual harassment cases.

Initially, Mexico did not have much response to the 2017 #MeToo movement. However, in March 2019, Mexican female media shared incidents of sexual harassment, physical attacks and psychological bullying in workplaces including newsrooms, publishing houses, literary fairs and debates. Shortly after, hundreds of reporters, photographers, camerawomen and university researchers had shared incidents of sexual harassment and abuse perpetrated by colleagues and bosses using hashtags like #MeTooCine (#MeTooCinema), #MeTooAcademicosMexicanos (#MeTooMexicanAcademics) and #YoTeCreo (#IBelieveYou). 73% of female workers have suffered sexual harassment, according to a recent survey of close to 400 reporters, editors, designers, photographers, illustrators and administrators who currently or previously worked in the media. An online survey conducted by United Mexican Journalists collective (*Periodistas Unidas Mexicanas,* or PUM) found that half of the women surveyed said they were harassed by their direct boss, and 43 percent by sources who they were working with on a story. The harassment negatively impacted their professional performance, according to 60 percent of respondents (Source: The Guardian, March 27, 2019. "#MeToo reaches Mexico: majority of women in media report harassment at work," by Nina Lakhani).

Legislation

- Federal Labor Law (FLL), 1970, as amended 2019

Title of legislation	Federal Labor Law (Ley Federal del Trabajo), 1970, as amended 2019

The *Federal Labor Law (*Ley Federal del Trabajo*), 1970,* as amended in 2019, requires that employers have proper considerations for their employees, abstaining from verbal or physical mistreatment, and that the work environment be free of treatment going against the dignity, integrity, and safety of the employees.

Amendments to the Federal Labor Law in 2012 added *sexual harassment* to the list of justifiable causes for termination of a labor relationship. *Sexual harassment* is a:

> ...form of violence in which, although there is no subordination, there is an abusive exercise of power that leads to a state of helplessness and risk to the victim, regardless of whether it takes place at one or several events.

The employer may rescind the employment relationship with its employees, without any liability, when the employees commit immoral acts or sexual harassment against any person at the facility or workplace.

As noted above, on May 1, 2019, Mexico's Federal Official Gazette published a decree setting forth major amendments to Mexico's Federal Labor Law. In relevant part, the decree requires that a company must implement, in agreement with its employees, an internal protocol to address sexual harassment cases.

BIBLIOGRAPHY

El Consejo Nacional para Prevenir La Discriminación, CONAPRED, 2014. Ley Federal Para Prevenir Y Eliminar La Discriminación Reforma del 20 de marzo de 2014. Available at: http://www.diputados.gob.mx/LeyesBiblio/pdf/262_210618.pdf. Accessed April 10, 2019

Legislatura. Federal Labour Law 1970, as Amended May 1, 2019. Available at: http://www.diputados.gob.mx/LeyesBiblio/ref/lft.htm. Accessed May 15, 2019

Official Gazette. Decree Whereby Various Provisions of the Federal Labor Law, the Organic Law of the Judicial Power of the Federation, the Federal Law of the Public Defender, the Law of the National Housing Fund Institute Are Reformed, Added and Repealed for Workers and the Social Security Law, in Matters of Labor Justice, Trade Union Freedom and Collective Bargaining. Available at: http://www.dof.gob.mx/nota_detalle.php?codigo=5559130&fecha=01/05/2019. Accessed May 15, 2019

The Guardian, March 27, 2019. #MeToo Reaches Mexico: Majority of Women in Media Report Harassment at Work, Nina Lakhani. Available at: https://www.theguardian.com/world/2019/mar/27/mexico-metoo-workplace-abuse-sexual-harassment-media. Accessed August 25, 2019

PANAMA

> Panama enacted Law 7 of February 14, 2018, to, in relevant part, prohibit sexual harassment in numerous environments, including the workplace.

The law establishes liability and penalties for any acts of violence against a person's honor, dignity, or physical or psychological integrity. It protects workers' human rights and their rights to dignity and respect and to work under equitable conditions.

Legislation

- Law 7 of February 14, 2018

Title of legislation	Law 7 of February 14, 2018

Law 7 prohibits sexual harassment at work. It defines *sexual harassment* as:

> ...any systematic, continuous, or persistent action or omission through which a person suggests, invites, asks, pursues, limits, or restricts the exercise of another person's rights, impairs their rights, insults or addresses them in a disrespectful manner, or humiliates them in order to obtain sexual favors or to affect the person's dignity.

Law 7 sets forth a new obligation for employers to implement an appropriate and effective internal procedure to process and resolve complaints. The procedure may be developed and implemented through the internal work regulation approved by the Ministry of Labor, collective bargaining agreements, or internal policies. Training, counseling, and orientation on the law must also be implemented.

The employer must implement an investigation process which is effective, confidential, and prompt and which cannot exceed a three-month period from receipt of the complaint. A written report of the investigation and its results must be issued.

Violations of Law 7 by an employer or supervisor are subject to a fine ranging from B/. 550.00 to B/.1000.00 per violation, notwithstanding the employee's right to bring a lawsuit against the employer for any damages arising from the organization's failure to conduct an effective investigation or to remedy the conduct once it has been reported.

An individual who is found to have carried out any of the acts described in the law may be terminated, and such conduct may also constitute a punishable act in accordance with the provisions of the Penal Code.

Employers were required to be in full compliance under the law by May 16, 2018.

BIBLIOGRAPHY

ASAMBLEA NACIONAL DE PANAMÁ, Law 7 of February 14, 2018. Available at: http://www.asamblea.gob.pa/APPS/LEGISPAN/PDF_NORMAS/2010/2018/2018_637_4056.pdf. Accessed May 6, 2019

PERU

Changes to Peru's sexual harassment law in 2018 set out a new definition of sexual harassment as well as defined a grievance procedure for victims of workplace sexual harassment. Sexual harassment in the workplace may now constitute both a labor infraction and a criminal offense.

Legislation

- Ley No. 27942 on Prevention and Punishment of Sexual Harassment, 2003, as amended
- Criminal Code

Title of legislation	Ley No. 27942 on Prevention and Punishment of Sexual Harassment, 2003, as amended

Sexual harassment in Peru is covered by *Law No. 27942: The Law of Prevention and Punishment of Sexual Harassment* and its regulations.

In September 2018, Peru's new decree amending its Law 27942 was published in the Official Gazette, El Peruano (Legislative Decree No. 1410, "Legislative Decree incorporating the offence of sexual harassment, sexual blackmail and dissemination of audiovisual or audio material with sexual content into the Criminal Code and modifying the procedure for punishing sexual harassment"). The stated purpose of the amendment was to reinforce current protections, especially for women, who tend to experience higher levels of harassment.

Sexual harassment and "environmental sexual harassment," under the 2018 amendment, are defined as follows:

> Sexual harassment is a form of violence enacted through behaviour, repeated or otherwise, of a sexual nature or with sexist connotations that is unwanted by the person against whom it is directed, which can create a hostile or humiliating environment, or affect their activity, work, or any teaching or training situation.

The following subsection was added to the list of behaviour and conduct that constitutes sexual harassment: "f) Other behaviours that fit within the concept of sexual harassment."

The law requires that the employer do the following:

- Promote and establish, at the workplace, prevention measures and punishment of sexual harassment in accordance with the obligations set out in Article 7 of the Act. (Article 19)
- Through the Office of Personnel or a substitute, train and sensitize workers about behaviors to punish sexual harassment in accordance with the law and present Regulation to promote a healthy work environment and change behavior contrary to it. (Article 20)
- Establish an internal preventive procedure that allows workers to file a complaint if they become a victim of sexual harassment. This procedure must be made known to all workers of the Center Labor, as well as for new labor contracts. (Article 21)
- Inform the Ministry of Labour and Employment Promotion on procedures established on sexual harassment and on penalties imposed within the following 30 calendar days from the date of resolution of the procedure laid down in this Regulation. (Article 22)

Under Article 23, if an employee believes he or she has experienced sexual harassment in an employment context, the victim may make a formal written request for the harassment to stop or demand payment as compensation for the harassment. Evidence must be submitted to prove that sexual harassment occurred.

The employer has six days to respond to this request. If the employer fails to investigate a claim of sexual harassment or to adopt the appropriate protective, prevention, and sanction measures, the employee may either sue the employer to compel him or her to deal with the harassment, or consider himself or herself to have been constructively dismissed, and sue for compensation.

The complaint procedure lasts approximately 20 days. Following thorough investigation and analysis of the evidence presented, the employer must issue a reasoned resolution stating that the complaint is founded or unfounded, and the penalty to be applied if applicable. The employer must adopt appropriate sanction measures, which may include a reprimand, suspension, or dismissal.

If the harasser is the employer, management personnel, senior employee, owner, or director, the harassed worker has the choice of requesting that the hostility is immediately stopped or demand the payment of an indemnity and a termination of the employment contract.

Title of legislation	Criminal Code

With passage of *Legislative Decree No. 1410* in September 2018, four new crimes were added to the *Criminal Code*, including sexual harassment, the dissemination of audiovisual or audio material with sexual content and sexual blackmail. *Sexual harassment* in the workplace is categorized as an aggravated criminal offense, which may result in a minimum of four and maximum of eight year in prison to the harasser.

BIBLIOGRAPHY

Ministry of Labor and Employment Promotion, Regulation of Law No. 27942 Act and Punishment of Prevention Sexual Harassment Supreme Decret No. 010–2003 (in Spanish). Available at: http://www.mimp.gob.pe/webs/mimp/herramientas-recursos-violencia/contenedor-dgcvg-recursos/contenidos/Legislacion/normas-nacionales/2003_Reglamento_Ley_hostigamiento_sexual.pdf. Accessed March 27, 2019

NORTH AMERICA

CANADA

Canada Federal

#MeToo in Canada: "The MeToo and Time's Up movements have helped women and other survivors from around the world to bring their stories forward and shine a spotlight on harassment and sexual violence," said Patty Hajdu, Canada's labor minister, while opening the debate on stronger sexual harassment protection legislation in the House of Commons, "and it's our responsibility to ensure that light does not fade" (Source: New York Times, January 29, 2018. "'Perfect storm' for a #MeToo reckoning").

Survey reveals more than half of Canadian women sexually harassed at work: "In the wake of the revelations of the #MeToo movement and Time Magazine naming the silence breakers the person of the year, a new survey reveals more than half of women in Canada have experienced sexual harassment at work." The public opinion survey entitled "#MeToo: moment or movement?" was conducted in February 2018, by the Angus Reid Institute. A total of 2,004 Canadian individuals were surveyed, with 979 male and 1025 female respondents. Overall, 52 percent of female respondents said they had been sexually harassed at work, while 28 percent said they had experienced sexual assault at work at some point. Of the female respondents who experienced sexual harassment and/or sexual assault in the workplace, approximately 75 percent stated that they did not report the behavior (Source: Global News, December 6, 2017. "Breaking the silence: new survey reveals more than half of Canadian women sexually harassed at work," by Danielle Carr).

Canada budget initiatives address workplace sexual harassment: in its 2018 budget, in the context of its goal of "eliminating gender-based violence and harassment," the Government of Canada responded to public and stakeholder concerns relating to workplace sexual harassment by proposing to invest 50 million CAD over five years in Government programs to address sexual harassment in the workplace. Of this amount, 25 million CAD will be dedicated to boosting legal aid funding across the country to support complainants of sexual harassment in the workplace, and 25 million CAD to developing a pan-Canadian outreach program to better inform workers, particularly those most vulnerable, about their rights and how they can access help if they have been harassed in the workplace (Source: Department of Justice, 2018. "Initiatives to address workplace sexual harassment anticipatory call for proposals").

Canada publishes draft of Work Place Harassment and Violence Prevention Regulations: On April 27, 2019, Canada published the *Work Place Harassment and Violence Prevention Regulations* for public comment which closed on May 26, 2019. The Regulations will support the recently passed Bill C–65 and will replace the current workplace violence obligations in the Canada Occupational Health and Safety Regulations.

The Government noted that:

> ...harassment and violence, including sexual harassment and sexual violence, continues to be pervasive in federally regulated workplaces. Many employees who have experienced harassment and violence in the workplace do not report it for fear of retribution, lack of support, or a belief that what they have experienced does not substantiate a complaint. The current legal framework is fragmented and not designed to adequately address occurrences of sexual harassment and sexual violence."

The regulations are proposed to support the goals of Bill C–65, discussed in the following section, which include the authority to make regulations to prevent and respond to harassment and violence in the workplace (Source: Canada Gazette, Part I, Volume 153, Number 17, April 27, 2019. Work Place Harassment and Violence Prevention Regulations).

Legislation

Canada is separated into several provinces and territories. The 10 provinces within Canada are Alberta, British Columbia, Manitoba, New Brunswick, Newfoundland and Labrador, Nova Scotia, Ontario, Prince Edward Island, Quebec, and Saskatchewan. The three territories are the Northwest Territories, Nunavut, and Yukon. The majority (approximately 90%) of employees in Canada are covered by provincial laws, with the remainder under the jurisdiction of Canada Federal law. Canadian *sexual harassment* laws and regulations involve both human rights codes and occupational health and safety laws, as well as the 1989 Supreme Court of Canada sexual harassment ruling in Janzen v. Platy Enterprises Ltd., 10 C.H.R.R. D/6205 (S.C.C.), which held that *sexual harassment is discrimination on the basis of sex.*

The Supreme Court of Canada has decided that in cases of proven sexual harassment, employers are responsible for the actions of their employees. Lack of awareness by management does not necessarily eliminate this liability (Source: Alberta Human Rights Commission Sexual Harassment Information Sheet, October 2017).

- Canada Labour Code, Part II R.S.C. 1985, c. L–2, as amended
- Canada Occupational Health and Safety Regulations (SOR/86–304) PART XX
- Canadian Human Rights Act (R.S., 1985, c. H–6), as amended

Title of legislation Canada Labour Code

The Canada Labour Code is a federal Act consolidating the labour (employment) statutes that govern any work, undertaking or business that falls under federal jurisdiction.

Division XV.1 of Part III of the Canada Labour Code establishes an employee's right to employment free of *sexual harassment*. Section 247.1 states:

> In this Division, sexual harassment means any conduct, comment, gesture or contact of a sexual nature (a) that is likely to cause offence or humiliation to any employee; or
>
> (b) that might, on reasonable grounds, be perceived by that employee as placing a condition of a sexual nature on employment or on any opportunity for training or promotion.

The employer is required to make every reasonable effort to ensure that no employee is subjected to sexual harassment and, after consulting with employees or their representatives, must issue a policy on sexual harassment.

The required policy statement under 247.4 may contain any term consistent with the tenor of this Division the employer considers appropriate but must contain the following:

- A definition of sexual harassment that is substantially the same as the definition in section 247.1;
- A statement to the effect that every employee is entitled to employment free of sexual harassment;
- A statement to the effect that the employer will make every reasonable effort to ensure that no employee is subjected to sexual harassment;

- A statement to the effect that the employer will take such disciplinary measures as the employer deems appropriate against any person under the employer's direction who subjects any employee to sexual harassment;
- A statement explaining how complaints of sexual harassment may be brought to the attention of the employer;
- A statement to the effect that the employer will not disclose the name of a complainant or the circumstances related to the complaint to any person except where disclosure is necessary for the purposes of investigating the complaint or taking disciplinary measures in relation thereto; and
- A statement informing employees of the discriminatory practices provisions of the Canadian Human Rights Act that pertain to rights of persons to seek redress under that Act in respect of sexual harassment.

The employer shall ensure that each person under the his or her direction is aware of the policy statement. The statement must also inform employees of the discriminatory practices' provisions of the *Canadian Human Rights Act* that pertain to rights of persons to seek redress under that Act with respect to sexual harassment.

The employer shall take disciplinary measures against any person under his or her direction who subjects any employee to sexual harassment, but shall not disclose the name of the complainant or the circumstances related to the complaint to any person unless disclosure is necessary for the purposes of investigating the complaint or taking disciplinary measures in relation to the complaint.

New: *Bill C–65*, an Act to amend the Canada Labour Code (harassment and violence), expands employer responsibilities regarding allegations of harassment and violence, including sexual harassment and sexual violence in federally regulated workplaces. It received royal assent on October 25, 2018 and is to come into force on a date to be fixed by an order of the Governor in Council (not determined as of August 19, 2019) but within two years following Royal Assent. To support implementation and goals of the Act, regulations will be enacted (Source: Parliament of Canada, C–65, An Act to amend the Canada Labour Code (harassment and violence), the Parliamentary Employment and Staff Relations Act and the Budget Implementation Act, 2017, No. 1).

Amendments to the Labour Code effected by *Bill 65* include the following:

- The addition of 0.1 Subsection 122(1) of the Canada Labour Code by adding the following:

  > harassment and violence means any action, conduct or comment, including of a sexual nature, that can reasonably be expected to cause offence, humiliation or other physical or psychological injury or illness to an employee, including any prescribed action, conduct or comment; (harcèlement et violence)

  which expanded the stated purpose of Part II of the Code (Occupational Health and Safety) from only preventing accidents and injuries to include prevention of harassment and violence and psychological injuries and illness;
- A duty on federally regulated employers to do the following:
  - Prevent and protect against occurrences of harassment and violence;
  - Investigate, in accordance with the regulations (which have not yet been finalized), occurrences of harassment and violence that are known to the employer, and to provide support to employees affected by harassment and violence in the workplace. This duty includes occurrences involving former employees if the occurrence becomes known to the employer within three months of the last date of employment. The Minister may also extend the three month period if a former employee applies for an extension;
  - Ensure that employees, including supervisors and managers, receive training in harassment and violence prevention and in relation to these new Code obligations;
  - Ensure that the employer representative who receives complaints of harassment and violence has knowledge, training and experience in these issues, and knowledge of the relevant legislation; and
  - Provide employees, in printed and electronic form, copies of Part II of the Code, any applicable regulations, the employer's general health and safety policy, and any other information prescribed by the regulations.

Involvement of the policy committee, workplace committee and health and safety representatives in harassment or violence complaints shall be limited. The employer shall be prohibited from providing identifying information about a person involved in an occurrence of harassment and violence to the policy committee, workplace committee, or health and safety representative unless that person consents to the disclosure.

Title of legislation	Canada Occupational Health and Safety Regulations (SOR/86–304)

Canada Occupational Health and Safety Regulations (SOR/86–304), PART XX, "Violence prevention in the work place," addresses violence prevention in the workplace but does not specifically refer to sexual harassment. The regulations contain employer responsibilities that include the developing and posting at a place accessible to all employees a workplace violence prevention policy, assessment of the workplace for potential workplace violence and procedures to prevent and respond to it. The regulations do not expressly mention sexual harassment but do state that "work place violence" constitutes any action, conduct, threat or gesture of a person towards an employee in their workplace that can reasonably be expected to cause harm, injury or illness to that employee. Further, the proposed Work Place Harassment and Violence Prevention Regulations, which would repeal these regulations, note that harassment includes sexual harassment.

New: on April 27, 2019, Canada introduced the *Work Place Harassment and Violence Prevention Regulations*. These proposed stand-alone Regulations:

> ...will apply to all federal workplaces covered under Part II of the Canada Labour Code (the Code), and replace Part XX (violence prevention) of the Canada Occupational Health and Safety Regulations, as well as portions of two other regulations that include violence prevention provisions. The proposed Regulations would include provisions to prevent harassment and violence through comprehensive prevention policies, training, and improved data collection; respond to occurrences when they do happen through a resolution process that requires employers to communicate regularly with parties and that provides multiple options for seeking resolution; and make available to employees information respecting support services.

These regulations will repeal the Canada Occupational Health and Safety Regulations, Part XX—Violence Prevention in the Work Place.

The Government noted that:

> ...harassment and violence, including sexual harassment and sexual violence, continues to be pervasive in federally regulated workplaces. Many employees who have experienced harassment and violence in the workplace do not report it for fear of retribution, lack of support, or a belief that what they have experienced does not substantiate a complaint. The current legal framework is fragmented and not designed to adequately address occurrences of sexual harassment and sexual violence.

The regulations are proposed to support the goals of Bill C–65, which includes the authority to make regulations to prevent and respond to harassment and violence in the workplace.

The proposed regulatory provisions to address harassment and violence were developed based on the following goals:

- Change the culture of harassment and violence in the workplace: Create a culture change in the workplace where civility and respect are the standard.
- Increase empowerment of affected employees: While early resolution is emphasized as a first step, in the case where that step does not complete the resolution process, the employee who is the object of the occurrence (principal party) will have a voice to decide on the next step for resolution, either conciliation or an investigation.
- Acknowledge a continuum of behaviours that qualify as harassment and violence: To support the concept of a continuum of inappropriate behaviours, all forms of harassment and violence, ranging from teasing and unwanted advances to assault, will be captured.
- Emphasize the importance of prevention: Prevention is the most critical step to effectively reduce the number of occurrences of harassment and violence. Prevention also alleviates the financial burden on employers by reducing the need for outside conciliators or investigators to be involved in the resolution process.
- Emphasize the importance of privacy and confidentiality: In an effort to encourage those who have witnessed harassment and violence in the workplace to come forward.
- Establish predictable time frames for resolution: In order to support all parties and minimize negative impacts on the workplace.

Title of legislation	Canadian Human Rights Act (R.S., 1985, c. H–6)

The Canadian Human Rights Act, R.S.C., 1985, c. H–6, employers shall not, directly or indirectly, in the course of employment, differentiate adversely in relation to an employee, on a prohibited ground of discrimination. (Part 1: Proscribed Discrimination)

Prohibited grounds of *discrimination* include sex (Article 3). *Sexual harassment* shall be deemed to be harassment on a prohibited ground of discrimination. Article 14 (2)

Discriminatory practices include:

- In matters related to employment, to harass an individual on a prohibited ground of discrimination. (Article 14 (1))
- For an employer or organization to establish or pursue a policy or practice, or to enter into an agreement affecting recruitment, referral, hiring, promotion, training, apprenticeship, transfer or any other matter relating to employment or prospective employment, that deprives or tends to deprive an individual or class of individuals of any employment opportunities on a prohibited ground of discrimination. (Article 10)

BIBLIOGRAPHY

Alberta Human Rights Commission Sexual Harassment Information Sheet, October 2017. Available at: https://www.albertahumanrights.ab.ca/publications/bulletins_sheets_booklets/sheets/hr_and_employment/Pages/sexual_harassment.asp.x. Accessed August 23, 2019

Breaking the Silence: New Survey Reveals More Than Half of Canadian Women Sexually Harassed at work, By Danielle Carr Global News December 6, 2017. Available at: https://globalnews.ca/news/3900443/breaking-the-silence-new-survey-reveals-more-than-half-of-canadian-women-sexually-harassed-at-work/. Accessed July 9, 2019

Canada Gazette, April 27, 2019. Work Place Harassment and Violence Prevention Regulations. Available at: http://www.gazette.gc.ca/rp-pr/p1/2019/2019-04-27/html/reg1-eng.html. Accessed May 16, 2019

Canada Gazette, Part I, Volume 153, Number 17: Work Place Harassment and Violence Prevention Regulations, 2019. Available at: http://www.gazette.gc.ca/rp-pr/p1/2019/2019-04-27/html/reg1-eng.html. Accessed July 9, 2019

Department of Justice, 2018. Initiatives to Address Workplace Sexual Harassment Anticipatory Call for Proposals. Available at: https://www.justice.gc.ca/eng/fund-fina/harassment-harcelement.html. Accessed April 10, 2019

Global News, December 6, 2017. Breaking the Silence: New Survey Reveals More Than Half of Canadian Women Sexually Harassed at Work, by Danielle Carr. Available at: https://globalnews.ca/news/3900443/breaking-the-silence-new-survey-reveals-more-than-half-of-canadian-women-sexually-harassed-at-work/. Accessed August 20, 2019

Government of Canada. Sexual Harassment, 2019. Available at: https://www.canada.ca/en/employment-social-development/services/labour-standards/reports/sexual-harassment.html. Accessed April 7, 2019

Government of Canada, Justice Laws Website, 1986. Canada Occupational Health and Safety Regulations (SOR/86-304), PART XX, Violence Prevention in the Work Place. Available at: https://laws-lois.justice.gc.ca/eng/regulations/sor-86-304/page-57.html#h-896613 and https://laws-lois.justice.gc.ca/eng/regulations/SOR-86-304/page-56.html#docCont. Accessed May 16, 2019

Government of Canada, 1985. Justice Laws Website, Canadian Human Rights Act (R.S.C., 1985, c. H-6). Available at: https://laws-lois.justice.gc.ca/eng/acts/H-6/page-2.html?txthl=harassment+sexual+harass#s-14. Accessed April 7, 2019

Government of Canada, 1985. Justice Laws Website, Canada Labour Code (R.S.C., 1985, c. L–2), Division XV.1, Sexual Harassment. Available at: http://laws-lois.justice.gc.ca/eng/acts/L-2/page-47.html#h-100. Accessed April 7, 2019

Parliament of Canada, 2018. C-65, An Act to Amend the Canada Labour Code (Harassment and Violence), the Parliamentary Employment and Staff Relations Act and the Budget Implementation Act, 2017, No. 1. Available at: https://www.parl.ca/LegisInfo/BillDetails.aspx?billId=9220285&Language=E. Accessed August 20, 2019

New York Times, January 29, 2018. 'Perfect Storm' for a #MeToo Reckoning. Available at: https://www.nytimes.com/2018/01/29/world/canada/metoo-sexual-harassment.html. Accessed June 5, 2019

New York Times, January 29, 2018. 'Perfect Storm' for a #MeToo Reckoning. Available at: https://www.google.com/search?q=NYT.+%E2%80%98Perfect+Storm%E2%80%99+for+a+%23MeToo+Reckoning&rlz=1C1CHZL_enUS708US708&oq=NYT.+%E2%80%98Perfect+Storm%E2%80%99+for+a+%23MeToo+Reckoning&aqs=chrome.69i57.5032j0j7&sourceid=chrome&ie=UTF-8. Accessed August 20, 2019

SELECT CANADIAN PROVINCES

Laws in a number of Canadian provinces require the employer to have sexual harassment prevention policies and procedures. Policies in most provinces require content similar to the Canada Labour Code to be included in their policy statements.

ALBERTA

Legislation

- Alberta Human Rights Act
- Occupational Health and Safety Act, 2018

Title of legislation Alberta Human Rights Act

Sexual harassment is a form of discrimination prohibited under the Alberta Human Rights Act. The Act protects employees against harassment in and away from the workplace, if harassment is based on one of the protected grounds and the incidents occur in connection with their employment.

The Alberta Human Rights Commission provides an information sheet on sexual harassment that is available on its website.

Title of legislation Occupational Health and Safety Act, 2018

On June 1, 2018, amendments pursuant to Bill 3, "An Act to Protect the Health and Well-being of Working Albertans," 2018, became effective, significantly expanding Alberta's Occupational Health and Safety Act.

Under the Act, "harassment" includes a sexual solicitation or advance.

3(1) An employer shall ensure, as far as it is reasonably practicable for the employer to do so, that none of the employer's workers are subjected to or participate in harassment or violence at the work site.

7(1) An employer who employs 20 or more workers shall establish, in consultation with the joint work site health and safety committee, a health and safety program that includes, at a minimum, the following elements: identification of existing and potential hazards to workers at the work site, including harassment, and measures that will be taken to eliminate, reduce or control those hazards.

Additional provisions added in June 2018 require the employer to develop and implement a harassment prevention plan that includes a harassment prevention policy and harassment prevention procedures in consultation with the joint work site health and safety committee or the health and safety representative, if the employer is required to establish a committee or designate a representative, or affected workers, if the employer is not required to establish a committee or designate a representative.

The employer must ensure that a harassment prevention policy under includes the following:

- A statement that the employer is committed to eliminating or, if that is not reasonably practicable, controlling the hazard of harassment;
- A statement that the employer will investigate any incidents of harassment and take corrective action to address the incidents;
- A statement that the employer will not disclose the circumstances related to an incident of harassment or the names of the complainant, the person alleged to have committed the harassment, and any witnesses, except where necessary to investigate the incident or to take corrective action, or to inform the parties involved in the incident of the results of the investigation and any corrective action to be taken to address the incident, or as required by law;
- A statement that the harassment prevention policy is not intended to discourage a worker from exercising rights pursuant to any other law, including the Alberta Human Rights Act.

The employer must ensure that the harassment prevention procedures include the following:

- The procedure to be followed by a worker when reporting harassment;
- The procedure to be followed by the employer when documenting, investigating and preventing harassment;
- The procedure to be followed by the employer when informing the parties involved in an incident of harassment of the results of an investigation of the incident, and any corrective action to be taken to address the incident.

Provision 390.7 requires that an employer must review the violence prevention plan and the harassment prevention plan, and revise the plans, if necessary. This review shall be carried out in consultation with the joint work site health and safety committee or the health and safety representative, if they are required, or affected workers, if the employer is not required to establish a committee or designate a representative.

BIBLIOGRAPHY

Alberta.ca. Alberta Human Rights Act. Available at: http://www.qp.alberta.ca/1266.cfm?page=A25P5.cfm&leg_type=Acts&isbncln=9780779744060. Accessed June 5, 2019

Alberta Government. Occupational Health and Safety Act and Code 2009. Available at: http://www.qp.alberta.ca/1266.cfm?page=O02P1.cfm&leg_type=Acts&isbncln=9780779800865&display=html and http://www.qp.alberta.ca/documents/OHS/OHSCode.pdf. Accessed March 10, 2019

Bill 30, 2017. An Act to Protect the Health and Well-Being of Working Albertans. Available at: http://www.assembly.ab.ca/ISYS/LADDAR_files/docs/bills/bill/legislature_29/session_3/20170302_bill-030.pdf. Accessed June 5, 2019

BRITISH COLUMBIA

Legislation

- Human Rights Code
- The Workers Compensation Act, RSBC 1996, c 492

Title of legislation Human Rights Code [Rsbc 1996] Chapter 210

The *Human Rights Code [Rsbc 1996] Chapter 210* prohibits discrimination in employment in Article 13, which states that a person must not refuse to employ or refuse to continue to employ a person, or discriminate against a person regarding employment or any term or condition of employment, because of grounds which include sex.

Title of legislation Workers Compensation Act, RSBC 1996, c 492

The *Workers' Compensation Act* deals with harassment, which includes sexual harassment, although sexual harassment is not expressly mentioned.

Under Article 5, a worker is entitled to compensation for a mental disorder that does not result from an injury for which the worker is otherwise entitled to compensation, only if the mental disorder

(a) either
  (i) is a reaction to one or more traumatic events arising out of and in the course of the worker's employment, or
  (ii) is predominantly caused by a significant work-related stressor, including bullying or harassment, or a cumulative series of significant work-related stressors, arising out of and in the course of the worker's employment,
(b) is diagnosed by a psychiatrist or psychologist as a mental or physical condition that is described in the most recent American Psychiatric Association's Diagnostic and Statistical Manual of Mental Disorders at the time of the diagnosis, and
(c) is not caused by a decision of the worker's employer relating to the worker's employment, including a decision to change the work to be performed or the working conditions, to discipline the worker or to terminate the worker's employment.

BIBLIOGRAPHY

British Columbia Government, B.C. Laws, Current to November 21, 2018. Human Rights Code, [RSBC 1996] Chapter 210. Available at: http://www.bclaws.ca/Recon/document/ID/freeside/00_96210_01. Accessed on April 14, 2019

British Columbia Government, B.C. Laws. Workers Compensation Act [Rsbc 1996] Chapter 492. Available at: http://www.bclaws.ca/civix/document/id/complete/statreg/96492_00. Accessed April 10, 2019

Legislative Assembly of British Columbia, 2011. Bill 14-2011 Workers Compensation Amendment Act. Available at: http://www.leg.bc.ca/39th4th/3rd_read/gov14-3.htm. Accessed April 14, 2019

MANITOBA

Manitoba's Human Rights Commission refers to harassment and sexual harassment together. It has issued guidelines under The Human Rights Code on harassment and sexual harassment in order to provide employers, unions, and service providers with information about harassment and sexual harassment under Manitoba's human rights laws.

Legislation

- Workplace Safety and Health Act and Regulations, 2016
- Human Rights Code, 1987, as amended

Title of legislation	Manitoba Workplace Safety and Health Act and Regulation, 2016

The Workplace Safety and Health Act and Regulation, 2016, as amended, protects workers from psychological harassment in the workplace under Part 10 (Harassment). *Sexual harassment* is not specifically mentioned but is grouped with harassment.

Conduct is:

- Objectionable, if based on sex; or
- Severe, if it could reasonably cause a worker to be humiliated or intimidated and is repeated, or in the case of a single occurrence, has a lasting, harmful effect on a worker. In this section and in the definition "harassment," conduct includes a written or verbal comment, a physical act or gesture or a display, or any combination of them. (Part 1)

The employer is obligated to do the following with regard to workplace harassment:

- Prepare and annually review policies respecting workplace-related harassment (see more in the next section on the harassment prevention policy);
- Take steps to prevent occurrences of workplace-related harassment;
- Require allegations of workplace-related harassment to be investigated;
- Give workers the right to refuse to work in certain circumstances after workplace-related harassment has occurred; and
- Provide training on how to prevent workplace-related harassment to every supervisor employed by the employer.

The harassment prevention policy must be developed in consultation with the committee at the workplace; the representative at the workplace; or when there is no committee or representative, the workers at the workplace. It must include information on how to make a harassment complaint; how a harassment complaint will be investigated; and how the complainant and alleged harasser will be informed of the results of the investigation.

Under the harassment prevention policy, the employer must ensure, so far as is reasonably practicable, that no worker is subjected to harassment in the workplace and will take corrective action respecting any person under the employer's direction who subjects a worker to harassment. The employer must post a copy of the harassment prevention policy in a conspicuous place at the workplace.

Title of legislation Human Rights Code, 1987, as amended

Under the *Human Rights Code,* effective 1987, as amended, *sexual harassment* is defined as a series of objectionable and unwelcome sexual solicitations or advances or a sexual solicitation or advance made by a person in authority, if that person should reasonably have known that their behavior would be unwelcome or retaliating against someone for rejecting a sexual solicitation or advance. *Sexual harassment* is prohibited in employment.

Harassment is defined as follows:

- A course of abusive and unwelcome conduct or comment undertaken or made on the basis of any characteristic referred to in subsection 9(2); or
- A series of objectionable and unwelcome sexual solicitations or advances; or
- A sexual solicitation or advance made by a person who is in a position to confer any benefit on, or deny any benefit to, the recipient of the solicitation or advance, if the person making the solicitation or advance knows or ought reasonably to know that it is unwelcome; or
- A reprisal or threat of reprisal for rejecting a sexual solicitation or advance. 19(2)

The unwanted behaviors may be physical or verbal and may include one of more of the following: unnecessary physical contact, such as touching, patting or pinching; demands for sexual favors in return for a promise of a reward or a threat of reprisal unwelcome sexual remarks or jokes that put down one's gender displaying insulting materials such as pictures, cartoons or printed matter.

BIBLIOGRAPHY

Manitoba Laws, Human Rights Code, C.C.S.M. c. H175, as Amended. Available at: https://web2.gov.mb.ca/laws/statutes/ccsm/_pdf.php?cap=h175. Accessed January 1, 2019

Safe Work Manitoba, 2016. Manitoba Workplace, Safety and Health Act, and Regulation. Available at: https://www.gov.mb.ca/labour/safety/pdf/1_2016_wsh_ar_oc.pdf. Accessed January 1, 2019

NEW BRUNSWICK (N.B.)

> Effective April 1, 2019, New Brunswick enacted new occupational health and safety law requirements specific to workplace violence and harassment. Violence and harassment in the workplace can include sexual harassment.

Legislation

- New Brunswick Regulation 2018–82 Under The Occupational Health And Safety Act (OC 2018–300)
- Human Rights Act, 2011

Title of legislation	New Brunswick Regulation 2018–82 Under the Occupational Health and Safety Act (OC 2018–300)

New Brunswick Regulation 2018–82 Under the Occupational Health and Safety Act (OC 2018–300) states that harassment:

> …in a place of employment, means any objectionable or offensive behaviour that is known or ought reasonably to be known to be unwelcome, including bullying or any other conduct, comment or display made on either a one-time or repeated basis that threatens the health or safety of an employee, and includes *sexual harassment*, but does not include reasonable conduct of an employer in respect of the management and direction of employees at the place of employment; (harcèlement).

Every employer, regardless of the number of employees, must undertake an assessment of the risk of violence at the place of employment.

Title of legislation New Brunswick Human Rights Act

The NB Human Rights Act defines sexual harassment as "engaging in vexatious comment or conduct of a sexual nature that is known or ought reasonably to be known to be unwelcome," and expressly prohibits sexual harassment in employment.

Section 10(2) states that "No employer, representative of the employer or person employed by the employer shall sexually harass a person employed by the employer or a person seeking employment with the employer."

BIBLIOGRAPHY

Laws.gnb.ca. Human Rights Act, 2011. Available at: http://laws.gnb.ca/en/ShowPdf/cs/2011-c.171.pdf. Accessed August 20, 2019

Laws.gnb.ca. New Brunswick Regulation 2018-82 Under The Occupational Health And Safety Act (O.C. 2018-300). Available at: https://www.gnb.ca/0062/acts/BBR-2018/2018-82.pdf. Accessed March 5, 2019.

ONTARIO

In 2016, Bill 132 Ontario amended the province's Occupational Health and Safety Act, defining what constitutes sexual harassment in the workplace: Bill 132, Sexual Violence and Harassment Action Plan Act (Supporting Survivors and Challenging Sexual Violence and Harassment). Effective on September 8, 2016, this Act is part of the Ontario Government's Action Plan known as "It's Never Okay: An Action Plan to Stop Sexual Violence and Harassment." Bill 132 amends various statutes with respect to *sexual violence and harassment,* including the Occupational Health and Safety Act (OHSA), as discussed below.

In 2018, Ontario published a comprehensive non-binding Code of Practice Code for employers to help meet their workplace harassment legal responsibilities under the Occupational Health and Safety Act.

Legislation

- Bill 132, Sexual Violence and Harassment Action Plan Act (Supporting Survivors and Challenging Sexual Violence and Harassment), 2016

- Occupational Health and Safety Act, R.S.O. 1990, as amended
- Ontario Human Rights Code, as amended 2012

Title of legislation	Bill 132, Sexual Violence and Harassment Action Plan Act (Supporting Survivors and Challenging Sexual Violence and Harassment), 2016

Ontario's *Sexual Violence and Harassment Action Plan Act (Supporting Survivors and Challenging Sexual Violence and Harassment), 2016*, effective on September 8, 2016, made changes to the Occupational Health and Safety Act (OHSA) to expand the definition of workplace harassment to include sexual harassment and create specific duties for all employers to develop policies and procedures to prevent *sexual harassment* in the workplace, including a duty to investigate incidents and complaints.

The definition of "workplace harassment" in the OHSA includes "workplace sexual harassment," which means:

- Engaging in a course of vexatious comment or conduct against a worker in a workplace because of sex, sexual orientation, gender identity or gender expression, where the course of comment or conduct is known or ought reasonably to be known to be unwelcome, or
- Making a sexual solicitation or advance where the person making the solicitation or advance is in a position to confer, grant or deny a benefit or advancement to the worker and the person knows or ought reasonably to know that the solicitation or advance is unwelcome; ("harcèlement sexuel au travail").

The employer's requirements include the following:

- In consultation with the committee or a health and safety representative, if any, develop and maintain a written program to implement the policy with respect to workplace harassment required;
- Include measures and procedures for workers to report incidents of workplace harassment to a person other than the employer or supervisor, if the employer or supervisor is the alleged harasser;
- Set out how incidents or complaints of workplace harassment will be investigated and dealt with;
- Set out how information obtained about an incident or complaint of workplace harassment, including identifying information about

any individuals involved, will not be disclosed unless the disclosure is necessary for the purposes of investigating or taking corrective action with respect to the incident or complaint, or is otherwise required by law;

- Set out how a worker who has allegedly experienced workplace harassment and the alleged harasser, if he or she is a worker of the employer, will be informed of the results of the investigation and of any corrective action that has been taken or that will be taken as a result of the investigation; and
- Include any prescribed elements.

The employer's duties also include protecting a worker from workplace harassment, by conducting an investigation into incidents and complaints of workplace harassment that is appropriate in the circumstances; informing the worker and alleged harasser in writing of the results of the investigation and of any corrective action that has been taken or that will be taken as a result of the investigation; reviewing the program developed under the Act as often as necessary, but at least annually, to ensure that it adequately implements the policy with respect to workplace harassment; and such other duties as may be prescribed are carried out.

The employer shall provide a worker with information and instruction that is appropriate for the worker on the contents of the policy and program with respect to workplace harassment; and any other prescribed information.

Title of legislation	Occupational Health and Safety Act, R.S.O. 1990, C. 0.1, as amended

Changes to *Ontario Occupational Health and Safety Act* (OHSA), known as Bill 168 amendments to the Occupational Health and Safety Act, 2010, is applicable to all workplaces covered by the OHSA. Its provisions have been incorporated into the OSHA.

Workplace sexual harassment means:

> ...engaging in a course of vexatious comment or conduct against a worker in a workplace because of sex, sexual orientation, gender identity or gender expression, where the course of comment or conduct is known or ought reasonably to be known to be unwelcome, or making a sexual solicitation or advance where the

person making the solicitation or advance is in a position to confer, grant or deny a benefit or advancement to the worker and the person knows or ought reasonably to know that the solicitation or advance is unwelcome; ("harcèlement sexuel au travail")

The employer is required to take action when a worker is threatened or is an abuser, to protect employees from psychological harassment, and workplace violence, including issues of domestic violence in the workplace. An employer with more than five workers must conduct an annual workplace risk assessment to identify workplace bullying and harassment.

Under Part III.0.1, *Violence and Harassment*: September 8, 2016 amendments pursuant to Bill 132, *Sexual Violence and Harassment* Action Plan Act (Supporting Survivors and Challenging Sexual Violence and Harassment), 2016, the employer must:

- Ensure an investigation into a workplace harassment complaint is conducted appropriately for the circumstances;
- Ensure the complainant and alleged harasser are informed of the results of the investigation and any corrective action, in writing; and
- Review the program as often as necessary, but at least once a year, to ensure it adequately implements the workplace harassment policy.

The employer shall provide a worker with information and instruction that is appropriate for the worker on the contents of the policy and program with respect to workplace harassment; and any other prescribed information. (32.0.7)

A 2018 Code of Practice Code has been published to address workplace harassment in order that employers can follow the practices set forth to help meet their workplace harassment legal responsibilities under the Occupational Health and Safety Act.

Title of legislation	Ontario Human Rights Code, 1990 as amended

Ontario employers are governed by the *Ontario Human Rights Code* (Code). Employers and employees are not permitted to "contract out" of the provisions of the Code.

Under the Code, every employee has a right to freedom from harassment in the workplace because of sex by his or her employer or agent of the employer or by another employee. Harassment is defined as engaging in a course of vexatious comment or conduct that is known or ought reasonably to be known to be unwelcome. (Article 10)

The Ontario Human Rights Commission issued a statement regarding *sexual harassment* and Ontario's Human Rights Code in November 2014. The Commission reiterated that employers have a legal duty to prevent and respond to sexual harassment in the workplace. The Commission stated that employers can prevent many cases of sexual harassment by:

- Having a clear, comprehensive anti-sexual harassment policy in place;
- Ensuring all employees have the policy and are aware of both their rights and their responsibility not to engage in harassment; and
- Training individuals in positions of responsibility on the policy and their related human rights obligations.

BIBLIOGRAPHY

Government of Ontario Website, 1990, last updated November 20, 2018. Health and Safety Act, R.S.O. 1990, c. O.1, Part III.0.1 Violence and Harassment. Available at: https://www.ontario.ca/laws/statute/90o01?_ga=1.211205525.1498100697.1462979171#BK50. Accessed April 10, 2019

Government of Ontario Website, 1990. Human Rights Code, R.S.O. 1990, c. H.19 as Amended. Available at: https://www.ontario.ca/laws/statute/90h19. Accessed December 28, 2018

Government of Ontario Website, January 9, 2018. Code of Practice Code of Practice to Address Workplace Harassment. Available at: https://www.ontario.ca/page/code-practice-address-workplace-harassment. Accessed August 26, 2019

Legislative Assembly of Ontario, 2016. Bill 132, Sexual Violence and Harassment Action Plan Act (Supporting Survivors and Challenging Sexual Violence and Harassment). Available at: http://www.ontla.on.ca/web/bills/bills_detail.do?locale=en&BillID=3535 Accessed May 10, 2019

Ontario Human Rights Commission, November 25, 2014. Sexual Harassment and the Ontario Human Rights Code. Available at: http://www.ohrc.on.ca/en/news_centre/sexual-harassment-and-ontario-human-rights-code. Accessed December 28, 2018

Ontario Ministry of Labour, 2016. Code of Practice to Address Workplace Harassment under Ontario's Occupational Health and Safety Act. Available at: https://www.ontario.ca/page/code-practice-address-workplace-harassment. Accessed December 28, 2018

QUEBEC

In June 2018, Quebec's government granted 6 million CAD to counter psychological and sexual harassment in the workplace.

Over the next three years, the Government of Quebec will provide a total of 6 million CAD for the implementation of a program to counter psychological and sexual harassment in the workplace. Half will be awarded for projects from employee associations (unionized or non-unionized), artists or cultural workers and self-employed groups, with the other half for projects submitted by employers' associations (Source: Quebec.ca., June 22, 2018. "The Quebec government grants $6 million to counter psychological and sexual harassment in the workplace").

Legislation

- Act Respecting Labour Standards, R.S.Q., c. N–1.1, June 2004, amending Labour Code, as amended 2018
- Charter of Human Rights and Freedom, 1975

Title of legislation	Act Respecting Labour Standards, R.S.Q., c. N–1.1, 2004, as amended 2018

Quebec's *Act Respecting Labour Standards,* R.S.Q., c. N–1.1, ("Act"), addresses psychological harassment in the workplace. It provides that every employee has a right to a work environment free from psychological harassment, as defined, and mandates that employers must take reasonable action to prevent psychological harassment and, whenever they become aware of such behaviour, to put a stop to it. (81.19)

In 2018, the National Assembly enacted Bill 176, entitled "An Act to amend the Act respecting labour standards," effective June 12, 2018. The existing Act had contained specific provisions on psychological harassment; it now specifically includes *sexual harassment,* explicitly recognizing it as a form of psychological harassment. Bill 176, a 2018 Act amending labour standards, specifies that conduct, verbal comments, actions or gestures of a sexual nature may be a form of psychological harassment. Section 81.18 of the Act is amended with addition of: "For greater certainty, psychological harassment includes such behaviour in the form of such verbal comments, actions or gestures of a sexual nature."

Changes from the amendment include the following:

- The legal definition of psychological harassment now specifically includes sexual harassment, which includes words, acts, or gestures of a sexual nature;
- An employer must adopt and make available to employees mechanisms for the prevention and treatment of complaints so that employees may file internal workplace harassment complaints;
- The employer should document and retain evidence of harassment; and
- The time limit to file a complaint of psychological harassment is two years (increased from 90 days) from the most recent occurrence of the offending conduct alleged by the complainant.

Title of legislation	Charter of Human Rights and Freedom, 1975

Quebec's Charter of Human Rights and Freedom prohibits discrimination in areas including training and conditions of employment of a person on the basis of sex. Section 10 states that no one may harass a person on the basis of any of these grounds.

BIBLIOGRAPHY

National Assembly, Bill 176 (2018, chapter 21) An Act to amend the Act respecting labour standards and other legislative provisions mainly to facilitate family-work balance. Available at: http://www2.publicationsduquebec.gouv.qc.ca/dynamicSearch/telecharge.php?type=5&file=2018C21A.PDF. Accessed December 31, 2018

Publications Quebec, 1975. Chapter C-12, Charter of Human Rights and Freedoms. Available at: http://www2.publicationsduquebec.gouv.qc.ca/dynamicSearch/telecharge.php?type=2&file=/C_12/C12_A.html. Accessed December 31, 2018

Publications Quebec, 2004. Act Respecting Labour Standards, Chapter N-1.1, 2004. Available at: http://www2.publicationsduquebec.gouv.qc.ca/dynamicSearch/telecharge.php?type=2&file=/N_1_1/N1_1_A.html. Accessed December 31, 2018

Quebec.ca, June 22, 2018. The Quebec Government Grants $ 6 Million to Counter Psychological and Sexual Harassment in the Workplace. Available at: http://www.fil-information.gouv.qc.ca/Pages/Article.aspx?idArticle=2606227438. Accessed August 23, 2019

SASKATCHEWAN

Legislation

- Saskatchewan Employment Act, 2014
- Occupational Health and Safety Regulations, 1996, as amended
- Human Rights Code, 2018

Title of legislation Saskatchewan Employment Act, 2014

The *Saskatchewan Employment Act* ("Act"), calls for promotion and maintenance of a working environment that is free of harassment.

Under the Act, harassment means any inappropriate conduct, comment, display, action, or gesture by a person that is either based on grounds which include sex, or, with some limitations, adversely affects the worker's psychological or physical well-being and that the person knows or ought reasonably to know would cause a worker to be humiliated or intimidated; and that constitutes a threat to the health or safety of the worker (Article 3-1 (l)).

The Government states that harassment referred to in the Act "also extends to *sexual harassment* which is conduct, comment, gesture or contact of a sexual nature that is offensive, unsolicited or unwelcome." This can include the following:

- A direct or implied threat of reprisal for refusing to comply with a sexually-oriented request; unwelcome remarks, jokes, innuendos, propositions, or taunting about a person's body, attire, or sex;
- Displaying pornographic or sexually explicit pictures or materials;
- Unwelcome physical contact;
- Unwelcome invitations or requests, direct or indirect, to engage in behaviour of a sexual nature; or
- Refusing to work with or have contact with workers because of their sex, gender, or sexual orientation.

The employer shall ensure, insofar as is reasonably practicable, that:

- The employer's workers are not exposed to harassment with respect to any matter or circumstance arising out of the workers' employment (Article 3–8).

- All workers under the supervisor's direct supervision and direction are not exposed to harassment at the place of employment. (Article 3–9)

Title of legislation	Occupational Health and Safety Regulations, 1996, RRS, c. O–1, r. 1 Part III, General Duties; Section 36, Harassment; Section 37, Violence, Bill 66, as amended

Occupational Health and Safety Regulations, 1996, RRS, c. O–1, r. 1 Part III, General Duties; Section 36, *Harassment*; Section 37, Violence, Bill 66—the Occupational Health and Safety (Harassment Prevention) Amendment Act, 2007—amends the 1993 Occupational Health and Safety Act.

The regulations prohibit harassment on grounds based on sex as well as personal harassment that adversely affects the worker's psychological or physical well-being where the harasser knows, or ought reasonably to know, the harassment would cause a worker to be humiliated or intimidated. The employer must ensure, insofar as is reasonably practicable, that his or her workers are not exposed to harassment with respect to any matter arising out of their employment.

Employer requirements addressing *harassment* (Article 36) require that an employer, in consultation with the committee, develop a policy in writing to prevent harassment that includes a definition and commitment that the employer will make every reasonably practicable effort to ensure that no worker is subjected to harassment. A copy of the policy must be posted in a conspicuous place that is readily available for reference by workers.

Title of legislation	Human Rights Code, 2018

The Human Rights Code, 2018, prohibits an employee from discriminating against another employee on the basis of sex.

BIBLIOGRAPHY

Government of Saskatchewan, 1979. Saskatchewan Human Rights Code, 2018. Available at: http://www.publications.gov.sk.ca/freelaw/documents/english/Chapters/2018/S24-2.pdf. Accessed December 31, 2018

Government of Saskatchewan, 1996. Occupational Health and Safety Regulations, 1996, as Amended. Available at: http://www.qp.gov.sk.ca/documents/English/Regulations/Regulations/O1-1R1.pdf. Accessed December 31, 2018

Government of Saskatchewan, 2014. Saskatchewan Employment Act, April 29, 2014, as Amended. Available at: http://www.publications.gov.sk.ca/freelaw/documents/English/Statutes/Statutes/S15-1.pdf. Accessed December 31, 2018

Government of Saskatchewan, n.d. Bullying and Harassment in the Workplace. Available at: http://www.saskatchewan.ca/business/safety-in-the-workplace/hazards-and-prevention/bullying-and-harassment-in-the-workplace#step-1. Accessed December 31, 2018

THE UNITED STATES OF AMERICA

#MeToo: sexual harassment in the workplace law has long been illegal under Title VII of the Civil Rights Act of 1964, as amended. Illegal does not mean it is not occurring as became clear following October 15, 2017, when Alyssa Milano tweeted #MeToo, as a show of support for those who asserted they were sexually harassed or assaulted by Harvey Weinstein and to seek to illustrate the magnitude of the problem. Within 24 hours, the tweet generated more than 12 million retweets, posts, and reactions.

A 2018 National Women's Law Center report states that the #MeToo movement has demonstrated that sexual harassment occurs in nearly every workplace and at every level of employment. (National Women's Law Center, 2018. "Out of the shadows, an analysis of sexual harassment charges filed by working women")

Federal: US Equal Employment Opportunity Commission (EEOC)

The US Equal Employment Opportunity Commission (EEOC) is responsible for enforcing federal laws that make it illegal to discriminate against an employee on a number of grounds including sex. Most employers with at least 15 employees are covered by EEOC laws. The agency addresses *sexual harassment* as follows:

> It is unlawful to harass a person (an applicant or employee) because of that person's sex. Harassment can include "sexual harassment" or unwelcome sexual advances, requests for sexual favors, and other verbal or physical harassment of a sexual nature. Harassment does not have to be of a sexual nature, however, and can include offensive remarks about a person's sex. For example, it is illegal to harass a woman by making offensive comments about women in general. Both victim and the harasser can be either a woman or a man, and the victim and harasser can be the same sex. Although the law doesn't prohibit simple teasing, offhand comments, or isolated incidents that are not very serious, harassment is illegal when it is so frequent or severe that it creates a hostile or offensive work environment or when it results in an adverse employment decision (such as the victim being fired or demoted). The harasser can be the victim's supervisor, a supervisor in another area, a co-worker, or someone who is not an employee of the employer, such as a client or customer.

The EEOC has stated that although quid pro quo and hostile environment harassment are theoretically distinct claims, the line between the two is not always clear and the two forms of harassment often occur together.

Both types of sexual harassment are actionable under section 703 of Title VII of the Civil Rights Act of 1964, 42 U.S.C. § 2000e–2(a), as forms of sex discrimination.

Notable Sexual Harassment Figures from the US Equal Employment Opportunity Commission (EEOC) include the following:

- FY 2018 EEOC Fiscal Year 2018 Enforcement and Litigation Data, released April 10, 2019, showed the EEOC received 7,609 sexual harassment charges—a 13.6 percent increase from FY 2017.
- EEOC obtained a record 56.6 million USD in settlements and awards for victims of sexual harassment.
- The EEOC increased the number of sexual harassment-related lawsuits it filed in fiscal year 2018 by more than 50 percent. Preliminary figures indicated that the agency filed 41 lawsuits which included allegations of sexual harassment.
- The EEOC recovered nearly 70 million USD for the victims of sexual harassment through administrative enforcement and litigation in fiscal year 2018, up from 47.5 million USD in fiscal year 2017.

Sexual harassment and mandatory arbitration agreements: the #MeToo movement has led to recent pressure to bar sexual harassment claims from mandatory employment arbitration agreements.

Many employers have instituted mandatory arbitration programs in their workplaces requiring employees to arbitrate workplace disputes, including employment discrimination or harassment disputes, rather than litigating them in court. The arbitrations generally are confidential, private proceedings and usually the decisions do not become part of the public record. With the prominent news stories and accompanying rise in the number of sexual harassment allegations following the growth of the #MeToo movement, commentators and advocates have questioned whether employers should be able to use mandatory arbitration requirements to prevent sexual harassment claims from becoming public.

Mandatory arbitration changes for Microsoft and Google: in 2017, Microsoft became the first major tech company to eliminate forced arbitration in sexual harassment disputes, followed by ride-sharing companies Uber and Lyft. After 20,000 Google employees staged a worldwide walkout over the company's handling of sexual abuse in 2018, the company ended the practice for sexual abuse cases. Alphabet Inc.'s Google stated it would change the way it handles sexual harassment claims, a week after the 20,000 workers walked off their jobs to protest its response to such issues. Arbitration will become optional for individual sexual harassment and sexual assault claims, enabling lawsuits on those matters. Employees who fail to complete mandatory sexual harassment training will also be docked in performance reviews. Facebook, Airbnb, and Uber have also said they would not force employees who filed sexual harassment claims to settle those cases in private arbitration. (Sources: The Hill, February 28, 2019. "Google employees join lawmakers pushing bills to end forced arbitration," by Emily Birnbaum; Reuters.com, November 9, 2018. "Google hears protesters, changes sexual harassment policies," by Arjun Panchadar and Paresh Dave)

Legislation

Federal legislation on sexual harassment

- Title VII of the Civil Rights Act of 1964, as amended

Title of legislation	Title VII of the Civil Rights Act of 1964, as amended

Title VII of the Civil Rights Act of 1964, as amended, ("Title VII"), applies to employers with 15 or more employees and also applies to employment agencies and to labor organizations, as well as to the federal government. Title VII is enforced by the Equal Employment Opportunity Commission (EEOC). It prohibits discrimination in hiring, promotion, discharge, pay, fringe benefits, job training, classification, referral, and other aspects of employment on bases which include sex.

Sexual harassment is a form of sex discrimination that violates Title VII. Section 703 Unlawful Employment Practices:

> Unwelcome sexual advances, requests for sexual favors, and other verbal or physical conduct of a sexual nature constitute sexual harassment when this conduct explicitly or implicitly affects an individual's employment, unreasonably interferes with an individual's work performance, or creates an intimidating, hostile, or offensive work environment.
>
> *(Source: EEOC, Facts about Sexual Harassment)*

The EEOC states that:

Sexual harassment can occur in a variety of circumstances, including but not limited to the following:

- The victim as well as the harasser may be a woman or a man. The victim does not have to be of the opposite sex.
- The harasser can be the victim's supervisor, an agent of the employer, a supervisor in another area, a co-worker, or a non-employee.
- The victim does not have to be the person harassed but could be anyone affected by the offensive conduct.
- Unlawful sexual harassment may occur without economic injury to or discharge of the victim.
- The harasser's conduct must be unwelcome.

The harasser can be the victim's supervisor, a supervisor in another area, a co-worker, or someone who is not an employee of the employer, such as a client or customer. Harassment outside of the workplace may also be illegal if there is a link with the workplace. For example, if a supervisor harasses an employee while driving the employee to a meeting.

BIBLIOGRAPHY

Code of Federal Regulations, 2016. Guidelines on Discrimination Because of Sex. Available at: https://www.gpo.gov/fdsys/pkg/CFR-2016-title29-vol4/xml/CFR-2016-title29-vol4-part1604.xml. Accessed March 10, 2019

EEOC. Facts about Sexual Harassment. Available at: https://www.eeoc.gov/eeoc/publications/fs-sex.cfm. Accessed August 25, 2019

Equal Employment Opportunity Commission, n.d. Sexual Harassment. Available at: https://www.eeoc.gov/laws/types/sexual_harassment.cfm. Accessed January 1, 2019

Equal Employment Opportunity Commission, n.d., Facts about Sexual Harassment. Available at: https://www.eeoc.gov/laws/types/sexual_harassment.cfm. Accessed June 7, 2019

Equal Opportunity Commission, 1964. Title VII of the Civil Rights Act of 1964. Available at: http://www.eeoc.gov/laws/statutes/titlevii.cfm. Accessed January 1, 2019

Govinfo.gov, 2016, Code of Federal Regulations Title 29-Labor, 1604.11 Guidelines on Discrimination because of Sex. Available at: https://www.govinfo.gov/content/pkg/CFR-2016-title29-vol4/xml/CFR-2016-title29-vol4-part1604.xml

National Women's Law Center, 2018. Out of the Shadows, An Analysis of Sexual Harassment Charges Filed by Working Women. Available at: https://nwlc-ciw49tixgw5lbab.stackpathdns.com/wp-content/uploads/2018/08/SexualHarassmentReport.pdf. Accessed July 9, 2019

Reuters.com, November 9, 2018. Google Hears Protesters, Changes Sexual Harassment Policies, by Arjun Panchadar, Paresh Dave. Available at: https://www.reuters.com/article/us-alphabet-google-harassment/google-hears-protesters-changes-sexual-harassment-policies-idUSKCN1ND2KJ. Accessed August 28, 2019

The Hill, February 28, 2019. Google Employees Join Lawmakers Pushing Bills to End Forced Arbitration, by Emily Birnbaum. Available at: https://thehill.com/policy/technology/432065-lawmakers-introduce-bills-to-end-forced-arbitration. Accessed August 26, 2019

U.S. Equal Employment Opportunity Commission. Policy Guidance Documents Related to Sexual Harassment. Available at: https://www.eeoc.gov/laws/types/sexual_harassment_guidance.cfm. Accessed August 27, 2019

STATE LEGISLATION ON SEXUAL HARASSMENT

The #MeToo movement has led numerous states in the United States to enact stricter and more comprehensive sexual harassment laws.

The #MeToo movement continues to be a top priority of state legislatures throughout the country, with a growing trend in State legislation in 2018 and early 2019 to curtail organizations from requiring employees to sign nondisclosure agreements as a condition of employment, to prohibit non-disclosure and settlement agreements that prevent employees from discussing, or to require a waiver of rights with respect to sexual harassment that they may have faced.

States that have proposed to exclude either mandatory arbitration agreements or sexual harassment claims from mandatory employment arbitration agreements include New York, California, and New Jersey. State laws are also mandating sexual harassment training while two States have passed laws requiring employers provide housekeepers and room service employees with panic buttons.

Although federal law covers employers with 15 or more employees with regard to sexual harassment, numerous states have enacted laws with lower applicability thresholds. Sexual harassment laws may apply to public and private employers with as few as one employee.

CALIFORNIA

California has had laws since 2005 involving mandatory harassment training and education in the workplace. Existing law requires California employers with 50 or more employees to provide all of their supervisory employees at least two hours of sexual harassment training every two years. However, in the wake of the #MeToo movement, the Governor signed a number of bills on September 30, 2018 to extend sexual harassment training requirements and address settlement agreements that prohibit disclosure of sexual harassment claims. These new laws took effect on January 1, 2019.

The bills are as follows:

- *Senate Bill 1300*, effective January 1, 2019, makes changes to the Fair Employment and Housing Act (FEHA), prohibiting employers in California after January 1, 2019, from forcing employees to sign a nondisparagement agreement to release the employer of claims, including for sexual harassment, as a condition for a raise or bonus, or as a condition of employment. Exceptions are provided when the employees voluntarily agree to waive their rights in an agreement. SB 1300 voids any agreement in which an employee forfeits his or her right to disclose unlawful acts in the workplace, including acts of sexual harassment. The bill also strengthens sexual harassment training, authorizing employers to provide bystander intervention training. SB 1300 also declares that a single incident of harassing conduct could be sufficient to create a triable issue regarding the existence of a hostile work environment in certain circumstances.

- *Assembly Bill 2770* protects people from the threat of a defamation lawsuit when a sexual harassment allegation to an employer is "based on credible evidence" and without malice. The law was passed after the state's defamation laws were identified as sometimes deterring victims and witnesses from making complaints or communicating information about harassers to others. Also, it protects companies with knowledge of the harassing activity and allows them to warn other potential employers without the threat of a defamation lawsuit.
- *Senate Bill 820* applies to private and public employers and prohibits secret settlements or nondisclosure agreements of factual information in cases involving allegations of sexual assault, harassment, or discrimination. The bill, effective January 1, 2019, also grants claimants in sexual abuse or sex discrimination cases the option to keep their name private. SB 820 prohibits settlement agreements from including a provision that prevents the disclosure of factual information related to claims of sexual assault and sexual harassment but does not prohibit confidentiality of the settlement amount.
- *Assembly Bill 3109 Contracts* is a waiver of right of petition or free speech, approved on September 30, 2018. It makes a provision in a contract or settlement agreement void and unenforceable if it waives a party's right to testify in an administrative, legislative, or judicial proceeding concerning alleged criminal conduct or sexual harassment.
- *Government Code 12950, as amended, 2018*: under California's Government Code, employers have an affirmative duty to take reasonable steps to prevent and promptly correct discriminatory and harassing conduct (Gov. Code, § 12940(k)). Every employer is required to act to ensure a workplace free of sexual harassment by implementing certain minimum requirements, including posting sexual harassment information posters at the workplace and obtaining and making available an information sheet on sexual harassment. *A 2018 amendment (SB–1343 Employers: sexual harassment training: requirements)* to Government Code, Section 12950, effective January 1, 2019 lowered the threshold for the state's sexual harassment training requirements for employers, requiring employers

with five or more workers to provide sexual harassment training to supervisors and non-supervisorial employees by January 1, 2020.

Additional requirements for employers pursuant to *SB 1343* include the following:

- The employer shall post a poster provided by the Department of Fair Employment and Housing (Department) on discrimination in employment with information on the illegality of sexual harassment in a prominent and accessible location in the workplace.
- The employer shall obtain from the Department an information sheet on sexual harassment and shall distribute this information sheet to its employees, unless the employer provides equivalent information to its employees as set forth in the amendment. An employer's compliance with this section does not insulate the employer from liability for sexual harassment of any current or former employee or applicant.

If an employer violates the requirements of this section, the Department may seek an order requiring the employer to comply.

Additionally, SEC. 2. *Section 12950.1 of the Government Code* requires changes addressing sexual harassment training and education, including for seasonal, migrant, or temporary workers, for January 1, 2020 as follows:

> 12950.1. (a) By January 1, 2020, an employer having five or more employees shall provide at least two hours of classroom or other effective interactive training and education regarding sexual harassment to all supervisory employees and at least one hour of classroom or other effective interactive training and education regarding sexual harassment to all nonsupervisory employees in California within six months of their assumption of a position. An employer may provide this training in conjunction with other training provided to the employees. The training may be completed by employees individually or as part of a group presentation, and may be completed in shorter segments, as long as the applicable hourly total requirement is met.
>
> An employer who has provided this training and education to an employee after January 1, 2019, is not required to provide training and education by the January 1, 2020, deadline. After January 1, 2020, each employer covered by this section shall provide sexual harassment training and education to each employee in California once every two years.

> The training and education required by this section shall include information and practical guidance regarding the federal and state statutory provisions concerning the prohibition against and the prevention and correction of sexual harassment and the remedies available to victims of sexual harassment in employment. The training and education shall also include practical examples aimed at instructing supervisors in the prevention of harassment, discrimination, and retaliation, and shall be presented by trainers or educators with knowledge and expertise in the prevention of harassment, discrimination, and retaliation. The department shall provide a method for employees who have completed the training to save electronically and print a certificate of completion.

An amendment to California Fair Employment and Housing Act Regulations on discriminatory and harassing conduct in the workplace: California law (called the Fair Employment and Housing Act or FEHA) prohibits discrimination and harassment. The law also requires that employers "take reasonable steps to prevent and correct wrongful (harassing, discriminatory, retaliatory) behavior in the workplace (Cal. Govt. Code §12940(k))." The Department of Fair Employment and Housing (DFEH) is the State's enforcement agency related to the obligations under the FEHA. As of April 1, 2016, an amendment to California Fair Employment and Housing Act Regulations elaborated on the employer's obligation under Government Code section 12940(k) to take reasonable steps to prevent and promptly correct discriminatory and harassing conduct. The amendment added the following section: § 11023, "Harassment and Discrimination Prevention and Correction," requiring all California employers with more than five employees to have written policies regarding *harassment, discrimination,* and retaliation. Employers must develop and distribute anti-discrimination and harassment policies to employees in English as well as in any additional languages that are spoken by at least 10% of the workforce.

Harassment is defined in the Act to include but not be limited to the following:

- Verbal harassment, e.g., epithets, derogatory comments or slurs on a basis enumerated in the Act;
- Physical harassment, e.g., assault, impeding or blocking movement, or any physical interference with normal work or movement, when directed at an individual on a basis enumerated in the Act;

- Visual forms of harassment, e.g., derogatory posters, cartoons, or drawings on a basis enumerated in the Act; or
- Sexual favors, e.g., unwanted sexual advances, which condition an employment benefit upon an exchange of sexual favors. [See also section 11034(f)(1)]

Employees includes unpaid interns, volunteers, and persons providing services under a contract.

- Harassment of an applicant or employee by an employee is unlawful if the employer or other covered entity, its agents, or supervisors knows of such conduct and fails to take immediate and appropriate corrective action. Proof of such knowledge may be direct or circumstantial.
- If the employer or other covered entity, its agents, or supervisors did not know but should have known of the harassment, knowledge shall be imputed unless the employer or other covered entity can establish that it took reasonable steps to prevent harassment from occurring. Such steps may include affirmatively raising the subject of harassment, expressing strong disapproval, developing appropriate sanctions, informing employees of their right to raise and how to raise the issue of harassment under California law, and developing methods to sensitize all concerned.
- An employee who has been harassed on the job by a co-employee should inform the employer or other covered entity of the aggrievement; however, an employee's failure to give such notice is not an affirmative defense. (Fair Employment and Housing Council, 2016)

BIBLIOGRAPHY

Assembly Bill 2770, 2018. Privileged communications: communications by former employer: sexual harassment' if this messes up pagination for index it is okay to only add the year. Available at: https://leginfo.legislature.ca.gov/faces/billTextClient.xhtml?bill_id=201720180AB2770. Accessed August 25, 2019

Assembly Bill 3109, 2018. Contracts: waiver of right of petition or free speech. Available at: https://leginfo.legislature.ca.gov/faces/billTextClient.xhtml?bill_id=201720180AB3109. Accessed April 14, 2019

California Department of Fair Employment and Housing Workplace Harassment Prevention Guide for California Employers. Available at: https://www.dfeh.ca.gov/wp-content/uploads/sites/32/2017/06/DFEH-Workplace-Harassment-Guide.pdf. Accessed April 10, 2019

California Legislative Information, 2014. Assembly Bill No. 2053, Chapter 306. Available at: http://leginfo.legislature.ca.gov/faces/billNavClient.xhtml?bill_id=201320140AB2053. Accessed March 10, 2019

California Legislative Information, 2018. References AB-3109 Contracts: Waiver of Right of Petition or Free Speech. Available at: https://leginfo.legislature.ca.gov/faces/billTextClient.xhtml?bill_id=201720180AB3109. Accessed April 14, 2019

Government Code, Section 12950, 2018. Available at: https://leginfo.legislature.ca.gov/faces/codes_displaySection.xhtml?sectionNum=12950.&lawCode=GOV. Accessed April 10, 2019

Section 12950 of the Government Code Amendment, SB–1343 Employers: sexual harassment training: requirements, 2018. Available at: https://leginfo.legislature.ca.gov/faces/billCompareClient.xhtml?bill_id=201720180SB1343. Accessed April 10, 2019

Senate Bill 820, 2018. Settlement Agreements: confidentiality. Available at: https://leginfo.legislature.ca.gov/faces/billTextClient.xhtml?bill_id=201720180SB820. Accessed August 25, 2019

Senate Bill 1300, 2018. Unlawful employment practices: discrimination and harassment. Available at: https://leginfo.legislature.ca.gov/faces/billTextClient.xhtml?bill_id=201720180SB1300. Accessed August 25, 2019

A 2018 Amendment (SB-1343 Employers: Sexual Harassment Training: Requirements) to Government Code, Section 12950. Available at: https://leginfo.legislature.ca.gov/faces/billTextClient.xhtml?bill_id=201720180SB1343. Accessed August 25, 2019

CONNECTICUT

Connecticut's Public Act No. 19–16 An Act Combatting Sexual Assault and Sexual Harassment ("Act") was passed on June 18, 2019. Effective October 1, 2019, Connecticut employers will have a host of new training, notice, and human resources requirements with which to comply—and will now face new, substantial categories of damages for violations.

The Act expands the sexual harassment prevention laws by requiring additional training for employees and imposing new notice and posting requirements. Employers with at least 50 employees had been required to give their supervisors two hours of training on State and federal sexual harassment laws and remedies; the new law requires employers of all sizes to give training to supervisors by October 1, 2020 (or within six months of their assumption of supervisory duties, after that time). Employers with three or more employees must provide training to all other employees by October 1, 2020 (or within six months of hire, after that time). Any employee trained since October 1, 2018 is exempt. The fine for failing to provide training will be 750 USD.

BIBLIOGRAPHY

State of Connecticut, Public Act No. 19-16. Available at: https://www.cga.ct.gov/2019/act/Pa/pdf/2019PA-00016-R00SB-00003-PA.PDF. Accessed July 9, 2019

DELAWARE

Delaware's HB 360, effective January 1, 2019, expands *sexual harassment* protections. It defines sexual harassment as an unlawful employment practice and mandates sexual harassment training. This law requires Delaware employers with 50 or more employees to provide interactive sexual harassment training to all employees. New employees must receive training within one year of hire, and current employees must receive training by January 1, 2020. Training must be repeated every two years.

BIBLIOGRAPHY

H.B. 360. Available at: https://legis.delaware.gov/BillDetail/26453 Accessed April 14, 2019

ILLINOIS

The Illinois Workplace Transparency Act (WTA), a legislative response to the #MeToo movement, limits unilateral nondisclosure agreements and mandatory arbitration agreements relating to sexual harassment claims. The WTA applies to all employment, separation, and settlement agreements, that have been entered into, extended, or modified on or after January 1, 2020, with no exception.

Pursuant to Article 5 of the Workplace Transparency Act, the Illinois' Hotel and Casino Employee Safety Act requires hotels and casinos to adopt anti-sexual harassment policies and make panic buttons available to employees working in isolated spaces. It prohibits retaliation against an employee for using a panic button, availing himself or herself of the protections afforded by an anti-sexual harassment policy, or disclosing, reporting, or testifying about violations of the Act. The Act provides remedies for noncompliance limits unilateral nondisclosure agreements and mandatory arbitration agreements relating to sexual harassment and employment discrimination claims. Employers are required to provide annual sexual harassment training for all employees. The Article becomes effective on July 1, 2020.

BIBLIOGRAPHY

Illinois General Assembly. Workplace Transparency Act, 2019. Available at: http://www.ilga.gov/legislation/101/SB/PDF/10100SB0075lv.pdf. Accessed August 19, 2019

MARYLAND

Maryland's Disclosing Sexual Harassment in the Workplace Act of 2018 ("Act"), effective on October 1, 2018, prohibits contractual waivers of *sexual harassment* claims and imposes reporting requirements for certain Maryland employers.

The Act adds the following requirements to current Maryland labor and employment law:

- Any provision in an employment contract or policy that waives any right or remedy to a future claim of sexual harassment or retaliation for reporting sexual harassment is void as against public policy. Retaliation based upon an employee's failure to enter into such a prohibited contract is prohibited. An employee is entitled to attorneys' fees and costs when defending against an employer's attempts to enforce a prohibited contract or policy. These provisions apply to all employers.
- Reporting of sexual harassment claims for employers with over 50 employees. On or before July 1, 2020, and again on or before July 1, 2022, covered employers must submit to the Maryland Commission on Civil Rights the number of settlements made after an allegation of sexual harassment; the number of times the employer paid to settle a sexual harassment claim against the same employee over a ten year period; and the number of sexual harassment settlements containing a confidentiality provision.

BIBLIOGRAPHY

General Assembly of Maryland, 2018. Disclosing Sexual Harassment in the Workplace Act of 2018. Available at: http://mgaleg.maryland.gov/2018RS/chapters_noln/Ch_738_hb1596E.pdf. Accessed June 7, 2019

NEVADA

AB 248 prohibits employers from including language in settlement agreements requiring an employee to keep confidential the facts and circumstances relating to a sexual harassment claim in a civil or administrative proceeding. The law became effective on July 1, 2019.

BIBLIOGRAPHY

AB 248. Available at: https://www.leg.state.nv.us/Session/80th2019/Bills/Amendments/A_AB248_303.pdf. Accessed July 9, 2019

NEW JERSEY

On March 18, 2019, New Jersey's Governor signed S121, amending the New Jersey Law Against Discrimination. This law bars provisions in employment contracts that waive rights or remedies and bars agreements that conceal details relating to discrimination claims. Its prohibitions are prospective and apply to all agreements entered into, renewed, modified, and amended after March 18, 2019. The new law covers not only sexual harassment, assault, and sex discrimination claims but also aims to prohibit disclosure of the details of all discrimination, retaliation, or harassment complaints in employment agreements and settlement agreements.

In the words of the law, S121 states:

A provision in any employment contract or settlement agreement which has the purpose or effect of concealing the details relating to a claim of discrimination, retaliation, or harassment (hereinafter referred to as a "non-disclosure provision") shall be deemed against public policy and unenforceable against a current or former employee (hereinafter referred to as an "employee") who is a party to the contract or settlement. If the employee publicly reveals sufficient details of the claim so that the employer is reasonably identifiable, then the non-disclosure provision shall also be unenforceable against the employer.

Every settlement agreement resolving a discrimination, retaliation, or harassment claim by an employee against an employer shall include a bold, prominently placed notice that although the parties may have agreed to keep the settlement and underlying facts confidential, such a provision in an agreement is unenforceable against the employer if the employee publicly reveals sufficient details of the claim so that the employer is reasonably identifiable.

Notwithstanding any other provision of law to the contrary, this section shall not be construed to prohibit an employer from requiring an employee to sign an agreement:

(1) in which the employee agrees not to enter into competition with the employer during or after employment; or
(2) in which the employee agrees not to disclose proprietary information, which includes only non-public trade secrets, business plan and customer information.

New Jersey has approved legislation on June 11, 2019 that will require hotels with 100 or more guest rooms to provide housekeepers and room service employees with panic buttons as of January 2020. Hotels will also have to keep records of accusations it receives of inappropriate conduct by guests, provide notice to other hotel employees assigned to a room where a guest's behavior has caused an employee to use the panic button, and maintain and distribute policies to their employees and guests regarding the panic buttons. New Jersey is the first state to mandate these devices.

BIBLIOGRAPHY

Legiscan.com, 2019. New Jersey Senate Bill 121. Available at: https://legiscan.com/NJ/text/S121/2018. Accessed April 16, 2019

Senate, P.L., 2019. Chapter 123. Available at: https://legiscan.com/NJ/text/S2986/id/2045811/New:Jersey-2018-S2986-Chaptered.html. Accessed August 26, 2019

NEW YORK

In August 2019, New York enacted a new law which lowers the threshold for filing a harassment complaint by eliminating the "severe or pervasive" standard for behavior. It also does the following:

- Provides increased protections for protected classes and special protections for employees who have been sexually harassed;
- Prohibits nondisclosure agreements related to discrimination;
- Prohibits mandatory arbitration clauses related to discrimination;

- Requires employers to provide employees notice of their sexual harassment prevention training program in writing in English and in employees' primary languages;
- Extends the statute of limitations for claims resulting from unlawful or discriminatory practices constituting sexual harassment to three years; requires review and update of the model sexual harassment prevention guidance document and sexual harassment prevention policy; and
- Protects independent contractors and others providing services in the workplace from sexual harassment in the workplace.

Required adoption of written sexual harassment policy: in 2018, New York expanded protections against sexual harassment by requiring all employers, regardless of size, to adopt a written sexual harassment policy, with explicit substantive and process protections for employees; to train all employees as soon as possible after their start date and thereafter, annually, on sexual harassment prevention using interactive training programs; and to provide access to a complaint form for reporting sexual harassment to the State Division of Human Rights.

The sexual harassment prevention policy must meet or exceed the State's new minimum standards. Employers do not have to use the model policies and training but must be sure that the training and policies are, at a minimum, compliant with the State's materials.

Minimum standards for the sexual harassment prevention policy:

- Prohibit sexual harassment consistent with guidance issued by the Department of Labor in consultation with the Division of Human Rights;
- Provide examples of prohibited conduct that would constitute unlawful sexual harassment;
- Include information concerning the federal and state statutory provisions concerning sexual harassment, remedies available to victims of sexual harassment, and a statement that there may be applicable local laws; a complaint form; and a procedure for the timely and confidential investigation of complaints that ensures due process for all parties;
- Inform employees of their rights of redress and all available forums for adjudicating sexual harassment complaints administratively and judicially;
- Clearly state that sexual harassment is considered a form of employee misconduct and that sanctions will be enforced against individuals engaging in sexual harassment and against supervisory

and managerial personnel who knowingly allow such behavior to continue; and
- Clearly state that retaliation against individuals who complain of sexual harassment or who testify or assist in any investigation or proceeding involving sexual harassment is unlawful.

New York State employers must train their employees on sexual harassment prevention on an annual basis, with the first training occurring no later than October 9, 2019. New employees should be trained as soon as possible after beginning employment.

BIBLIOGRAPHY

New York State, 2018. Model Sexual Harassment Policy. Available at: https://www.ny.gov/combating-sexual-harassment-workplace/employers. Accessed June 7, 2019

New York State Assembly, 2019. Bill A08421. Available at: https://nyassembly.gov/leg/?default_fld=&leg_video=&bn=A08421&term=2019&Summary=Y&Text=Y. Accessed August 28, 2019

New York State Assembly, Bill No S06577(Same as A08421). Available at: https://nyassembly.gov/leg/?default_fld=&leg_video=&bn=S06577&term=2019&Summary=Y&Actions=Y&Memo=Y&Text=Y. Accessed August 28, 2019

New York State, n.d. Sexual Harassment Policy for All Employers in New York State. https://www.ny.gov/sites/ny.gov/files/atoms/files/SexualHarassmentPreventionModelPolicy.pdf. Accessed August 28, 2019

OREGON

Oregon's Workplace Protection Act makes it an "unlawful employment practice for employer to enter agreement that would prevent employee from disclosing or discussing conduct that constitutes unlawful discrimination, including sexual assault." The legislation prohibits requiring nondisclosure agreements for employees or applicants that prohibits them from revealing sexual assault, harassment or discrimination. It makes it an unlawful employment practice for an employer to enter into an agreement with an employee or prospective employee, as a condition of employment, continued employment, promotion, compensation or benefits, that includes a nondisclosure provision or any other provision with the purpose or effect of preventing the employee from disclosing or discussing conduct related to sexual harassment (unless it is the employee's preference). Additionally, the law requires employers to implement a written anti-harassment policy which must be provided to all current employees and new employees upon hire. The Act also lengthens the statute of limitations for filing complaints of harassment from one year to five years. The law generally became effective on June 30, 2019, with the limitations on nondisclosure agreements effective on October 1, 2020.

BIBLIOGRAPHY

Oregon State Legislature, 2019. Relating to Unlawful Conduct in the Workplace; and Prescribing an Effective Date. Available at: https://olis.leg.state.or.us/liz/2019R1/Measures/Overview/SB726. Accessed July 10, 2019

WASHINGTON

Senate Bill 5996, effective June 7, 2018, prohibits an employer from preventing its employees from publicly disclosing sexual harassment or sexual assault occurring in the workplace. However, the bill states that it does not prevent confidentiality provisions in settlement agreements, even as they relate to sexual assault or harassment allegations.

Senate Bill 6313, also effective June 7, 2018, voids provisions of employment contracts requiring employees to waive their right to "publicly pursue" a discrimination complaint under Washington or federal law. It also voids provisions of employment agreements that "require an employee to resolve claims of discrimination in a dispute resolution process that is confidential."

BIBLIOGRAPHY

State of Washington, 65th Legislature. Senate Bill 5996, 2018. Available at: http://lawfilesext.leg.wa.gov/biennium/2017-18/Pdf/Bills/Senate%20Passed%20Legislature/5996-S.PL.pdf. Accessed June 17, 2019

State of Washington, 65th Legislature. Senate Bill 6313, 2018. Available at: http://lawfilesext.leg.wa.gov/biennium/2017-18/Pdf/Bills/Senate%20Passed%20Legislature/6313-S.PL.pdf. Accessed June 17, 2019

6 Sexual harassment laws in Middle East and African countries

MIDDLE EAST

ISRAEL

> Israel's Prevention of Sexual Harassment Law, enacted in 1998, establishes a duty for employers to prevent and treat sexual harassment. Based on this law, the Voluntary Code Against Sexual Harassment in Workplaces provides concrete details and guidelines on how to implement the regulations.

Israel's Prevention of Sexual Harassment Law establishes a special duty for employers to prevent and treat sexual harassment. To implement this duty, the Association of Rape Crisis Centers and the Israel Standards Institute launched the *Voluntary Code for the Prevention of Sexual Harassment in Workplaces* ("Code"). The Code expands and translates the sexual harassment law into clearer and more applicable guidelines and provides concrete details on how to implement the regulations, focusing on prevention. It is suitable for large and small organizations in any industry.

The Code addresses the length, content, and frequency of sexual harassment training, handling of a complaint, conducting an annual management review, and the performance of an internal examination by the organization in the field of treatment and prevention. A certificate of adoption of the code will be given to organizations that have been tested by the Standards Institution of Israel and found to meet the requirements of the Code, pursuant to an organization's signing a commitment to be tested every two years. The granting of the certificate will attest to the organizations preventing and treating sexual harassment and may be published by the organization. The municipality of

Ra'anana was the first to adopt the voluntary code for its thousands of workers, followed by EIM, a high-tech company.

The Code may be downloaded from this page: https://www.1202.org.il/centers-union/activity/voluntary-code.

Legislation

- Prevention of Sexual Harassment law, 5758–1998, as amended
- Employment Equal Opportunities Law, 1988/Employment (Equal Opportunities) Law, 5748–1988, as amended

Title of legislation	Prevention of Sexual Harassment Law, 5758–1998, as amended

The *Prevention of Sexual Harassment Law, 5758–1998*, as amended, 2014, covers *sexual harassment* in the workplace, although the law is not limited to employer–employee relations. Its stated purpose is "to prohibit sexual harassment in order to protect human dignity, liberty and privacy and to promote equality between the sexes."

The law prohibits all forms of *sexual harassment* (verbal and physical) at the workplace. It prohibits intimidation or retaliation that accommodates sexual harassment. Intimidation or retaliation related to sexual harassment is defined by the law as "prejudicial treatment." *Sexual harassment* is interpreted broadly, and prohibited as a discriminatory practice, a restriction of liberty, an offence to human dignity, a violation of every person's right to elementary respect, and an infringement of the right to privacy.

Sexual harassment includes:

- Blackmail by way of threats, where the act demanded to be performed by the person is of a sexual character;
- Indecent acts, as defined in sections 348 and 349 of the Penal Law;
- Repeated propositions of a sexual character to a person, where that person has shown to the harasser that he is not interested in the said propositions;
- Repeated references directed towards a person, which focus on his sexuality, where that person has shown to the harasser that he is not interested in the said references;
- An intimidating or humiliating reference directed towards a person concerning his sex, or his sexuality, including his sexual tendencies;

- Propositions or references as described above where the person harassed has not shown the harasser that he is not interested in the said propositions or references.

An employer is required to do the following:

- Take such steps as are reasonable in the circumstances to prevent sexual harassment or adverse treatment, on the part of his employee or on the part of a person in charge on the employer's behalf, even where such a person is not his employee; an employer is also obliged to deal with cases of sexual harassment and adverse treatment;
- Prescribe an efficient procedure for filing a complaint in respect of sexual harassment and for the examination of the complaint; deal efficiently with a case of sexual harassment or of adverse treatment which has come to his notice and do everything within his power to prevent the recurrence of the said acts and to rectify the harm caused to the complainant as a result of sexual harassment or adverse treatment; and
- Where more than 25 workers are employed, a code of practice which includes these procedures and the main provisions of the Prevention of Sexual Harassment Law, 5758–1998 must be published. It shall detail the procedures prescribed by the employer for filing complaints in respect of sexual harassment or adverse treatment and for dealing with such complaints. The employer shall publish the code of practice among his employees. An employer who has failed to publish a code of practice is liable to a fine.

Responsibility is placed on the employer to take preventive measures against *sexual harassment* in the workplace. An employer who fails to meet these preventive requirements is liable both on the criminal and civil level. Employers who are found guilty of sexual harassment are liable to imprisonment for a term of up to four years.

The law establishes two stages of proof. First, the employee must show that he or she was sexually harassed by the employer, a supervisor, or another employee. If this burden is met, the employer is then required to prove he or she was not responsible and has taken all reasonable steps to prevent this from happening.

The law allows for compensation of up to 50,000 NIS (approximately 10,000 USD) without proof of actual injury.

The provisions of the law in relation to employers and employees also apply to a person who in practice employs another through a manpower contractor and to a person so employed.

Israel Amendment to the Sexual Harassment Prevention Law: the Sexual Harassment Prevention Law (Amendment No.10), 5774–2014 (Amendment) was published on January 8, 2014. The Amendment provides that the publication of a photograph, film or recording of a person without his or her consent, including the editing or combination of any of the above, that focuses on such person's sexuality (provided that such person can be identified) and under the circumstances is likely to degrade or embarrass such person, is considered sexual harassment.

The employer may be subject to a criminal fine or civil lawsuit for sexual harassment. (Ministry of Economy and Industry. Sexual Harassment at Work)

Title of legislation	Employment Equal Opportunities Law 1988, as amended

The *Employment Equal Opportunities Law* 1988, as amended, protects workers from *sexual harassment* at the workplace. An employer found liable for sexual harassment may be imprisoned.

Section 7. (a) states that:

> the employer or an appointed person acting on his behalf shall not harm an employee or a successor to work in the matters enumerated in section 2 or in any other manner, where the source of the injury is one of the following: (1) sexual harassment of the employee or of the work-seeker done by the employer, by the person in charge of him or by another employee.

In this Law, "sexual harassment" within its meaning in the Prevention of Sexual Harassment Law, 5758–1998 (Prevention of Sexual Harassment Law), provided that in respect of an offense resulting from sexual harassment under section 3 (a) (3) and (4), only one proposal or reference is sufficient:

(2) A complaint or claim by the employee for an injury as stated in this section;

(3) The assistance of an employee to another employee in connection with a complaint or claim in respect of an injury as provided in this section.

This section shall apply, for the purposes of an employer and an employee and also to a person who actually employs a person through a manpower contractor, and to a person employed as aforesaid.

BIBLIOGRAPHY

Association of Rape Crisis Centers, n.d., Voluntary Code for the Prevention of Sexual Harassment in Workplaces. Available at: https://www.1202.org.il/centers-union/activity/voluntary-code. Accessed September 8, 2018

Israel 21c, March 28, 2018. UN Likes Israel's Voluntary Code against Sexual Harassment, Abigail Klein Leichman. Available at: https://www.israel21c.org/un-likes-israels-voluntary-code-against-sexual-harassment/. Accessed September 8, 2018

Ministry of Economy and Industry, 2014. Employment Equal Opportunities Law 1988, as amended. Available at: https://www.nevo.co.il/law:html/law01/p214m1_001.htm#Seif6. Accessed March 21, 2019

Ministry of Justice. 1998. Prevention of Sexual Harassment Law, 5758–1998, as amended 2014. Available at: http://www.jewishvirtuallibrary.org/jsource/Politics/PrventionofSexualHarassmentLaw.pdf. Accessed September 8, 2018

Ministry of Justice, 1998. Prevention of Sexual Harassment Law, 5758–1998, as amended 2014. Available at: http://www.jewishvirtuallibrary.org/jsource/Politics/PrventionofSexualHarassmentLaw.pdf. Accessed March 21, 2019

Ministry of Labor, Social Affairs and Social Services, n.d.. Sexual Harassment at work. Available at: http://economy.gov.il/Employment/Shivyon/Employees/Pages/SexualHarassment.aspx. Accessed September 8, 2018

SAUDI ARABIA

Saudi Arabia enacted an anti-harassment law in 2018, which defines sexual harassment as words or actions that hint at sexuality towards one person from another, or that harms the body, honor or modesty of a person in any way. The legislation criminalizes harassment, protects both genders and is applicable both inside and outside of the workplace.

Legislation

- Royal Decree No. 96/M of May 31, 2018

Title of legislation	Royal Decree No. 96/M of May 31, 2018

Saudi Arabia's anti-harassment law, enacted by Legal Gazette on 24 Ramadan 1439 H, (June 8, 2018), Decision 488 dated 14/9/1439H, includes *sexual harassment.* Although harassment was already unlawful under Sharia law, the introduction of the Anti-Harassment Law reinforces this position and introduced penalties for violating the law. The law criminalizes harassment and imposes requirements on employers to implement measures to combat workplace harassment.

The Anti-Harassment Law applies to harassment both inside and outside the workplace, and to all individuals regardless of gender. Harassment is defined as "any words, act or sign of sexual implication made by a person towards any other person, in a way that affects the other person's body or honor or taints the modesty, by any means whatsoever, including modern technology means."

Anyone who incites others, agrees with them or assists them in any way to commit harassment is given the same penalty prescribed for the offender, while anyone who attempts to harass will be given up to half of the maximum punishment.

The employer's responsibilities include implementing an internal mechanism and procedure for receiving harassment complaints; implementing measures to investigate complaints validity and ensure their confidentiality; taking remedial action with regard to any breaches of these policies; and publishing the above procedures and ensuring employees are familiar with them.

The employer must not seek to prevent or replace (e.g. through trying to replace the criminal process under the law with an internal process) a victim's right to raise a complaint to the authorities regarding any harassment. Employers must also discipline employees for any breaches of the Anti-Harassment Law.

Breach of the Anti-Harassment Law is punishable by up to five years imprisonment and/or a fine of 300,000 SAR if the crime is committed in certain aggravating circumstances, which includes where the perpetrator was in a position of power or influence over the victim and where the harassment happens at a place of work. These penalties apply without prejudice to any more severe penalties that may apply under Sharia law.

Any person who incites, agrees or otherwise assists a person to commit a harassment crime may also be subject to the above penalties as an accessory to the crime.

BIBLIOGRAPHY

Arab News, June 3, 2018. Justice for All': How Saudi Arabia's Sexual Harassment Law will Work, by Noor Nugali. Available at: http://www.arabnews.com/node/1314546/saudi-arabia. Accessed July 19, 2019

Arab News, September 29, 2107. Saudi Society Welcomes New Law Criminalizing Sexual Harassment. Available at: http://www.arabnews.com/node/1169576/saudi-arabia. Accessed July 21, 2019

https://www.uqn.gov.sa Royal Decree No. (M / 96), 2018. Available at: https://www.uqn.gov.sa/articles/1528406489385942200/. Accessed June 3, 2019

Library of Congress. Saudi Arabia: Shura Council Approves Anti-harassment Bill, 2018. Available at: https://www.loc.gov/law/foreign-news/article/saudi-arabia-shura-council-approves-anti-harassment-bill/. Accessed July 21, 2019

TURKEY

> There has not been a significant #MeToo movement in Turkey. Under the law, sexual harassment is considered a type of discrimination which includes harassment.

Legislation

- Law on Turkish Human Rights and Equality Institution No. 6701, 2016
- Code of Obligations No. 6098, 2011
- Labour Act, Law No. 4857, 2003
- Criminal Code, 2004

Title of legislation	Law on Turkish Human Rights and Equality Institution, No. 6701, 2016

The *Law on Turkish Human Rights and Equality Institution, No. 6701*, effective April 20, 2016, aims to protect and improve human rights on the basis of human dignity, ensure the right of individuals to be treated equally, and prevent discrimination against the exercise of rights.

Under this law, *sexual harassment* is considered a type of discrimination which includes harassment. Specifically, harassment means "Any painful, degrading, humiliating and disgraceful behaviour which intend to tarnish human dignity or lead to such consequence based on one of the grounds cited in this Law including psychological and *sexual harassment*."

Article 6 (1) sets forth employer prohibitions as follows:

> An employer or a person authorized by the employer shall not discriminate against an employee or applicant for a job, a person gaining applied work experience or an applicant for that kind of work and anyone wishing to receive information about the workplace or the work in order to be an employee or gain applied work experience, while being informed of the work, during the application process, selection criteria, work and termination of work and in terms of conditions for recruitment.

This prohibition includes workplaces, working conditions, and training.

An administrative fine of minimum 1,000 TRY and maximum 15,000 TRY is prescribed for violation of the law. The law is applicable to employment contracts not within the scope of the Turkish Employment Law No. 4857. Other exclusions are also set forth.

Title of legislation	Turkish Code of Obligations (Law No. 6098 of January 11, 2011)

The *Turkish Code of Obligations (Law No. 6098 of January 11, 2011)*, effective July 1, 2012, is termed the new Code of Obligations (New TCO). It does not remove or repeal Labor Law regulations. The new regulations only apply in circumstances where the New TCO governs employment.

Sexual harassment is addressed in Article 417 by stating, as translated, that the employer shall maintain and respect the personality of the worker in the service relationship and honesty in the workplace in order to ensure that the workers are not subjected to psychological and sexual harassment, in particular and to take the necessary measures in order to prevent further damage.

Title of legislation	Labour Act of Turkey Law No. 4857, 2003

Although the *Labor Act Law No. 4857, 2003* does not contain a special section concerning *sexual harassment*, it is defined among the just causes that entitle an employee and employer to terminate a contract. A worker who has been sexually harassed by the employer, a fellow worker, or by a third person in the workplace may instantly terminate the labor contract. Similarly, an employer may instantly lay off a worker who has sexually harassed him or her, a family member or a fellow worker.

Title of legislation	Criminal Code, 2004

The *Criminal Code* Law Nr. 5237, 2004, states: if a person is subject to *sexual harassment* by another person, the person performing such act may be sentenced to punishment for up to three years upon complaint of the victim. In case of commission of these offenses by undue influence based on hierarchy or public office or by using the advantage of working in the same place with the victim, the punishment to be imposed according to the above subsection is increased by one half. If the victim is obliged to leave the business place for this reason, the punishment to be imposed may not be less than one year. Article 105 (1) (2)

BIBLIOGRAPHY

Official Gazette, 2004. Criminal Code, No. 25611 dated 12.10.2004. Available at: http://www.legislationline.org/documents/action/popup/id/6872/preview. Accessed March 22, 2019

Official Gazette, 2011. p. 42. Code of Obligations (Law No. 6098 of January 11, 2011) Available at: (in Turkish) http://www.ilo.org/dyn/natlex/docs/ELECTRONIC/88938/101882/F1326871879/TUR88938.pdf. Accessed March 21, 2019

Official Gazette, 2016. Law on Turkish Human Rights and Equality Institution. Available at: (in Turkish) http://www.resmigazete.gov.tr/eskiler/2016/04/20160420-1.pdf. Accessed March 22, 2019

Ministry of Labour and Social Security, 2003. Labour Act, of Turkey Law No. 4857, 2003. Available at: (in Turkish) https://kms.kaysis.gov.tr/Home/Goster/34576. https://www.ilo.org/dyn/natlex/docs/ELECTRONIC/64083/77276/F75317864/TUR64083%20English.pdf. (in English) Accessed March 21, 2019

AFRICA

Slower and smaller #MeToo movement in Africa: providing a comprehensive cross-continental picture of workplace sexual harassment and the #MeToo movement in Africa is impossible, but articles indicate the #MeToo movement has been slower and smaller in Africa. Reasons include the role and treatment of women, fear of backlash and being shamed for speaking out about sexual harassment, and claims of sexual harassment not being taken seriously. Further, many countries do not have laws specifically against sexual harassment in the workplace, while most corporations do not have guidelines (Source: Reuters, March 8, 2019. "Why Africa's #MeToo is more a murmur than an outcry," by Nita Bhalla and Inna Lazareva).

The *Protocol to the African Charter on Human and Peoples' Rights on the Rights of Women in Africa*, published in July 2003, obligates State Parties, in relevant part, to take appropriate measures to protect women from all forms of abuse (including sexual harassment); and to ensure transparency in recruitment, promotion and dismissal of women, and combat and punish sexual harassment in the workplace (Source: refworld.org, July 2003. "Protocol to the African Charter on Human and Peoples' Rights on the Rights of Women in Africa").

BIBLIOGRAPHY

refworld.org. Protocol to the African Charter on Human and Peoples' Rights on the Rights of Women in Africa, July 2003. Available at: https://www.refworld.org/docid/3f4b139d4.html. Accessed June 25, 2019

Reuters, March 8, 2019. Why Africa's #Metoo Is More a Murmur Than An Outcry. By Nita Bhalla, Inna Lazareva. Available at: https://www.reuters.com/article/us-womens-day-africa-metoo-feature/why-africas-metoo-is-more-a-murmur-than-an-outcry-idUSKCN1QP1VO. Accessed August 20, 2019

KENYA

Kenya's Employment Act addresses sexual harassment in the workplace. Although Section 23 of the Sexual Offences Act, 2006 makes sexual harassment a crime, it only applies to holders of a public office.

There has not been much activity in the workplace around the #MeToo movement. In 2017, sexual harassment claims were brought against Ushahidi, a global crisis-mapping platform headquartered in Kenya. The charges led to the executive director of the Kenyan software company Ushahidi being fired by the board following an investigation into sexual harassment claims lodged by a former company employee (Source: Quartz Africa, July 22, 2017. "Ushahidi has fired its executive director accused of sexual harassment," by Abdi Latif Dahir).

Legislation

- Employment Act, 2007, as amended

Title of legislation	Employment Act, 2007, as amended

Kenya's Employment Act, 2007, as amended, addresses *sexual harassment* in the workplace in Part 6, which states as follows:

(1) An employee is sexually harassed if the employer of that employee or a representative of that employer or a co-worker—

(a) directly or indirectly requests that employee for sexual intercourse, sexual contact or any other form of sexual activity that contains an

implied or express—

(i) promise of preferential treatment in employment;

(ii) threat of detrimental treatment in employment; or

(iii) threat about the present or future employment status of the employee;

(b) uses language whether written or spoken of a sexual nature;

(c) uses visual material of a sexual nature; or

(d) shows physical behaviour of a sexual nature which directly or indirectly subjects the employee to behaviour that is unwelcome or offensive to that employee and that by its nature has a detrimental effect on that employee's employment, job performance, or job satisfaction.

An employer who employs 20 or more employees shall, after consulting with the employees or their representatives if any, issue a policy statement on *sexual harassment.*

The policy statement required may contain any term the employer considers appropriate for the purposes of this section and must include the definition of sexual harassment; as well as a statement that every employee is entitled to employment that is free of sexual harassment; that the employer shall take steps to ensure that no employee is subjected to sexual harassment and shall take such disciplinary measures as the employer deems appropriate against any person under the employer's direction, who subjects any employee to sexual harassment.

The policy must also include an explanation of how complaints of sexual harassment may be brought to the attention of the employer; and that the employer will not disclose the name of a complainant or the circumstances related to the complaint to any person except where disclosure is necessary for the purpose of investigating the complaint or taking disciplinary measures in relation.

The employer shall bring the required policy statement to the attention of each person under the employer's direction.

BIBLIOGRAPHY

Kenya Law, 2007. Employment Act. Available at: http://www.kenyalaw.org/kl/fileadmin/pdfdownloads/Acts/EmploymentAct_Cap226-No11of2007_01.pdf. Accessed June 3, 2019

Quartz Africa. Ushahidi Has Fired Its Executive Director Accused of Sexual Harassment, by Abdi Latif Dahir July 22, 2017. Available at: https://qz.com/africa/1036430/ushahidis-exec-director-daudi-were-has-been-fired-following-a-sexual- harassment-case/. Accessed June 3, 2019

NIGERIA

> Although the Nigerian Labour Act 2004 has no provision prohibiting sexual harassment in the workplace, Nigeria's National Industrial Court has applied a provision of the Constitution to find sexual harassment at Work:

The Constitution of the Federal Republic of Nigeria 1999, as amended, Section 34, states in relevant part: "Every individual is entitled to respect for the dignity of his person, and accordingly (a) no person shall be subject to torture or to inhuman or degrading treatment."

The National Industrial Court of Nigeria applied this provision of the Constitution to find sexual harassment at work as follows:

National Industrial Court of Nigeria, Ejieke Maduka v. Microsoft, 19 December 2013, Case No. NICN/LA/492/2012: the Court found that the Respondent consistently touched Ms. Maduka, an employee, and some other female workers in the office, against their will. It ruled that the sexual harassment of Ms. Maduka was an infringement on her fundamental right to dignity of the human person and freedom from discrimination. Specifically, the Court referred to the *Convention on the Elimination of All Forms of Discrimination against Women and ILO Convention No. 111* to rule on the sexual harassment charge, stating that this instrument had been ratified by Nigeria and was applicable to construe the fundamental rights of the applicant expressly guaranteed in the 1999 Constitution as amended. The Court held that the interpretation and meaning of CEDAW General Recommendation 19, ILO Convention No. 111, and Respondents' Microsoft Nigeria and Microsoft Corporation anti-harassment and anti-discrimination policy was that sexual harassment is a form of discrimination based on gender.

BIBLIOGRAPHY

Constitution of the Federal Republic of Nigeria, 1999. as amended. Available at: https://www.ilo.org/dyn/natlex/docs/ELECTRONIC/54097/71263/F728467428/NGA54097.pdf. Accessed June 3, 2019

National Industrial Court of Nigeria, Ejieke Maduka v. Microsoft, 19 December 2013. Case No. NICN/LA/492/2012. Available at: http://compendium.itcilo.org/en/compendium-decisions/national-industrial-court-of-nigeria-ejieke-maduka-v-microsoft-19-december-2013-case-no-nicn-la-492-2012. Accessed June 3, 2019

SOUTH AFRICA

A 2018 survey, "Too much #MeToo: sexual harassment in the South African workplace, found that approximately 30 percent of South Africa's women and 18 percent of its men have been victims of unwanted sexual advances in the workplace, with 57 percent of women and 47 percent of men claiming that the unwanted advances came from a workplace peer, while 26 percent of women reported that a boss or superior was the source of the harassment. The survey was conducted by Columinate, and engaged 1,000 research participants, representative of urban South Africa, to investigate sexual harassment in the workplace (Source: Columinate Insites Consulting, 2018. "Too much #MeToo: sexual harassment in the South African workplace").

In Rustenburg Platinum Mines Limited vs UASA obo Pietersen and Others, a 2018 case in the Johannesburg Labour Court, the Court held that there was no requirement that for a valid sexual harassment claim to be present, the accused employee must have been aware or should have reasonably been aware that his conduct was unwanted, or that the recipient must have made it clear that the behavior was considered offensive. The Court noted the 2005 Code clearly states that verbal conduct includes unwelcome innuendos, suggestions, and hints, among others, all of which require the conduct complained of to be assessed objectively. (South Africa, 2018. Johannesburg Labour Court)

Legislation

- Employment Equity Act, 1998/Employment Equity Amendment Act 2013/Code of Good Practice on Handling Sexual Harassment Cases
- Protection from Harassment Act, 2010 (No. 17 of 2011)

Title of legislation	Employment Equity Amendment Act, 2013, as amended

The *Employment Equity Act, 1998,* as amended, and the *Employment Equity Amendment Act, 2013* apply to all employers and workers and protect workers and job seekers from unfair discrimination on grounds which include sex. Section 6 provides that no person may unfairly discriminate against another and that "harassment of an employee is a form of unfair discrimination and is prohibited on any one, or a combination of grounds of unfair discrimination."

The employer may be liable if it is shown that the employee (the harasser) contravened the Act and the employer failed to take the necessary steps to eliminate the sexual harassment. In this case, the employer may be liable to pay damages or compensation to the victim of the sexual harassment. However, the employer will not be liable if he or she is able to prove that he or she did all that was reasonably practicable to ensure that there was no sexual harassment in the workplace.

The Employment Equity Act provides measures for handling *sexual harassment* cases, primarily through the Code of Good Practice on the Handling of Sexual Harassment, issued under the Employment Equity Act. The Code includes guidelines as to what type of conduct will be considered to be sexual harassment. Under the Employment Equity Act 55 of 1998 Code of Good Practice: Sexual Harassment, employers must adopt a sexual harassment policy and ensure all employees are aware of this policy.

The *Code of Good Practice on Handling Sexual Harassment Cases*, 2008, ("Code") aims to eliminate *sexual harassment* in the workplace. The Code provides appropriate procedures to deal with sexual harassment and encourages and promotes the development and implementation of policies and procedures that will lead to the creation of workplaces free of sexual harassment. Provisions addressing the employer's responsibilities include reporting, informal and formal complaint procedures, and disciplinary sanctions.

Perpetrators and victims of sexual harassment may include owners, employers, managers, supervisors, employees, clients, suppliers, contractors, and others having dealings with a business. A non-employee who is a victim of sexual harassment may lodge a grievance with the employer of the harasser where the harassment has taken place in the workplace or in the course of the harasser's employment. Sexual harassment of employees may lead to direct liability on the employer's part on the basis that the employer could be held vicariously liable for the conduct of its employees who committed the acts of sexual harassment against a colleague.

Sexual harassment is defined as unwanted conduct of a sexual nature. Sexual attention becomes sexual harassment if the behavior is persisted in, although a single incident of harassment can constitute sexual harassment; and/or the recipient has made it clear that the behavior is considered offensive; and/or the perpetrator should have known that the behavior is regarded as unacceptable.

Sexual harassment may include unwelcome physical, verbal or nonverbal conduct, but is not limited to the examples listed as follows:

- Physical conduct of a sexual nature includes all unwanted physical contact, ranging from touching to sexual assault and rape.
- Verbal forms of sexual harassment include unwelcome innuendoes, suggestions and hints, sexual advances, comments with sexual overtones, sex-related jokes or insults or unwelcome graphic comments about a person's body made in their presence or directed toward them, unwelcome and inappropriate enquiries about a person's sex life, and unwelcome whistling directed at a person or group of persons.
- Non-verbal forms of sexual harassment include unwelcome gestures, indecent exposure, and the unwelcome display of sexually explicit pictures and objects.
- Quid pro quo harassment occurs where an owner, employer, supervisor, member of management or co-employee undertakes or attempts to influence the process of employment, promotion, training, discipline, dismissal, salary increment or other benefit of an employee or job applicant, in exchange for sexual favors.
- Sexual favoritism exists where a person who is in a position of authority rewards only those who respond to his or her sexual advances, whilst other deserving employees who do not submit themselves to any sexual advances are denied promotions, merit rating or salary increases.
- Employers/management must take appropriate action when instances of sexual harassment which occur within the workplace are brought to their attention.

Sexual harassment policies should substantially comply with the provisions of this code and include at least the following statements, pursuant to 7.4.1:

- Sexual harassment is a form of unfair discrimination on the basis of sex and/or gender and/or sexual orientation which infringes the rights of the complainant and constitutes a barrier to equity in the workplace.
- Sexual harassment in the workplace will not be permitted or condoned.
- Complainants in sexual harassment matters have the right to follow the procedures in the policy and appropriate action must be taken by the employer.
- It will be a disciplinary offence to victimize or retaliate against an employee who in good faith lodges a grievance of sexual harassment.

- The procedures to be followed by a complainant of sexual harassment and by an employer when sexual harassment has occurred, should be outlined in the policy.

Note: At one time, sexual harassment cases were dealt with in terms of the Employment Equity Act (EEA), read together with the Code of Good Practice in the Handling of Sexual Harassment Cases in the Workplace published in 1998. In 2005, the Amendment to the Code of Good Practice on the Handling of Sexual Harassment Cases in the Workplace was published but it did not repeal the 1998 Code and both codes continued to apply at the same time. However, on December 19, 2018, the Minister of Labour issued a notice formally repealing the 1998 code.

Title of legislation	Protection from Harassment Act (Act No. 17 of 2011)

The *Protection from Harassment Act (Act No. 17 of 2011)*, effective April 27, 2013, provides for the issuing of protection orders against *harassment* and affords victims of harassment with an effective remedy against such behavior.

Sexual harassment is defined in Article 1 in the words of the law as follows:

(a) Unwelcome sexual attention from a person who knows or ought reasonably to know that such attention is unwelcome;
(b) Unwelcome explicit or implicit behaviour, suggestions, messages or remarks of a sexual nature that have the effect of offending, intimidating or humiliating the complainant or a related person in circumstances, which a reasonable person having regard to all the circumstances would have anticipated that the complainant or related person would be offended, humiliated or intimidated;
(c) Implied or expressed promise of reward for complying with a sexually oriented request; or
(d) Implied or expressed threat of reprisal or actual reprisal for refusal to comply with a sexually oriented request.

Under the Act an employee may obtain a protection order against an abusive employer or colleague. This protection is in addition to provisions in the Employment Equity Act.

BIBLIOGRAPHY

Columinate Insites Consulting, 2018. Too Much #Metoo: Sexual Harassment in the South African Workplace. Available at: https://www.columinate.com/2018/09/04/too-much-metoo-sexual-harassment-in-the-south-african-workplace/. Accessed May 9, 2019

Department of Justice, 2000. Promotion of Equality and Prevention of Unfair Discrimination Amendment Act, 2000 as amended. Available at: http://www.justice.gov.za/legislation/acts/2000-004.pdf. Accessed March 22, 2019

Department of Justice, 2011. Protection from Harassment Act. Available at: http://www.justice.gov.za/legislation/acts/2011-017.pdf. Accessed March 22, 2019

Department of Labour, 1995. Labour Relations Act and Amendments, 1995, as amended. Available at: https://www.gov.za/sites/default/files/gcis_document/201409/act42of1996.pdf and https://www.gov.za/documents/labour-relations-amendment-act. Accessed May 8, 2019

Department of Labour, 2005. Amended Code of Good Practice on the Handling of Sexual Harassment Cases in the Workplace. Available at: https://www.gov.za/sites/default/files/gcis_document/201409/278650.pdf. Accessed May 8, 2019

South Africa, 2018. Johannesburg Labour Court. Available at: http://www.saflii.org/za/cases/ZALCJHB/2018/72.html. Accessed June 3, 2019

http://www.labour.gov.za Employment Equity Act, 1998. Available at: http://www.labour.gov.za/DOL/downloads/legislation/acts/employment-equity/eegazette2015.pdf. Accessed June 3, 2019 and http://www.labour.gov.za/DOL/downloads/legislation/acts/employment-equity/eegazette2015.pdf. Accessed May 9, 2019

http://www.labour.gov.za Employment Equity Amendment Act, 2013. Available at: http://www.labour.gov.za/DOL/downloads/legislation/acts/employment-equity/eea_amend2014.pdf. Accessed March 23, 2019

Index

For Product Safety Concerns and Information please contact our EU
representative GPSR@taylorandfrancis.com
Taylor & Francis Verlag GmbH, Kaufingerstraße 24, 80331 München, Germany

www.ingramcontent.com/pod-product-compliance
Ingram Content Group UK Ltd.
Pitfield, Milton Keynes, MK11 3LW, UK
UKHW020939200926
475569UK00011B/31

* 9 7 8 0 3 6 7 1 9 2 7 6 1 *